Caldera® OpenLinux™ For Dummies®

vi (1) Commands

vi *filename*	Invokes vi text editor on the *filename* file
i	Enter insert mode, inserting before the current position
I	Enter insert mode, inserting at the beginning of the current line
a	Enter insert mode, inserting after the current position
A	Enter insert mode, inserting at the end of the current line
<Esc>	Return from insert mode to command mode
x	Delete a character while in command mode
cw	Delete the word behind the current position and put the editor in input mode
:w	Write out the file
:q	Quit with no additional writes to the disk
:wq	Write back the file, and then quit
:q!	Quit the file with impending changes unwritten
/string	Search forward through the file for *string*
?string	Search backward through the file for *string*
n	Find the next string (either forward or backward)
u	Undo the last command

D1608396

A Few System Administration Commands

mount	Mount a file system, connecting a disk or a floppy section to the tree
unmount	Unmount a file system, making the file system ready to be removed from the system
fsck	File-system check of the structure and integrity of the specified file system
mkfs	Put a directory structure on the low-level formatted disk
shutdown now	Shut down the system now, instead of waiting for a message to be sent; Ctrl+Alt+Del does the same thing
vmstat	Look at the virtual memory performance
procinfo	Gather information about processes

File Permissions

rwxrwxrwx	Read, write, and execute permissions for user, group, and other (the world) — mode 777
drwxr-xr-	A directory that is completely open to its owner and can be read and searched by the group and read (but not searched) by the world — mode 754
crw-r-dr-	A character-special file that the owner can read or write to but that the group and the world can read only — mode 644
brw-------	A block-special file; only the owner can read or write to it — mode 600

For Dummies®: Bestselling Book Series for Beginners

Caldera® OpenLinux™ For Dummies®

Cheat Sheet

A Few Good Commands

cd *directory*	Change the current directory to *directory*
ls	List the directory
ls -l	List the directory, along with sizes, permissions, ownerships, and dates of files
ls -a	List all files, including invisible files (files whose name begins with a period)
pwd	Print the working directory (the one you are in)
rm *file*	Remove *file*
mkdir	Make a new (empty) directory
rmdir	Remove an empty directory
cp	Copy a file
mv	Move (or rename) a file
cat	Concatenate files
more	Paginate a file
less	Paginate a file
touch	Make a new (empty) file, changing the access date of an existing file
chown	Change the owner of a file or a directory
chgrp	Change the group of a file or a directory
chmod	Change the permissions of a file or a directory
sort	Sort a file in a particular order (depending on the option)
echo	Echo back to the screen what's typed after the command
date	Read the date and time (without an argument); set the date and time (with an argument)
cut	Break a wide file into multiple narrow files
sed	Stream editor for large files or real-time editing
ln	Link a filename to another file
grep	Searching program that uses general regular expressions to find data and then prints matching data as the output of grep

Caldera is a registered trademark and OpenLinux is a trademark of Caldera Systems, Inc. The IDG Books Worldwide logo is a registered trademark under exclusive license to IDG Books Worldwide, Inc., from International Data Group, Inc. The For Dummies logo is a trademark, and For Dummies is a registered trademark of IDG Books Worldwide, Inc. All other trademarks are the property of their respective owners.

For Dummies®: Bestselling Book Series for Beginners

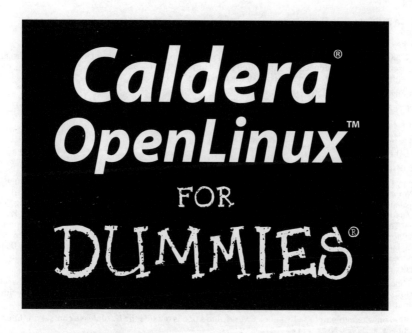

by Jon "maddog" Hall and Nicholas Wells

IDG Books Worldwide, Inc.
An International Data Group Company

Foster City, CA ◆ Chicago, IL ◆ Indianapolis, IN ◆ New York, NY

Caldera® OpenLinux™ For Dummies®

Published by
IDG Books Worldwide, Inc.
An International Data Group Company
919 E. Hillsdale Blvd.
Suite 400
Foster City, CA 94404
www.idgbooks.com (IDG Books Worldwide Web site)
www.dummies.com (Dummies Press Web site)

Library of Congress Catalog Card No.: 99-67524

ISBN: 0-7645-0679-X

Printed in the United States of America

10 9 8 7 6 5 4 3 2 1

1B/QX/QR/QQ/IN

Distributed in the United States by IDG Books Worldwide, Inc.

Distributed by CDG Books Canada Inc. for Canada; by Transworld Publishers Limited in the United Kingdom; by IDG Norge Books for Norway; by IDG Sweden Books for Sweden; by IDG Books Australia Publishing Corporation Pty. Ltd. for Australia and New Zealand; by TransQuest Publishers Pte Ltd. for Singapore, Malaysia, Thailand, Indonesia, and Hong Kong; by Gotop Information Inc. for Taiwan; by ICG Muse, Inc. for Japan; by Intersoft for South Africa; by Eyrolles for France; by International Thomson Publishing for Germany, Austria and Switzerland; by Distribuidora Cuspide for Argentina; by LR International for Brazil; by Galileo Libros for Chile; by Ediciones ZETA S.C.R. Ltda. for Peru; by WS Computer Publishing Corporation, Inc., for the Philippines; by Contemporanea de Ediciones for Venezuela; by Express Computer Distributors for the Caribbean and West Indies; by Micronesia Media Distributor, Inc. for Micronesia; by Chips Computadoras S.A. de C.V. for Mexico; by Editorial Norma de Panama S.A. for Panama; by American Bookshops for Finland.

For general information on IDG Books Worldwide's books in the U.S., please call our Consumer Customer Service department at 800-762-2974. For reseller information, including discounts and premium sales, please call our Reseller Customer Service department at 800-434-3422.

For information on where to purchase IDG Books Worldwide's books outside the U.S., please contact our International Sales department at 317-596-5530 or fax 317-572-4002.

For consumer information on foreign language translations, please contact our Customer Service department at 1-800-434-3422, fax 317-572-4002, or e-mail rights@idgbooks.com.

For information on licensing foreign or domestic rights, please phone +1-650-653-7098.

For sales inquiries and special prices for bulk quantities, please contact our Sales department at 800-762-2974 or write to the address above.

For information on using IDG Books Worldwide's books in the classroom or for ordering examination copies, please contact our Educational Sales department at 800-434-2086 or fax 317-572-4005.

For press review copies, author interviews, or other publicity information, please contact our Public Relations department at 650-653-7000 or fax 650-653-7500.

For authorization to photocopy items for corporate, personal, or educational use, please contact Copyright Clearance Center, 222 Rosewood Drive, Danvers, MA 01923, or fax 978-750-4470.

is a registered trademark under exclusive license to IDG Books Worldwide, Inc. from International Data Group, Inc.

About the Author

Jon "maddog" Hall is the Executive Director of Linux International, a vendor organization dedicated to promoting the use of the Linux OS. He has been in the computer industry for over a quarter century. While working for DEC, "maddog" met Linus Torvalds, and Linux entered and changed his life, mostly by providing him with 22-hour workdays. You usually can find Jon speaking at various Linux conferences and events, and he has also been known to travel long distances to speak to local Linux-user groups.

Nicholas Wells is a full-time author and training consultant who has written numerous titles on Linux, Linux applications, and related Internet subjects. His work for IDG Books Worldwide, Inc. includes *Linux Web Server Toolkit* and *OpenLinux Secrets*. He has a degree in linguistics (which, sadly, is rarely used) and an MBA (which, fortunately, is rarely used). Nicholas has worked in the software industry since 1980 at companies like Novell and, most recently, as a director at Caldera Systems. He trains, consults, and writes from his home in Utah.

ABOUT IDG BOOKS WORLDWIDE

Welcome to the world of IDG Books Worldwide.

IDG Books Worldwide, Inc., is a subsidiary of International Data Group, the world's largest publisher of computer-related information and the leading global provider of information services on information technology. IDG was founded more than 30 years ago by Patrick J. McGovern and now employs more than 9,000 people worldwide. IDG publishes more than 290 computer publications in over 75 countries. More than 90 million people read one or more IDG publications each month.

Launched in 1990, IDG Books Worldwide is today the #1 publisher of best-selling computer books in the United States. We are proud to have received eight awards from the Computer Press Association in recognition of editorial excellence and three from Computer Currents' First Annual Readers' Choice Awards. Our best-selling ...*For Dummies*® series has more than 50 million copies in print with translations in 31 languages. IDG Books Worldwide, through a joint venture with IDG's Hi-Tech Beijing, became the first U.S. publisher to publish a computer book in the People's Republic of China. In record time, IDG Books Worldwide has become the first choice for millions of readers around the world who want to learn how to better manage their businesses.

Our mission is simple: Every one of our books is designed to bring extra value and skill-building instructions to the reader. Our books are written by experts who understand and care about our readers. The knowledge base of our editorial staff comes from years of experience in publishing, education, and journalism — experience we use to produce books to carry us into the new millennium. In short, we care about books, so we attract the best people. We devote special attention to details such as audience, interior design, use of icons, and illustrations. And because we use an efficient process of authoring, editing, and desktop publishing our books electronically, we can spend more time ensuring superior content and less time on the technicalities of making books.

You can count on our commitment to deliver high-quality books at competitive prices on topics you want to read about. At IDG Books Worldwide, we continue in the IDG tradition of delivering quality for more than 30 years. You'll find no better book on a subject than one from IDG Books Worldwide.

John Kilcullen
Chairman and CEO
IDG Books Worldwide, Inc.

Steven Berkowitz
President and Publisher
IDG Books Worldwide, Inc.

*Eighth Annual
Computer Press
Awards ≥ 1992*

*Ninth Annual
Computer Press
Awards ≥ 1993*

*Tenth Annual
Computer Press
Awards ≥ 1994*

*Eleventh Annual
Computer Press
Awards ≥ 1995*

Dedication

Jon "maddog" Hall

To Mom&Pop (TM), whose aversion to things electronic is well known, and who still call their son Jon rather than "maddog."

Nicholas Wells

To Anne, always.

Publisher's Acknowledgments

We're proud of this book; please register your comments through our IDG Books Worldwide Online Registration Form located at http://my2cents.dummies.com.

Some of the people who helped bring this book to market include the following:

Acquisitions, Editorial, and Media Development

Editorial Manager/Project Editor: Rev Mengle

Senior Acquisitions Editor: Laura Lewin

Copy Editor: Pam Wilson-Wykes

Technical Editor: Allan Smart

Media Development Editor: Marita Ellixson

Associate Permissions Editor: Carmen Krikorian

Media Development Manager: Heather Heath Dismore

Editorial Assistant: Candace Nicholson

Production

Project Coordinator: E. Shawn Aylsworth

Layout and Graphics: Amy Adrian, Karl Brandt, Barry Offringa, Jill Piscitelli, Tracy Oliver, Jacque Schneider, Brian Torwelle, Erin Zeltner

Proofreaders: Laura Albert, Corey Bowen, John Greenough, Betty Kish, Marianne Santy, Charles Spencer

Indexer: Becky Hornyak

Special Help
Korina Wilbert

General and Administrative

IDG Books Worldwide, Inc.: John Kilcullen, CEO

IDG Books Technology Publishing Group: Richard Swadley, Senior Vice President and Publisher; Walter Bruce III, Vice President and Associate Publisher; Joseph Wikert, Associate Publisher; Mary Bednarek, Branded Product Development Director; Mary Corder, Editorial Director; Barry Pruett, Publishing Manager; Michelle Baxter, Publishing Manager

IDG Books Consumer Publishing Group: Roland Elgey, Senior Vice President and Publisher; Kathleen A. Welton, Vice President and Publisher; Kevin Thornton, Acquisitions Manager; Kristin A. Cocks, Editorial Director

IDG Books Internet Publishing Group: Brenda McLaughlin, Senior Vice President and Publisher; Diane Graves Steele, Vice President and Associate Publisher; Sofia Marchant, Online Marketing Manager

IDG Books Production for Dummies Press: Debbie Stailey, Associate Director of Production; Cindy L. Phipps, Manager of Project Coordination, Production Proofreading, and Indexing; Tony Augsburger, Manager of Prepress, Reprints, and Systems; Laura Carpenter, Production Control Manager; Shelley Lea, Supervisor of Graphics and Design; Debbie J. Gates, Production Systems Specialist; Robert Springer, Supervisor of Proofreading; Kathie Schutte, Production Supervisor

Dummies Packaging and Book Design: Patty Page, Manager, Promotions Marketing

◆

The publisher would like to give special thanks to Patrick J. McGovern, without whom this book would not have been possible.

◆

Contents at a Glance

Cartoons at a Glance

By Rich Tennant

The 5th Wave — By Rich Tennant

"Whoa there, boy! You think you're gonna install Caldera OpenLinux on that Windows 98 box?! Well you'd better hope to high heaven she's in a good mood today."

page 33

The 5th Wave — By Rich Tennant

"Okay - this is an example of some of the bootup problems you'll incur with Caldera OpenLinux unless you maintain your system properly."

page 227

The 5th Wave — By Rich Tennant

Look, all I said was, 'FTC for Mr. Gates,' and this nerdy guy with big glasses comes out and tells me he's not afraid of me, I can investigate him all I want, and he'll see me in court with his attorneys.

Flying Turkey Courier

Microsoft

page 9

The 5th Wave — By Rich Tennant

"It's called 'Caldera OpenLinux Poker.' Everyone gets to see everyone else's cards, everything's wild, you can play off your opponents' hands, and no one loses except Bill Gates, whose face appears on the Jokers."

page 257

The 5th Wave — By Rich Tennant

BRAD WAS BEGINNING TO FEEL PRESSURED TO FIND A WAY HIS CALDERA OPENLINUX USERS COULD TALK OVER A PEER-TO-PEER NETWORK

page 113

The 5th Wave — By Rich Tennant

MODERN MARRIAGE

WE'RE AGREED ON THE SILVER PATTERN, WALLPAPER AND CARPET SCHEME, BUT WE'RE STILL HASHING OUT THE OPERATING SYSTEM.

page 309

The 5th Wave — By Rich Tennant

"I don't think it's so much the Caldera OpenLinux OS she's fascinated with, as much as the association it has with a small flightless bird."

page 289

Fax: 978-546-7747
E-mail: richtennant@the5thwave.com
World Wide Web: www.the5thwave.com

Table of Contents

Introduction

Other books about OpenLinux contain fascinating information for UNIX system administrators, as well as long lists of unpronounceable commands with confusing options. This book is different. In *Caldera OpenLinux For Dummies,* the fascinating information is for you, and the descriptions and directions are written in plain English.

Use this book as an entertaining and informative reference to OpenLinux. Or buy a whole stack of *Caldera OpenLinux For Dummies* books and use them to press flowers. (Hey, you still can use the top book as a reference for OpenLinux.)

About This Book

This book is designed to be a helping-hands reference. *Caldera OpenLinux For Dummies* provides a place to turn for help and solace in those moments when, after two hours of fruitlessly typing *xstart* and twice reloading X Window System, your five-year-old tells you that the *x* goes at the end of the word.

We've tried to fill this book with the things you need to know, such as:

- Installing OpenLinux
- Exploring the KDE graphical desktop
- Issuing important commands
- Working with files and directories
- Using text editors and other interesting applications
- Getting online to surf the Web
- Finding help

You see troubleshooting tips throughout the book. Actually, OpenLinux isn't all that much trouble — we just want your experience to be as trouble-free as possible.

Foolish Assumptions

You know what they say about people who make assumptions, but this book never would have been written if we didn't make a few. This book's for you, if

- ✔ You have an OpenLinux operating system. Surprise — the CD-ROM in the back of this book has one.
- ✔ You have a computer.
- ✔ You want to put the OpenLinux operating system and your computer together and using duct tape hasn't worked.
- ✔ You don't need to become an OpenLinux guru — at least not yet.

Conventions Used in This Book

At computer conventions, thousands of computer people get together and talk about deep issues, such as:

- ✔ Is Coke better than Pepsi?
- ✔ Are Tim-Tams the ultimate junk food?
- ✔ What's the best hardware for running OpenLinux?

But these conventions aren't the types of conventions we're talking about in this section. The conventions we use are shorthand ways of designating specific information, such as what is and isn't a command, or the meaning of certain funny-looking symbols.

Typing code

Commands in the text are shown `like this`. Commands not in the text, but set off on lines by themselves, look like this:

```
pwd
```

If we boldface a command in text — as in **pwd** — that means you should type that part. We often show examples of commands and their returned text that look something like this:

```
[maddog@shamet maddog]$pwd
/home/maddog
```

The stuff exclusive of the command — in this case, everything but `pwd` — is either what the computer had on-screen before or what the command returned. So, in this example, after you type **pwd** (and press Enter), the computer displays `/home/maddog`. Is that all? Well, not quite. Notice the `[maddog@shamet maddog]` in the preceding example? You won't see that on your system, unless you're also known as maddog. But you will see something similar. The same goes for `/home/maddog`; the `maddog` is replaced with your system's directory name.

Now, for some further complications. Check out the following:

```
[root@localhost /root]# passwd <name>
```

⟨name⟩ is in *italic,* which means you should replace *⟨name⟩* with a name. In this case, you replace *⟨name⟩* with your login name. How are you supposed to know that? Don't worry. We tell you so in the text.

Here's a rundown of the command syntax in OpenLinux:

- ✔ Text *not* surrounded by [ ], { }, or ⟨ ⟩ must be typed exactly as shown.
- ✔ Text inside brackets [ ] is optional.
- ✔ Text inside angle brackets ⟨ ⟩ must be replaced with appropriate text.
- ✔ Text inside braces { } indicates that you must choose one of the values inside the braces and separated by the | sign.
- ✔ An ellipsis (. . .) means *and so on,* or to repeat the preceding command line as needed.

Don't concern yourself too much right now with this information. For most of the book, you don't need to know these particulars. And if you do need to know something about a particular syntax, come back here for a refresher course.

Keystrokes and such

Keystrokes are shown with a plus sign between the keys. For example, Ctrl+Alt+Delete means that you press the Ctrl key, the Alt key, and the Delete key all at the same time. (No, we don't make you press any more than three keys simultaneously.)

You also see something like this from time to time:

```
[maddog@localhost maddog]$ vi quagmire
a
echo Report of login names and users on the Linux system
date
echo =========================================
cut -f 1,5 -d: /etc/passwd | sed -e 's/:/ - /'
<ESC>
:wq
```

Now, you know from reading the "Typing code" section that the stuff in bold-face needs to be typed as shown. But in this case, the stuff inside angle brackets and in code — <ESC> — means you're being told to press the Escape key, not to type the E S C characters.

How This Book Is Organized

Like all proper *For Dummies* books, this book is organized into independent parts. Well, that's not quite true. This book is an almost-proper *For Dummies* book. If you don't have OpenLinux installed, then you really have to go through Part II before you can do much with OpenLinux, aside from framing the CD or using it as a neat Frisbee.

For all other parts, you can read them in any order. Heck, try reading the parts backwards for a real challenge. In this section, we tell you what each part contains.

Part I: Introducing OpenLinux

In Part I, you find out about the birth of Linux and how Caldera Systems OpenLinux fits into that fascinating history.

Part II: Installing OpenLinux

In Part II, you get your answer to the age-old question: How the heck do I install OpenLinux? We give you detailed, step-by-step instructions. You also get lots of help installing the X Window System and KDE, the graphical part of OpenLinux. You may want a double espresso or a can of Jolt soda (lots of sugar and caffeine!) by your side for this one.

Part III: Using OpenLinux

In Part III, you get the glorious particulars on actually doing something with OpenLinux. We take you through the history of text editors and how to use them. You find out that not all shells are found on the ocean floor; OpenLinux has a shell just for you. You can also take KDE through its paces, by moving, resizing, hiding, and closing windows and using a few of the many applications that are included with KDE.

Part IV: Maintaining Your System

OpenLinux isn't a high-maintenance operating system, but it does need some care. (Chocolate helps, too.) In Part IV, you find out how to manage the OpenLinux file system, which is the biggest part of the care and feeding of OpenLinux. You also get some hints on boosting the performance of OpenLinux. Vroom. Vroom.

Part V: Going Online

Everyone's online these days, and OpenLinux users like to lead the way. In Part V, you find out how to contact an Internet service provider to get an account for accessing the Internet, how to set up your OpenLinux system to interact with that account, and how to use the Netscape Communicator browser with that account to surf the Web.

Part VI: The Part of Tens

A *For Dummies* book just isn't complete without a Part of Tens. And that's Part VI. You find ten all-important OpenLinux resources in Chapter 17. In Chapter 18, we provide answers to the ten most bothersome questions people have after installing OpenLinux.

Part VII: Appendixes

Finally, the appendixes. In Appendix A, we list all the hardware that Caldera Systems says is compatible with OpenLinux. In Appendix B you find out all you need to know about the OpenLinux man pages. And in Appendix C, we tell you where in the book you can get information on installing the CD-ROM.

Other uses for CD-ROMs

Where computers and computer programmers abound, lots of CD-ROMs arrive in the mail or as part of the software that somebody buys. Eventually, these CD-ROMs become obsolete or are never installed — that's the case with software products that arrive as unwanted advertising. What can ecologically minded programmers do with these CD-ROMs so that they don't fill up landfills?

One group of programmers we know uses discarded CD-ROMs as drink coasters. Another group makes mobiles out of the CD-ROMs. (The sun shining off the CD-ROMs makes wonderful rainbows on the wall.) Still others use the CD-ROMs as clocks, by purchasing inexpensive quartz-crystal clock motors (complete with hands) and using the CD-ROM as the face of the clock. (Maddog has four of these clocks made out of Windows NT CD-ROMs — hey, can you imagine a better use for them?)

More exotic uses of CD-ROMs require high heat to melt them around the base of a water tumbler, creating either a nice flowerpot or, with the hole plugged, an ashtray. As you can imagine, doing this causes some consternation among management at these facilities, particularly after they find out that one of the more expensive programs they've purchased has ended up at the bottom of a flowerpot.

For right now, please keep your *Caldera OpenLinux For Dummies* CD-ROM in a safe place, such as the sleeve in the back of the book, when you're not using it.

What You're Not to Read

Heck, you don't have to read any of the book if you don't want to, but why did you buy it? (Not that we're complaining.) Part I has background information. If you don't want it, don't read it. Also, text in sidebars is optional, although often helpful. If you're on the fast track to using OpenLinux, you can skip the sidebars and the text with a Technical Stuff icon. But we do suggest instead that you slow down a bit and enjoy the experience.

Icons in This Book

This icon pinpoints particularly nerdy, technical information. You may skip this stuff.

This icon flags discussions that relate to the CD-ROM. The CD-ROM is a copy of Caldera Systems OpenLinux 2.3, the latest distribution available at publishing time.

Don't let this happen to you! We hope that our experiences in UNIX and Linux help you avoid making the same mistakes your first time around.

Nifty little shortcuts and timesavers. OpenLinux is a powerful operating system, and you can save unbelievable amounts of time and energy by utilizing the tools and programs in OpenLinux. We hope our tips show you how.

Maddog is something of an icon (icon: an object of uncritical devotion) in the Linux world, and this icon (icon: a little round circle in the margin with a representation of the subject's likeness) indicates a story or opinion from his vast experience.

Nick (like Maddog) has an impressive set of Linux credentials, and this symbol indicates an experience or opinion that Nick's had on his road to OpenLinux wizardry.

Where to Go from Here

You're about to join the legions of people who've been using and developing OpenLinux. We've both been using Linux for more than five years (and computers for nearly twenty). We've found OpenLinux to be a flexible, powerful operating system, capable of solving most problems even without buying a lot of additional software. The future of the OpenLinux operating system is bright. The time and energy you expend in becoming familiar with OpenLinux will be worthwhile. Carpe Linuxum.

Part I
Introducing OpenLinux

The 5th Wave   By Rich Tennant

Look, all I said was, "FTC for Mr. Gates," and this nerdy guy with big glasses comes out and tells me he's not afraid of me, I can investigate him all I want, and he'll see me in court with his attorneys.

Flying Turkey Courier

Microsoft

In this part . . .

Check out this part if you want to know what Linux in general and OpenLinux in particular are all about. First, we delve into a little history (not nearly as much as we'd like to). Then you find out why Linux is faster, smaller, less expensive, and prettier than other systems. Plus, you get a few pointers on the different ways you can use OpenLinux.

We also tell you about the different Linux varieties (*distributions* in Linux lingo) and why OpenLinux is a great choice for jumping into the world of Linux. You also get some examples of programs that are useful with OpenLinux — some come with OpenLinux and others you have to buy — to show what great things you can do with the operating system.

Chapter 1

OpenLinux and You

In This Chapter

▶ Finding out what Linux is all about

▶ Discovering why OpenLinux outperforms other systems

▶ Figuring out how you can use OpenLinux

*I*n 1991, Linus Torvalds, an undergraduate student at the University of Helsinki, got a brand-new IBM 386 PC. Dissatisfied with the operating system that came with the hardware, Linus wanted to run the UNIX operating system instead. UNIX, however, was too expensive, so Linus and a team of talented programmers tackled the daunting task of creating a new version of UNIX. They created a core operating system, or *kernel,* named Linux. Since those early days, Linus Torvalds has been on the cover of *Forbes* magazine, given keynote addresses at major computer trade shows, and been referred to as the nemesis of Bill Gates. Who knows what the next five years may bring!

Why Is This Stuff Free?

One of the most important decisions Linus Torvalds made early on about the Linux kernel was that all the code would be freely distributable. So several organizations accumulated huge amounts of freely distributable software, added that software to the Linux kernel, and then created a way to install the software on the computer. This process is called creating a *distribution*.

To learn more about many of the free software components included with OpenLinux, you may want to check out the Free Software Foundation Web site at www.fsf.org.

Distributions were available in several forms: the Internet, CD-ROMs from software publishers (who charged a distribution fee), and bundled with other programs (also charged for by organizations). In every case, however, the base Linux kernel and other freely distributable code had to be identified and made available without a charge.

Let's be open about Linux

Linux is the first operating system in major use today that got its start outside the United States of America. All other operating systems, although they have received some support and construction from non-U.S. participants, were conceived and maintained in the United States. People from all over the world — and increasingly from countries not globally recognized as technology countries — contribute to Linux.

When people ask me why I think Linux and the Open Source Code development projects are so important, I answer that I'm not so egotistical as to think that all good programmers come from the United States. I tell them that the next Albert Einstein of computer science may come from Korea, or China, or Venezuela, or even Helsinki, Finland, and the world can't afford to miss the opportunity of finding him. I stated this opinion while standing with the president of the University of São Paulo, Brazil, in front of his school's supercomputer that was running Linux. He answered my observation with "We, too, considered that point."

The importance of the operating system's source code's availability can't be overstressed. The result of freely distributable source code is a Linux operating system that continues to improve rapidly. Every developer can build on the efforts of an earlier developer, which benefits everyone — including you.

Linux kernel development started in 1991. By early spring of 1994 (not long before Caldera's start), the first version of Linux (V1.0) became available for public use. Even then, Linux was an amazing operating system, running in less than 2MB of RAM on Intel systems at awesome speeds. This free system included the following features, which were found in operating systems costing users hundreds of dollars:

- Multitasking (running more than one job simultaneously)
- Multiple users simultaneously
- High-performance virtual-memory system allowing OpenLinux to use hard-disk space as an extension to RAM

An estimated 125 thousand people were active users in 1994. (Because no licenses are issued for individual users, a more precise number can't be determined.) In 1997, just three years later, the estimated number of Linux users was 3 million and climbing rapidly. By the fall of 1999, the estimates were more than 10 million.

Where does Caldera come in? Caldera was founded in 1994 by Bryan Sparks to create a complete desktop and server operating system using Linux. Caldera created a distribution called OpenLinux, the focus of which is to provide a Linux system that benefits businesses and new users. To that end, OpenLinux includes the easiest installation and the most commercial add-ons among the Linux distributions as of this writing. Version 2.3 of OpenLinux is described in this book and included on the CD-ROM as well.

Adding the Other Pieces

Companies that gather Linux software from the Internet and then package that software for users like you and us provide a great service. But that service by itself doesn't make a great business; the margins are too small, because anyone with a CD-writer can join the fray. So companies like Caldera Systems, Inc., add all sorts of other things to their Linux product — things that you can't get on the Internet. That's why people pay good money for a box of stuff they otherwise can download for free. OpenLinux's highlights include

- ✔ An easy-to-use graphical-installation program that can be started from a bootable CD-ROM or from an existing Windows system.

- ✔ PartitionMagic, from PowerQuest, integrated into the installation program to help new users create hard-disk space for a new Linux installation. This feature allows a single computer with one hard disk to use either Windows or OpenLinux each time the system boots.

- ✔ A printed manual to guide you through installing and using the system (of course, you don't need that, because you have this book).

- ✔ Technical support options, including telephone support for those who really need support (and are willing to pay extra for it) and Web-based information searches.

- ✔ Commercial Office Suites — StarOffice 5 for Linux and WordPerfect for Linux.

- ✔ Commercial backup software (called BRU).

- ✔ Three CD-ROMs full of Linux software and source code.

Although this book doesn't include three CD-ROMs and commercial products like WordPerfect (because Caldera saves something to sell in its box of software), the graphical installation is included, so that you can get started without any difficulty!

Using OpenLinux in Different Ways

OpenLinux is a versatile operating system. Although Linux was initially the sole domain of computer-science students, OpenLinux is now used by businesses and governments to cut costs and improve performance. You can use OpenLinux in a variety of ways: as a desktop workstation, as a server system, as the basis of an embedded system (such as a smart VCR or a robot), or even as a supercomputer. The installation options described in Chapter 5 let you select the type of system for which you intend to use Linux. Your options include a home system, server, development workstation, and business server.

Another popular use for Linux is with Internet service providers (ISPs) that use Linux to provide information and services to the Internet and the World Wide Web. And thanks to the thousands of people working on different parts of Linux, the system becomes more flexible and more capable with each passing day.

The sections that follow describe some of the ways that you can use OpenLinux.

Personal workstation

With the power of OpenLinux, you can run many programs at the same time, handle the needs of more than one user at a time, and use high-quality graphics. OpenLinux can handle files and programs of immense size. OpenLinux uses a sophisticated windowing system called the X Window System (also known as X Windows, X11, or simply X) and can share files not only with most UNIX systems but also with Microsoft Windows, OS/2, and other operating systems.

The default graphical environment of OpenLinux is called KDE, which uses the X Window System as an underlying toolkit. (See Chapter 11 for KDE interface details.) KDE provides you with drag-and-drop features, graphical-file management, icons for your favorite applications, and browsable online help.

OpenLinux also includes the following:

- ✔ Netscape Web browsers that include e-mail and newsgroup readers
- ✔ Complete networking with the Internet-standard TCP/IP protocol
- ✔ Software-development tools, including numerous compilers, debuggers, and scripting languages
- ✔ Other useful programs, such as image editors, faxing software, system administration tools, multimedia utilities, and personal time managers

If the number of programs included with OpenLinux doesn't satisfy you, then additional commercial applications are available. These applications include databases, such as Oracle and Sybase; specialized scientific programs; and office suites, such as WordPerfect and Applixware. With OpenLinux, you can have the same environment on your notebook computer, desktop workstation, and large server system.

File and print server

Because of its multitasking capability, virtual memory, and powerful file system, OpenLinux works well as a file and print server for Microsoft Windows systems. A software product called Samba allows PCs that are running Windows to communicate with the file system and with printers attached to an OpenLinux machine. AppleTalk allows the same file- and printer-sharing for Apple computers. And, of course, OpenLinux can share files and printers with UNIX systems. By using OpenLinux to manage sharing files and printers, you can save a lot of money because the operating system and the layered software that provide these services are included with the basic OpenLinux product on the CD-ROM in this book.

Internet/intranet service provider

Many capabilities of the Internet (the worldwide network) and intranets (mini-Internets used within a single business) are possible because of HTML (HyperText Markup Language) and the World Wide Web. UNIX systems were at the forefront of these developments, and OpenLinux shares many benefits of that heritage. Both the Internet and intranets require similar services, such as:

- Firewalls to guard Internet servers against attacks from the bad guys
- FTP (File Transfer Protocol) so that the good guys can upload and download data files and software
- Telnet so that people can log in from other computers onto your local network and remotely use your machine
- Web servers so that people can see your Web pages
- NFS (Network File System) to share hard disks over a network

Many Internet service providers (ISPs) use OpenLinux to deliver these services to their customers, not only because OpenLinux is cost effective but also because the source code for the core of the operating system is available. If a problem occurs, ISPs can correct the problem quickly by downloading a program patch from Caldera's Web site or by working on the problem themselves. The alternative is to wait for a traditional software vendor to correct the problem, which easily can take months.

How critical is a timely correction? Well, in 1997, a problem with TCP/IP resulting from a deliberate misuse of a program called `ping` affected almost every UNIX system in the world. This problem allowed bad guys (called crackers) to shut down other people's UNIX systems. The world needed new software updates to repair this problem — and quickly! An update for OpenLinux (and all other Linux systems) was on the Internet within four hours after the problem was identified, and people could easily download the software update and then apply it to their systems. Various commercial UNIX vendors took weeks to develop a similar update for their operating systems and then sent it to their customers.

Three-tier client/server

Whoa! What the heck is a three-tier client/server? A three-tier client/server simply means that most large computer tasks can be broken down into three, separate, smaller tasks, or tiers:

- ✔ Data presentation
- ✔ Data manipulation
- ✔ Data storage and retrieval

If you break a problem down into these three levels, the problem typically is easier to solve and easier to change later, as necessary. Until recently, the data-presentation level consisted of Microsoft Windows systems running on the desktop (perhaps using Visual Basic to develop the interface). The data-manipulation level and the data-storage-and-retrieval level consisted of UNIX (or older systems) communicating over the network.

Now, however, the data-presentation level can be an OpenLinux system that's running a freely distributed Web browser or a freely distributed Java system (a portable environment for applications). By using OpenLinux, some firms can save thousands of dollars on operating-system costs yet still receive required security and operating-system robustness.

As with most UNIX systems, OpenLinux also has sophisticated data-manipulation tools that make OpenLinux a good second-tier system. OpenLinux can extract data from several types of databases or reports that are kept in files from older systems, and then sort, search, combine, process, and otherwise manipulate the data, passing the newly created results to the presentation level on the desktop.

Finally, OpenLinux has the facilities to act as a good data-storage-and-retrieval level. Several commercial database packages run on OpenLinux. These packages include DB2, Oracle, Informix, Sybase, and Interbase. But if you can't afford a commercial database package, you can use one of the freely available packages, such as Postgres.

The three-tier concept is to divide work logically, and after you do, then you can put all three pieces of functionality onto one computer — an OpenLinux system.

Turnkey system

A turnkey system is put together once and then duplicated in hundreds or thousands of places. Typical turnkey systems are information kiosks, hotel-reservation systems, doctors' and lawyers' office systems, and automotive-diagnostic systems. OpenLinux is perfect for turnkey-systems' work because OpenLinux provides the security, protection, and stability that turnkey systems need, while not requiring huge payments for many copies of the operating system. For example, suppose an application was needed on 4,000 hotel systems. If the business had to pay, say, $500 for the operating system, then the project would cost $2,000,000 extra, just to cover the operating system.

Linux all over

Standard PCs — the kind found in most offices — use 32-bit Intel processors. Don't want to limit yourself to an Intel processor? No problem. Linux has been *ported* (converted to run on) to a number of other architectures, including Alpha, StrongARM, and SPARC, to give users a choice of manufacturers and keep the Linux kernel flexible for new processors. Caldera joined this movement; OpenLinux for SPARC was announced in mid-1999. OpenLinux also supports symmetric multiprocessing (more than one CPU in the same computer). In the Linux community as a whole, projects are in the works to continue development of sophisticated processing capabilities (such as the following that are available already with OpenLinux).

✔ Real-time programming, typically to control machinery or test equipment

✔ High availability, which is having the computer run reliably at all times

✔ Scalability, that is, the ability to work on systems ranging from old PCs to the latest, fastest microprocessors

✔ Clustering, which allows multiple OpenLinux computers to be tied together into one supercomputer

This last capability — known as *Extreme Linux* systems or *Beowulf* systems — is enabling research organizations to create machines with supercomputer capabilities at a fraction of the price of supercomputers. In certain cases, Extreme Linux systems are made from obsolete PCs, costing the organizations that make them nothing in material costs.

Chapter 2

Accessorizing OpenLinux

· ·

· ·

*T*he *Caldera OpenLinux For Dummies* CD-ROM provides a copy of Caldera Systems OpenLinux 2.3. Many Linux distributions are available, but OpenLinux is a great choice, especially for new users or those focused on the business uses of Linux. This chapter highlights some of the tools included with OpenLinux, such as text editors and mail interfaces — just to whet your appetite. We tell you where else in the book you can look for more information.

Be Your Own Software Lawyer

Linus Torvalds and the Linux development team created the Linux operating system kernel. The *kernel* includes the software for managing memory, files, programs that are running, networking, and various hardware devices. Think of the kernel as a cop directing traffic.

The compilers and other programs that go into making up what most people think of as Linux are from a variety of people who distribute the programs over the Internet or on CD-ROM. Typically, these people add an installation technique, system management tools, some applications (either freeware or commercial), and a distribution medium, just as Caldera does with OpenLinux. In every case, the Linux license requires that the base Linux system is able to be copied freely, even if value-added components are not.

Different Linux systems are . . . well . . . different!

To describe other Linux distributions in depth would take a lot of space, but the following information gives you some idea of what the Linux world contains, besides the OpenLinux product that you hold in your hands.

One of the early distributions was the **Yggdrasil** distribution. After an easy installation, Yggdrasil started X Window System, displayed some mpeg videos, and croaked "Hello" through the computer's console speaker.

Another early distribution was **Slackware.** Distributed and still actively maintained by Patrick Volkerding and various resellers, such as Walnut Creek CD-ROM (www.cdrom.com), Slackware is divided into packages that are copied onto floppies from the Net or a CD-ROM. You can contact the Slackware people directly at www.slackware.com.

The **Debian** (www.debian.org) distribution was put together by a group of volunteers, who now distribute Debian over the Internet and on CD-ROM.

Red Hat Software (www.redhat.com) is an early distribution from a collaboration of three Linux enthusiasts who were later joined by ACC, Red Hat's largest distributor.

S.u.S.E. GmbH (www.suse.com) is a German firm (now with offices in California) that puts out its own distribution in German and English. S.u.S.E. GmbH also carries other people's distributions and products.

InfoMagic (www.infomagic.com) puts out a collection of Linux distributions, as well as various Linux products.

Pacific HiTech, Inc. (www.pht.com) is a company that provides translated copies of Linux, including Japanese and Chinese translations. Pacific HiTech recently changed its name to **Turbo Linux** and started selling specialized high-end Linux server solutions.

OpenLinux is one of many Linux distributions, and many Linux applications are available as well. These distributions differ widely in cost, appearance — and legal ramifications. A Linux application may be classified as any of the following, depending on the author/owner's decision:

- Freely available software
- Shareware
- Commercial applications

Freely available software is available for free use by the end user. Although software may be freely available, such software is often not the same as public domain software (or software you can do absolutely anything with because no one owns it). Freely available software is often owned and copyrighted by the author or authors, who then allow people to use their software or make modifications to it. Many different licenses are used with freely available software. The best known license for free software is probably the Gnu General Public License (the GPL), also called OpenSource software (see www.fsf.org and www.opensource.org).

Freely available software can be further divided into software that you can either *freely copy* or *freely distribute.* Some people make their software freely available, but only if you copy the software directly from a particular site or from a noncommercial distribution. Other people let you copy their software from anyplace. Copying restrictions usually apply to people making a commercial distribution, not to the end-user of that distribution. A company creating a product based on freely available software has the responsibility to be in compliance with the package's copying restrictions, which are usually outlined in the source code of a program or in the program's About or Help section.

Being free isn't always the best thing. One system administrator came to us when I worked at Caldera because his manager was upset about his using Linux. "We're not running this company on free software!" the manager insisted. We offered to help. We charged him for a copy of Linux (with documentation and support, of course), and everyone was happy.

Many freely available applications have been ported from UNIX to OS/2, Windows 3.1, 95, 98, and NT, and other operating systems. If you use an application that's been ported to many operating systems, such as the emacs(1) editor, you're more likely to be able to use the same application in more than one operating system.

When you see a word, such as *emacs,* followed by a number in parentheses, the name refers to a Linux command. The number is the section of the Linux manual set that contains information on how to use that command. For example, emacs(1) is a text editor that you can use to manipulate text in files, and emacs(1) documentation is located in section 1 of the manual pages. lpd(8) is a command found in the eighth section of the reference manual. After your Linux system is up and running, you can type the following commands:

```
man emacs
man lpd
```

to the information about how to use the commands.

Nonfree applications consist of commercial applications and shareware applications. *Commercial applications* are sold outright. *Shareware applications* may be tried out or used for personal use. If you use the shareware program a lot or want to use the program commercially, then you should pay the author. The amount is usually nominal ($25 is typical; $200 is the high end).

For a list of nonfree applications — after you install your Linux system and get your KDE Desktop going — look at the Commercial HOWTO by typing the following in a terminal-emulator window:

```
netscape file:/usr/doc/HOWTO/other-formats/html/Commercial-
         HOWTO.html
```

This file was pulled off your *Caldera OpenLinux For Dummies* CD-ROM when you installed the system. The file on the *Caldera OpenLinux For Dummies* CD-ROM is probably an older version of what you can find on the Internet. So, for an up-to-date list of nonfree applications, you can use a Web browser to look at the Linux Commercial HOWTO at the following URL:

```
www.linuxhq.com/tbm/Commercial-HOWTO
```

You can also poke around in some of the Linux application directories. These Web sites include information about freely available programs and commercial applications. Try `www.linuxapps.com` or `SAL.KachinaTech.com` (for scientific applications on Linux).

More and more commercial software programs are available for Linux. A good way to find software programs is to look in magazines, such as *Linux Journal* (or in Germany or Poland, *Linux Magazin* or *LinuxPlus,* respectively).

Interfaces: Pretty or Quick?

OpenLinux applications can be classified as free and nonfree, and also as character-cell and graphical applications. *Character-cell applications* are textual types of applications in which you type a command and the system responds. MS-DOS is an example of a character-cell operating system. In a *graphical application,* you use the mouse as well as the keyboard to tell the computer what to do. Microsoft Windows is a ubiquitous example of a graphical operating system.

UNIX started out as a character-cell operating system and then added graphical window systems. OpenLinux inherited both character-cell and graphical features from UNIX.

You'll probably spend most of your time using OpenLinux in its graphical mode — that's the default startup mode after you install OpenLinux. The graphical portion of OpenLinux is called the *KDE Desktop,* or just *KDE.* KDE looks great, but using a graphical window system has a few disadvantages:

- ✔ Many character-cell applications were created before the age of the X Window System (the OpenLinux windowing system upon which KDE sits) and KDE. Some just work better in character-cell mode. In Chapter 10, you see a bunch of applications that work very well in character-cell mode.

- ✔ Managing a graphical interface is always a lot more work for your computer.

If your system seems to slow down to the point of annoying you, then add memory, buy a faster computer, or try some character-cell applications. Also, if you're using a laptop for short periods of time (to take notes in a meeting, for example) and find that the startup time for X Window System and its associated programs is too long, then you may want to opt (as we both often do) for character-cell mode.

The sections that follow show you some character-cell and graphical applications.

Text Editors

OpenLinux comes with several different text editors. *Text editors* are programs that typically enable you to type and manipulate alphanumeric characters. Some text editors can do simple word-processing tasks, such as word wrap, but most text editors can't perform most word-processing functions, such as spell checking or italicizing text. In fact, a plain-text file can't store information about text formatting, such as large fonts, bold, and italic. Plain-text files only store the plain characters that you type.

Text editors are good for simple text-editing tasks and for writing simple or even complex programs. Most editors have built-in help functions, and some have full-scale documentation built in or available online. In addition, you can find books about a few editors, such as vi(1) and emacs(1).

In this section, we describe character-cell text editors and graphical-based text editors that are included with OpenLinux. We also mention some commercial text editors.

Character-cell text editors

The editor-of-editors on all Linux systems is called vi(1), for visual editor. (Believe it or not, vi(1) is more "visual" than its predecessors.) Written in the mid-1970s, vi(1) allowed people to see a whole screen of text at one time! Although vi(1) is challenging to use, learning a little about it is a good idea, because vi(1)'s the text editor that is generally available on any Linux system you work with. Using vi(1) also makes you feel really smart — that's one reason we show you some vi(1) basics in Chapter 9. Many Linux systems ship with a new version of vi(1) called vim(1), for vi improved.

Another character-cell text editor is emacs(1), one of the shining stars of the Free Software Foundation. Devotees of emacs(1) claim that emacs(1) is not just a text editor; but an interface to reading mail, debugging programs, reading news from the Internet, and a variety of other text-oriented activities. The emacs(1) program can also emulate several character-cell editors and has made the jump to a graphical mode. Memory size and the use of a fair amount of disk space are the downsides to emacs(1).

Remember, you can start any character-cell editor within the graphical environment (KDE) by starting it from a command-line window. The program runs as if in character-cell mode.

Graphical text editors

In addition to all the character-cell editors that come with OpenLinux, two excellent text editors are built into the KDE Desktop.

The first editor, called Kedit, is a basic text editor but adds features, such as spell checking and keyboard control. You start Kedit by choosing Editor on the Applications submenu in KDE (you find out about that in Chapter 9). Unless you're writing programs, Kedit is a good choice. The basic Kedit window with a menu bar, toolbar, and status line is shown in Figure 2-1.

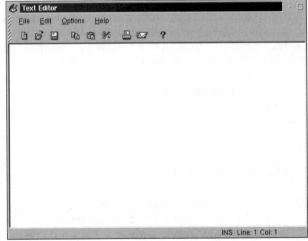

Figure 2-1:
The Kedit
graphical
text editor.

The more advanced editor in KDE, intended to replace Kedit eventually, is Kwrite. Kwrite is designed for programmers with color coding for program code but no spell checking. You start Kwrite by choosing Advanced Editor on the Applications submenu in KDE.

Commercial text editors

Several commercial text editors are available, and some of them come with significant value added — particularly for software developers — when compared
to simple text editors. Two of the most popular commercial text editors are:

- ✔ **Visual Slick Edit** by MicroEdge, an X11-based editor that also runs on
  Windows 3.1, 95, 98, and NT platforms. The editor is language sensitive,
  so if you're programming in C, C++, Java, HTML, Perl, AWK, Pascal, FOR-
  TRAN, BASIC, dBASE, Modula-2, COBOL, Ada, or several other languages,
  Visual Slick Edit knows about these languages and tries to help make the
  text more readable and searchable. Visual Slick Edit emulates several
  other editors (such as vi, emacs, and Brief) and integrates with other
  programs that help keep track of your program's code. Visual Slick Edit
  is definitely a programmer's editor but can be useful for nonprogram-
  mers, too.

- ✔ **Crisp** by Vital, another language-sensitive, cross-platform editor. Cross-
  platform editors run on many different UNIX and Linux systems, as well
  as on Windows 3.1, 95, 98, and NT.

E-Mail Tools

E-mail consists of two main parts: a *front end* (or interface) that you use to
compose or read messages, and a *back end* that delivers your messages. In
addition to the mail-specific programs described in this section, note that
some Web browsers can read mail and Internet News (a series of information
postings accessible over the Internet), handle FTP downloads of files, and
perform other Internet-related tasks.

Character-cell interfaces

The first mail interfaces were available only in character-cell mode. Some
character-cell interfaces follow:

- ✔ **mail(1):** One of the first mail interfaces. Was a character-cell interface for
  early versions of UNIX. mail(1) remains a powerful interface and is still a
  useful program, when working in character-cell mode and wanting to
  send a quick mail message or scan recent mail messages.

- ✔ **elm(1):** An interactive screen-oriented mailer that can be used in place
  of mail(1) as a front end. elm(1) is easy to use and presents a vim(1)-like
  editor for creating mail messages. pine(1) (which now means *program
  for Internet news and email* but previously was known by the friendlier
  name, *pine is not elm*) is another full-screen mail interface.

✔ **pine(1):** Has several features found in elm(1), plus a few of its own. pine(1) uses a simple editor called pico for composing mail and also handles MIME (Multipurpose Internet Mail Extensions), for sending pictures, computer programs, and other nontext items through the mail.

pine(1) runs on DOS and Windows systems, as well as on many UNIX systems. pine(1) includes a built-in spell checker (always nice when writing messages to your boss); can read NNTP, can be used to access Internet News; and can handle IMAP mail, which sends mail to a holding place accessed from anywhere on the Internet — especially nice when traveling with Linux on your notebook computer, because you can connect to your Internet service provider (ISP) and then take care of your e-mail.

✔ **mh(1):** Also known as the RAND Message Handling System, mh(1) is a series of commands that enable mail manipulation at the command-line level. mh(1) is a comprehensive mail interface that enables you to create different folders for mail, scan the mail in those folders in several ways, and reply, forward, and otherwise manage your mail. Because it consists of these different commands, mh(1) was used to build two useful graphical mail interfaces: xmh(1) and exmh(1), which are described next.

Graphical mail interfaces

Graphical mail programs offer a powerful and easy-to-use interface to read and manipulate mail. Graphical mail interfaces, like graphical text editors, require the X Window System and can be run in KDE.

xmh(1) is a graphical interface written for the character-cell-oriented mh(1) commands, mentioned in the preceding section. As such, you can alternate between using mh(1) in the character-cell environment and xmh(1) in the graphical environment. xmh(1) is a simple interface written mostly to demonstrate early versions of the X Window System.

I prefer the exmh(1) graphical mailing program, because it's freely distributable, so I can use the same interface on systems at work, at home, and in notebooks when I'm traveling. exmh(1) is powerful — with MIME and POP (an earlier version of IMAP) capabilities, folder support, and easy ways to tailor printing, your editor, and a series of other parameters. The exmh(1) mailing program also highlights URLs (addresses of World Wide Web pages) in the text of your mail; when you click the URL, exmh(1) calls up your Web browser and displays the URL. exmh(1) has a comprehensive search facility for looking for mail messages sorted in folders.

KDE includes an e-mail interface called Kmail. Kmail can be launched from the Internet submenu in KDE. The initial screen (with a few messages already shown) appears in Figure 2-2.

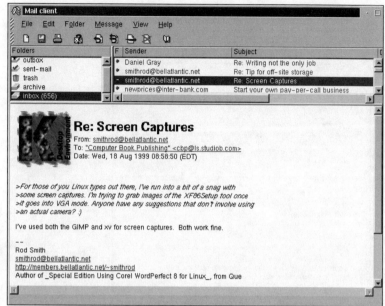

Figure 2-2:
The Kmail
graphical
e-mail inter-
face in KDE.

Kmail includes many advanced features, such as MIME attachments, e-mail filters, multiple mail folders, and support for all three popular e-mail protocols: POP, IMAP and SMTP. The message composition window in Kmail should look familiar to you if you've used any Web-browser-based e-mail readers (as shown in Figure 2-3).

Commercial mail interfaces

As with the text editors, several commercial mail-interface programs are available. Some programs are sold separately; others are part of application suites. One such product is Zmail from NetManage Software. Zmail has been ported to most UNIX systems and also to Windows 3.1, 95, 98, and NT. Because Zmail works across so many systems, you can use the same mail interface on all of your platforms.

Another commercial mail interface is found in Applixware, produced by Applix, Inc. This product is an office suite consisting of a WYSIWYG (what-you-see-is-what-you-get) text processor, an integrated spreadsheet, a presentation package, a graphical editor, and a mail front end. In Figure 2-4, you're shown some Applixware components. A demonstration copy of Applixware is included in the full commercial version of OpenLinux.

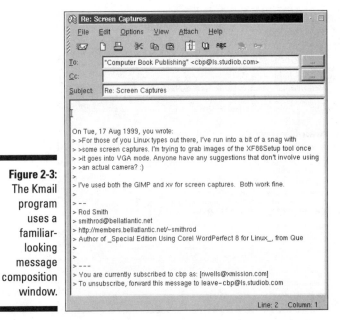

Figure 2-3:
The Kmail
program
uses a
familiar-
looking
message
composition
window.

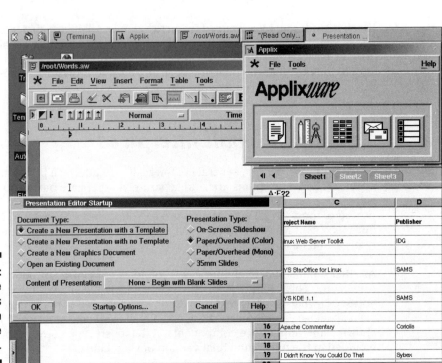

Figure 2-4:
Some of the
applications
in
Applixware
Office Suite.

Another commercial product with complete e-mail capabilities is StarOffice. This complete office suite is included in the full version of OpenLinux. The e-mail client in StarOffice is integrated into a desktop environment with the word processor, spreadsheet, and many Internet features, such as Web browsing and FTP site access. Figure 2-5 shows the StarOffice e-mail interface.

For more about StarOffice, check out *StarOffice For Linux For Dummies,* by Michael Meadhra (IDG Books Worldwide, Inc.).

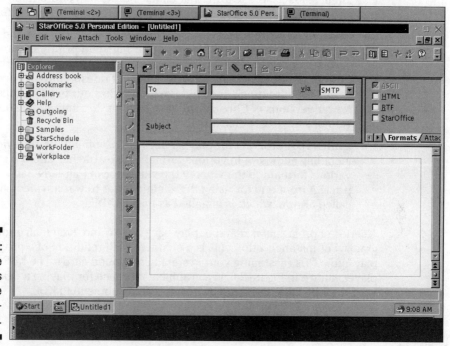

Figure 2-5:
StarOffice
includes
complete
e-mail func-
tionality.

A Multimedia Toolbox

OpenLinux comes with numerous programs for simple drawing and painting, as well as image viewing, conversion, and manipulation. OpenLinux can display still and animated images and can record, manipulate, and play back audio (given that your hardware has a supported sound card). This section gives you a sampling of some multimedia programs that you can use in OpenLinux.

- **kpaint:** A simple drawing and paint program used to read an image and then perform simple manipulations of the image.

- **ImageMagick:** A freely distributed program for graphical image manipulation that reads many types of images, makes the images larger or smaller, cuts image portions, transforms several still images into an animation, and stores the images back to disk in a different format (if desired).

- **gimp:** A graphical image-manipulation program based on plug-ins that extend a program's capabilities. One powerful feature of gimp is the intelligent-scissors feature that enables parts of a photo to be cut out and then pasted onto another photo (as in the movie *Forrest Gump*).

- **Ghostview:** A program for viewing files from PostScript, an industry-standard page-description language for high-end printers. Ghostview uses a program called Ghostscript (Aladdin Enterprises) to print PostScript files to a dumb printer (one that doesn't have a PostScript program built into it) or to put PostScript files out to a FAX machine. Newer versions of Ghostscript have distribution limitations, but older versions are freely distributable.

- **xanim(1):** A program for playing back stills, animations, and videos — including audios — in various formats. Also attaches audio streams of various formats to the video if the video doesn't already have an audio track. A front end for using the xanim viewer to watch video clips is called aKtion, which is installed as part of KDE.

A series of programs mix audio, play back audio, and even mail audio programs. For instance, cdplay(1) is a character-cell rendition of a program to play audio CDs (assuming your system has a sound card). The KDE CD player, shown in Figure 2-6, is a graphical interface for playing a CD. You can start the KDE CD player from the Multimedia submenu in KDE.

Figure 2-6:
The KDE CD player is part of the KDE multimedia package.

What Else Can I Have?

So far in this chapter you've been shown all sorts of different software that is available for OpenLinux (much of it included on the CD-ROM in this book). If the tool you need isn't already mentioned, don't despair. Whatever your need, a program that fulfills that need probably already exists for Linux — and may even be freely available on the Internet. Some very specialized stuff is available for Linux (from chemical and numeric analysis to educational software, from development tools to video-editing packages).

Do you need a good scientific calculator? Choose Calculator, shown in Figure 2-7, from the KDE Utilities submenu. Want to try illustrating a project? Choose KIllustrator from the Graphics submenu (as shown in Figure 2-8). Simply want to while away the day watching the clock? Try choosing World Clock from the Toys submenu, as shown in Figure 2-9, to make life interesting.

Figure 2-7: KDE includes a scientific calculator.

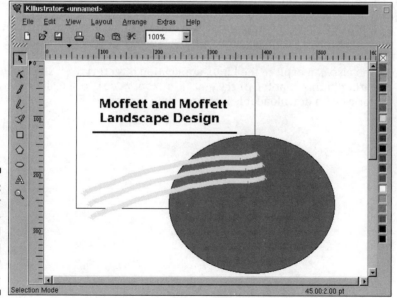

Figure 2-8: KIllustrator is a vector-based drawing program like CorelDRAW.

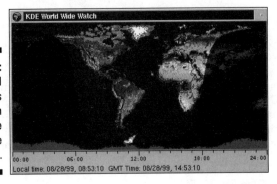

Figure 2-9:
The World
Clock lets
you watch
around the
world as the
day passes.

These programs, plus many more, are available for OpenLinux:

- ✔ Netscape Communicator, a full-featured Web browser and e-mail client, which you find more about in Chapter 16.

- ✔ KOrganizer, a day planner that helps you track appointments and task lists, which we discuss in Chapter 12.

- ✔ Kedit, a handy basic text editor that you can begin using without memorizing any commands (we explain the details in Chapter 9).

- ✔ Integrated tools for configuring a wallpaper graphic, color schemes, and a screen saver on your desktop. Chapter 11 describes how to set these up.

- ✔ A CD player, a graphics viewer, a scientific calculator, and a few other useful desktop gadgets. (All this stuff is covered in Chapter 12.)

You also can explore the Linux-application directory Web sites mentioned earlier in this chapter, or try www.linuxberg.com to see all types of categories with downloadable free programs for you to try.

Part II
Installing
OpenLinux

The 5th Wave   By Rich Tennant

"Whoa there, boy! You think you're gonna install Caldera OpenLinux on that Windows 98 box?! Well you'd better hope to high heaven she's in a good mood today."

In this part . . .

You're about to embark on a journey through the OpenLinux installation program. (If your OpenLinux system is already installed, you can skip this part and peruse another one.) Perhaps you know nothing about setting up the operating system on your computer. That's okay. OpenLinux is smart, and reasonable. Plus, you have us to guide you.

In Chapter 3, you find out what OpenLinux needs as well as what your system has in terms of hardware. In Chapter 4, you do more all-important preparation, such as creating a boot floppy disk. You also find out how to squeeze the data on your hard disk so that you can fit OpenLinux there, too.

Chapter 5 shows you how to do what you've been waiting for ever since you bought this book: Install OpenLinux. Like park rangers, we guide you along the various trails of the installation process, pointing out pitfalls and cautioning you about hazards. You get to enjoy the views, too, as you move screen-by-screen through your trek.

Your travels through the installation may not be over yet, however. Installing the graphical desktop (the X Window System and KDE) can be tricky, which is why we provide an entire troubleshooting chapter on it. So, if you have any troubles with this part of the installation, Chapter 6 is for you. If you installed the X Window System without a hitch, break out the trail mix and enjoy a well-deserved rest.

Finally, in Chapter 7, you reap the benefits of all your efforts and use OpenLinux for the very first time. Happy trails.

Chapter 3

Discovering What's in Your System

- -

In This Chapter

▶ Figuring out the resources OpenLinux requires
▶ Unearthing your type of hardware

- -

The sole function of this chapter (and the three chapters that follow) is to help you install your system. If your OpenLinux system is already installed, then count yourself lucky and check out the chapters in Part III. If you haven't installed your system, then console yourself with the fact that you'll find out a lot in this chapter and be the better for doing so later on. Your computer won't seem like such a stranger because you'll find out what's inside it.

A word of caution to begin with: You may not need to delve into all the hardware details described in this chapter. The OpenLinux installation wizard (affectionately called the Lizard) is fairly sharp and may do everything for you without much effort on your part. Still, this chapter helps you find out about your hardware so that you'll be prepared to handle any hiccups along the way.

We'd like to dispel a myth that Linux is more difficult to install than Microsoft Windows. Experience shows that OpenLinux is no harder to install than any other operating system — and considerably easier than many.

I've tried on several occasions to install Windows 95 from the beginning and have met with frustration over plug-and-play (often considered plug-and-pray) hardware components or drivers that were always on the "other" floppy disk (no matter which floppy disk I had). Windows *seems* easy to install because it's usually preinstalled, most people only update it, and people who do install Windows have the hardware documentation.

You can buy OpenLinux preinstalled if you prefer. Then all you do is turn it on. If that's how you obtain the OpenLinux operating system, then OpenLinux is as easy to "install" as Windows!

The next easiest way to install OpenLinux is to buy OpenLinux preinstalled on a hard disk. You then put the hard disk in your system, boot the system, and OpenLinux is installed.

If you're the rare reader who buys a system simply for OpenLinux, then look up a hardware supplier on the World Wide Web or in a Linux magazine and ask the supplier to build a system for you.

If you're like most readers, however, you

- ✔ Want to install OpenLinux on your existing hardware
- ✔ Want to use your existing hard disks
- ✔ Want to keep MS-DOS, or Windows, or both, on your system

Installing OpenLinux on your existing system is the most difficult type of installation. Don't worry, though, because we're here to guide you through it.

Hardware Supported by OpenLinux

Generally, OpenLinux runs on any Intel or compatible processor that is a 386 or newer (including AMD K6 and Cyrix chips). Most systems are Pentium-class (586), which is great, but if you still have an old 386SX system lying around, you can install OpenLinux on it and create a router, e-mail server, or something more useful than a doorstop (which is all a 386 can do without Linux).

OpenLinux supports *symmetric multiprocessing (SMP),* which means you can have more than one CPU inside one computer. In fact, OpenLinux supports several processors per system box. If your system has more than one CPU, OpenLinux can utilize those CPUs also, either by speeding up a specific program written to take advantage of multiple CPUs or by allowing more programs to execute at one time.

But the processor isn't the only piece of hardware that you need to know something about before you install OpenLinux. You also should know about the items in the following list:

- ✔ **RAM:** Without graphics, OpenLinux runs very well with 32MB. With graphics, OpenLinux runs (er, walks) with 16MB; with 32MB, the graphics get much faster. With 64MB, OpenLinux screams, and the speed of applications (particularly graphics-oriented programs) increases dramatically.

  Some OpenLinux developers have 128MB in their systems, because they tend to run many programs at a time, and each program takes a certain amount of RAM when running. This amount of memory isn't necessary for most users, but is always nice to have. After all, you can never be too rich or have too much hardware backing you up.

✔ **Hard disk:** An OpenLinux minimal installation requires about 200MB of hard disk space, but for the standard installation (which includes the graphical desktop interface) you need about 650MB. By the time you install all the goodies, such as WordPerfect, a few games and utilities, and other stuff you download from the Internet, you'll be glad if you have a total of 1GB or more to hold it all. When considering whether your system needs more hard-disk space or more RAM, remember that as a general rule, more is usually better.

Available space isn't the only hard-disk issue you should be aware of. You also need to know how many hard drives you have, and what is each drive's size and order (which one is first, second, and so on?). We discuss other hard-disk concerns in "Disk drives," later in this chapter.

✔ **Disk controllers:** How many do you have, and what are their types (IDE, SCSI)? Which hard-disk drives are connected to which controllers? If a SCSI controller is installed in your machine, what is its make and model number? We discuss this in greater detail in "Disk controllers," later in this chapter.

✔ **CD-ROM:** You usually install OpenLinux from a CD-ROM by booting your computer directly from the CD-ROM drive. OpenLinux can detect and use standard IDE/ATAPI and SCSI CD-ROM drives (the device interfaces found in most recent computers), as well as most of the early, non-IDE drives that attached directly to sound cards and other devices.

Some computers don't allow you to boot from a CD-ROM drive, so you have to create a floppy diskette to boot the Linux installation or use one of the other methods described in the following sections.

✔ **Mouse:** What type of mouse do you have — a bus mouse, a PS/2 mouse, or a serial mouse? How many buttons does your mouse have? If you have a serial mouse, which COM port is it attached to and what protocol does it use (such as Microsoft or Logitech)? The installation program normally detects your mouse, but you may have to select a serial port if the mouse cannot be detected.

✔ **Monitor:** What is the make and model of the monitor? You can normally choose your monitor from a very large list of monitor manufacturers and models. If yours is not listed, you need to know the monitor's vertical and horizontal refresh rates.

✔ **Video card:** What is the make and model number of the video card or video-chip set and the amount of video RAM? OpenLinux supports hundreds of video cards. Even if your card isn't supported directly, OpenLinux may support your card as a VGA, XGA, SVGA, or other graph-ical hardware standard video card. Most video cards that have been available for a while are supported, and many of the latest models include at least basic support (although support for some of the fancy 3D features may be missing on some cards).

OpenLinux also supports a variety of keyboards, sound cards, serial line cards (for attaching a lot of serial printers or modems to a system), and other peripherals. The hardware components supported by the OpenLinux product on your *Caldera OpenLinux For Dummies* CD-ROM are listed in Appendix A.

To install OpenLinux on some systems, you may not need any of the information in the preceding list; for other systems, you need most or all this information. Of course, you can attempt an installation first and see if you're missing things you need to know. Just in case, the last half of this chapter delves a bit more into how to locate and capture the information that you need.

You can install OpenLinux, after booting from an OpenLinux boot diskette, by copying files over the network. This method of copying files is a viable way of installing OpenLinux on local area networks used at colleges or businesses or if you have a friend who has an OpenLinux system, a CD-ROM drive, and a networking card the same as yours. However, if the network is not fast (that is, the network can't transfer lots of data quickly), then the easiest way to install OpenLinux is by using a CD-ROM drive attached to your system.

You can install OpenLinux on a notebook or laptop computer by using the notebook's built-in CD-ROM drive (if it has one), a CD-ROM drive attached to the notebook's docking station, or a SCSI CD-ROM drive attached to a PCMCIA (Personal Computer Memory Card Interface Adapter) SCSI controller. If you don't have any of these, you can try to get a PCMCIA Ethernet controller and do a network installation, as long as another OpenLinux system on the network has a CD-ROM drive installed to provide the data to your laptop.

Laptops before PCMCIA support

Early laptops had no built-in CD-ROMs; and before Linux had PCMCIA support, Linux had to be installed by using floppies. Imagine sorting out 100 or more floppy diskettes containing all the data on a CD-ROM. Some later laptops that didn't allow the floppy and CD-ROM drives to be installed at the same time weren't much better for installing Linux.

I still remember the day I got both my new notebook and the new release of Linux that had

PCMCIA support. I ran out and bought a PCMCIA SCSI controller that night, so I could use my SCSI CD-ROM to do the installation. My life has been better ever since. Having used floppies to install Linux on various notebooks — not once or twice, but seven times — I would have paid ten times that amount for the PCMCIA card.

Hard disk controllers

The two main types of hard disks are IDE and SCSI, and each type has its own controller. IDE is more common in PCs, and newer PCs usually have two IDE controllers rather than one. For each IDE controller, your system can have only two hard disks: a master and a slave. Therefore, a PC with two IDE controllers can have up to four hard disks. You should know which hard disk is connected to which controller, and which is the master and the slave hard disk on each controller. Also, if you have a Windows system that you want to preserve, you should know the partition number and IDE device where Windows is stored. Normally, on a Windows system:

✔ The first controller's master hard disk is called C.

✔ The next hard disk is called D and is the slave disk on the first controller.

✔ The next hard disk is E and is the master hard disk on the second controller. (A CD-ROM drive that uses the IDE/ATAPI interface is often the first device on the second IDE controller.)

✔ The last hard disk is called F and is the slave disk on the second controller.

Normally, Windows is located on your C hard disk, and data is on your other hard disks. However, this lettering scheme is just one possibility; your hard disks could be set up differently and even include CD-ROMs as drives on your IDE controllers, as mentioned in the preceding list.

Some high-end PCs have a SCSI controller on the motherboard or on a separate SCSI controller board, either in addition to or instead of the IDE controllers. Older SCSI controllers can have up to eight devices on them, numbered 0–7, including the controller. Newer SCSI controllers (known as wide controllers) can have up to 16 devices, including the controller itself.

If you only have a SCSI hard disk, then usually your C disk is disk 0 or disk 1 and any others disks follow in order.

If you have a mixture of IDE and SCSI controllers, then your C disk can be on any of the controllers. Later in this chapter the sections, "Getting Information from Windows 95/98" and "Getting Information from MS-DOS or Windows 3.1," show you how to identify the number of hard disks that you have, what type of hard disks they are, and the controllers to which the hard disks are attached.

Disk drives

You need to decide if you want to put OpenLinux on a separate hard disk from MS-DOS and Windows or have the two operating systems share one disk.

Most people think of Windows (either Windows 3.1, Windows 95, or Windows 98) as an operating system. The later versions, such as Windows 98 and Windows 2000, simply try to hide the fact that MS-DOS is running things behind the scenes, managing the disks and most other hardware components of your PC. From here on, unless we mention a particular system, consider MS-DOS and all versions of Windows to be the same thing.

Windows NT is another matter, because it doesn't use MS-DOS underneath the graphical interface. Also, Windows NT uses different methods of controlling your PC hardware. Still, you may be able to use some of the steps outlined in this chapter to use Windows NT to discover information about your PC.

Different hardware systems have different ways to enter the BIOS setup. Usually, you can enter the BIOS setup when you turn on the power and start to boot, or when you press the Reset button on the front of the system and start to reboot, or when you go through the normal shutdown of your Windows system and then ask the system to reboot.

If you decide to purchase a second hard disk on which you will install OpenLinux, put the new disk as the second disk on the first IDE controller or as disk 1 on your SCSI controller, assuming that your existing Windows disk is either the first disk on your IDE controller or ID 0 on your SCSI controller. Adding disks is a hardware thing; the folks where you buy the disk should be able to add the disk to your system for you. And while you're there, you can ask them to tell you the details about the other hardware in your system.

If you've taken apart your computer looking for other information (a pox on manufacturers who don't supply such useful information), you may as well write down all the disk information you can find. You can look for the number of heads, cylinders, and sectors. This information is used to tell the operating system where to put data with respect to the beginning of the disk. If you have trouble, then check out the "Getting Information from Windows 95/98" and "Getting Information from MS-DOS or Windows 3.1" sections later in this chapter. SCSI disk users don't have to supply this information because the SCSI controller and device drivers calculate the information on-the-fly. SCSI disk owners should, however, know the size of their disks, which is printed on the disks or is available through the sections just mentioned.

Finding Out What You Have

An extremely useful preliminary step for a successful installation of OpenLinux is identifying the type of hardware that you have. You can find most of this information in the manuals that came with your computer, but the manuals won't be much help if

- ✔ You threw the manuals out.
- ✔ You lost the manuals.
- ✔ You bought your computer secondhand from someone who threw away or lost the documentation.
- ✔ You bought your PC with Windows already installed (so it included almost zero useful documentation).

The last reason is the most insidious, because it means the company you bought the PC from didn't bother to buy the documentation for each part of the PC when assembling it for you. That would have cost the company more money. Instead the company used OEM parts (read that "sans documentation and colorful box") and bought only one copy of the documentation for its use. With Windows already installed, the company reasons, "Why would an end user need any documentation about the system?"

Contact the company where you bought your system. Perhaps you can obtain a copy of the documentation from the dealer.

If that doesn't work, open your system and look at its components. For instance, one source of information about your disk is the label on top of the disk drive. If you don't feel comfortable opening your system, then you may want to take the system back to where you bought it — assuming you didn't buy it by mail order — and perhaps the dealer can open the system and tell you what you have.

You can also look to the World Wide Web for information. Many vendors use their Web sites to provide technical data about their devices. To find information about your device, you need to know your equipment's manufacturer, make, and model number.

Another source of information is either Windows 95 or Windows 98. Step-by-step instructions in the following sections show you exactly how to use these operating systems to get all the information you need.

If you don't have any literature about your system, and you don't have Windows on your system (perhaps you like to run FAT free), and no dealer is within hundreds of miles of your system, don't give up hope. OpenLinux is good at sniffing out and identifying hardware during installation.

Getting Information from Windows 95/98

If you have Windows 95 or Windows 98, you can use the msd program in MS-DOS mode, as described in the next section, to find out about the hardware in your system. Much more information is available, however, through the Control Panel in Windows 95 or Windows 98. The Steps that follow are designed for a Windows 98 system, with notes to help you accomplish the same task on Windows 95.

With pencil and paper handy, it's time to access the Windows Control Panel and all that information. Follow along with these steps:

1. **Click Start⇨Settings⇨Control Panel.**

   That's a shorthand method we use that means, "Click the Start button, then click the Settings menu item, and then click the Control Panel item."

2. **Double-click the System icon.**

   The System Properties dialog box opens.

3. **Click the Device Manager tab.**

4. **At the top of the screen, select the View devices by connection option.**

   This view shows all the components and how they relate to each other. The screen looks similar to Figure 3-1.

   If you have a printer attached to your system, then you now can click Print on the Device Manager tab. Then in the Print dialog box that appears, select the All devices and system summary option. Click OK. This procedure prints a full report about your system. You may not have all the information you need, such as which hard disk goes with which controller, but you'll save yourself a lot of writing.

5. **In the list, click Computer.**

6. **Click the Properties button.**

   The Computer Properties dialog box appears.

7. **Select the View Resources tab of the Computer Properties dialog box.**

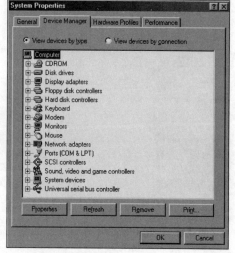

Figure 3-1:
Use the
Device
Manager
tab to
discover
hardware
details.

8. **Click to select the Interrupt request (IRQ) option and write down the displayed information.**

   The left column, Setting, lists interrupt requests, as shown in Figure 3-2. The hardware using a particular IRQ is listed in the right column. Note that no two devices can use the same IRQ.

9. **At the top of the screen, click to select the Direct memory access (DMA) option and copy the displayed information.**

10. **At the top of the screen, click the Input/output (I/O) option and copy the pertinent information.**

    Look for and write down entries regarding a sound card (if you have one) and a parallel port (LPT).

11. **Click Cancel.**

    You are returned to the Device Manager tab of the System Properties dialog box.

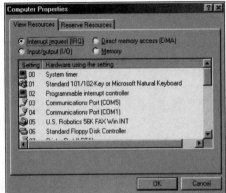

Figure 3-2:
Viewing
interrupt
request
(IRQ)
numbers.

Now you need to find out about the other devices in your system. This process takes some time, so you may want to pause here and grab something to drink, fix something to eat, and put on some tunes before following these steps:

1. **On the Device Manager tab of the System Properties dialog box, select the View devices by type option.**

   In the list, notice how a plus or minus sign precedes some icons. A plus sign indicates that the entry is collapsed. A minus sign indicates the entry is expanded to show all subentries.

2. **In the list, make sure that all items are expanded, as shown in Figure 3-3.**

   Expanded simply means that a minus sign precedes the icon. If a plus sign appears instead, click it, and the plus sign changes to a minus sign. As you expand some entries, you may see more plus signs. Click each plus sign to expand the item. You may need to use the scroll bar to the right of the window to bring additional items into view.

3. **Look through the list for Standard IDE/ESDI Hard Disk Controller or SCSI Host Adapter.**

   Write down the complete label, which tells you what type of hard disk controller you are currently investigating.

4. **Look at the first subentry under the IDE hard disk controller or SCSI adapter you have selected (if a subentry is shown). Write down the type of disk. Now double-click that disk entry.**

   The General tab of the Properties dialog box for that device appears.

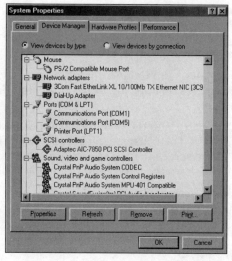

Figure 3-3:
If upper-
level entries
are
preceded
by a minus
sign, as
they are
here,
you can
see their
subentries.

Note: If the controller has no entries, don't despair. Some systems have extra hard disk controllers (particularly if you are using SCSI hard disks) that aren't connected to any hard disks. Also, be aware that the first con- troller may have some other type of device connected to it, such as a tape drive or a CD-ROM. If no hard disks are attached to this IDE con- troller or SCSI adapter, simply go on to the next IDE or SCSI item in the list of devices.

5. **Click the Settings tab, write down the drive type, and then click Cancel.**

   The screen returns to the Device Manager tab of the System Properties dialog box.

6. **Write down the highlighted information, which is the type of hard disk.**

7. **For each hard disk subentry for that controller, repeat Steps 4 through 6.**

8. **Follow the same general steps for any other hard-disk controller entries.**

9. **For the Display adapters entry, simply write down each subentry.**

   Don't bother clicking Properties because it won't supply you with any useful information for installing Linux.

10. **For the Keyboard entry, write down each subentry.**

11. **Likewise for the Monitor entry.**

12. **Like-likewise for the Mouse entry.**

13. **Like-like-likewise for the Ports (COM & LPT) entry.**

14. **Finally, for the Sound, Video, and Game Controllers entry, copy the information that appears on both the General tab and the Resources tab.**

    Double-click the first subentry, and the General tab appears (as usual). Write down the information. Then, instead of clicking Cancel, click Resources at the top of the screen to display the Resources tab, as shown in Figure 3-4. Write down the information and then click Cancel.

15. **Back on the Device Manager tab, click Cancel.**

    The screen returns to the Control Panel.

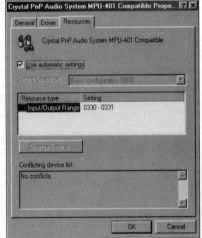

Figure 3-4:
The Resources tab of the Sound, Video, and Game Controllers entry.

Whew. That was a lot of copying, and you aren't finished yet. Follow these steps for fascinating facts about your monitor:

1. **Make sure that the Control Panel is displayed.**

    If it isn't, choose Start⇨Settings⇨Control Panel.

2. **Double-click the Display icon.**

    The Display Properties dialog box appears.

3. **Click the Settings tab.**

    The screen displays your monitor's settings.

4. Copy the information under Color and Screen Area.

If you're using Windows 95, the information is labeled Color Palette and Desktop Area.

The Color information is High Color (16 bit) or True Color (24 bit). The Desktop Area information is 640x480 pixels, 800x600 pixels, 1,024x768 pixels, or some higher numbers.

Windows 95 also has options for 16 color and 256 color.

5. Click Cancel.

You return to the Control Panel.

And now, it's time to check the time:

1. In the Control Panel, click the Date/Time icon.

The Date/Time Properties dialog box appears.

2. Click the Time Zone tab.

3. Copy the text at the top of the screen.

The text begins with *GMT,* which stands for Greenwich Mean Time, which is the world standard. The number after GMT indicates the difference between your time and the GMT. Be sure to copy the words that indicate your time zone, such as Eastern Time (United States and Canada).

4. Click Cancel.

Tired of this yet? You're almost finished. Next, you discover delightful details about your printer:

1. In the Control Panel, click the Printers icon.

2. Double-click to select the first non-networked Printer icon (one without a wire underneath it).

Another window appears. This new window has the same name as the printer you double-clicked. Don't click the icon labeled Add Printer.

3. In the menu bar at the top of the window, choose Printer⇨Properties and then click the Details tab.

4. Copy the make and model and the communications port that the printer is attached to.

The make and model appears at the top of the screen, next to the printer icon. The communications port is listed after Print to the Following Port.

5. Click Cancel.

6. **Double-click the next Printer icon and repeat Steps 3 through 5.**

   If you have only one printer, then skip this step.

7. **Close any open windows by clicking the Close button.**

   The Close button is the one with the X in the upper-right corner of a window.

The following — we promise — is the last set of steps. Here's how you get the hard facts about your hard drives:

1. **Double-click the My Computer icon on the Windows 98 desktop.**

2. **Select the first hard drive by clicking its icon. Copy down the capacity and the free space remaining.**

3. **Repeat Step 2 for all other hard drives.**

This information will be useful later as you make decisions about how much space to leave for Windows 98 (if any) and how much space you have for OpenLinux on each hard disk.

Getting Information from MS-DOS or Windows 3.1

If you're running MS-DOS or Windows 3.1, you have a program on your system called Microsoft Diagnostics, or msd. This program gives you information about the hardware on your system, which you can use to determine how to set up OpenLinux.

If you have a printer attached to your system, then you're in luck. You can avoid writer's cramp by following these steps:

1. **Make sure that your system is in DOS or MS-DOS mode.**

   If you've just booted, then you may already be in MS-DOS mode. The screen will be mostly black with a prompt like this c:\>.

   If you've booted and are in Microsoft Windows 3.1, then press Alt+F+X, which exits Windows and returns you to DOS. Then you see the c:\> prompt.

2. **Type msd to start the program.**

   The main screen appears, with categories such as computer and memory, as shown in Figure 3-5.

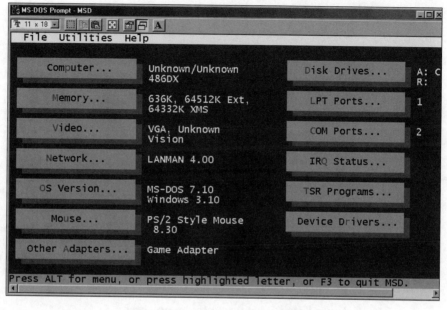

Figure 3-5:
The
Microsoft
Diagnostics
program's
initial
screen.

3. **Press Alt+F+P.**

4. **Press the spacebar and select Report All.**

5. **Press the Tab key until the cursor is in the Print To: section.**

6. **Use the up and down arrow keys on the keyboard to select the port your printer is attached to or to create a file to hold the information.**

7. **Press Tab until the cursor is on the OK button.**

8. **Press the Enter key.**

9. **Fill in the Customer Information, if you want.**

10. **Press the Tab key until the cursor is on the OK button.**

11. **Press the Enter key to print the report or create the file.**

If you're creating a file, then you may want to press the Tab key to move to the text box that contains the name of the file that will be holding the report and change the file extension to .txt, so that the file will be easier to print later from Windows.

Although you may not get all the information you need from this printout, you get a great deal of information, which is probably more accurate than recording the information by hand.

If you don't have a printer, then grab some paper and your favorite pen or pencil and prepare to copy some information:

1. **Make sure that your system is in DOS or MS-DOS mode.**

   See Step 1 in the preceding set of steps for more information.

2. **Type** msd **to start the program.**

   The main screen appears, with categories such as computer and memory (refer to Figure 3-5).

3. **Press P (for processor) and then copy the information on the screen.**

   The screen displays the type of processor in your system (usually a 386, 486, or some other type of Intel chip).

4. **Press Enter to return to the main screen.**

5. **Press V (for video screen) and then copy the displayed information.**

   You see your system's video adapter type (usually VGA, XGA, or SVGA). Also look for the display type (such as VGA Color or SVGA Color), manufacturer, and video BIOS version. Pay particular attention to the video BIOS version because this version may also list the computer chip set used to make the video controller, which in turn is used to set up the graphical part of Linux.

6. **Press Enter to return to the main screen.**

7. **Press N (for network) and then copy the displayed information.**

   If your system has no networking capability or none that msd knows about, you may see a message that says no network.

8. **Press Enter.**

9. **Press U (for mouse) and then copy the displayed information.**

   Look for entries for mouse hardware, the driver manufacturer, the DOS driver type, and the number of mouse buttons. Well, you don't really need to refer to the screen to figure out that last one.

10. **Press Enter.**

11. **Press D (for disk drives) and copy the pertinent information.**

    Now it gets interesting, as you can see in Figure 3-6. Copy your floppy drive's capacity and number of cylinders. (For a floppy drive, these values are usually 1.44MB and 80 cylinders, respectively.) Then look for your hard disk drives, usually designated as C, D, E, and so on. Each disk drive should have a Total Size entry and a number, such as 400M, which stands for 400 megabytes. You should also see an entry, such as CMOS Fixed Disk Parameters, followed by something like 731 Cylinders, 13 heads, 26 sectors/track. This information is useful when setting up your hard disks for OpenLinux.

12. **Press Enter.**

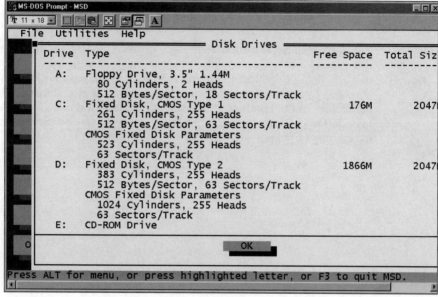

13. **Press L (for parallel ports) and then write down the pertinent information.**

    The screen displays entries, such as LPT1 and LPT2. OpenLinux usually finds out about these ports all by itself. In case it doesn't, then write down the port address, which is usually a number, such as 0378H.

14. **Press Enter.**

15. **Press C (for the COM ports) and then write down the pertinent information.**

    The COM ports are your serial ports, which are typically used for a modem, a serial printer, and other interesting gadgets. Copy the port address, baud rate, parity, data bits, stop bits, and UART chip used. Usually, you don't need any of this information for OpenLinux but having a complete record of your system is useful.

16. **Press Enter.**

17. **Press Q (for IRQ list) and then copy the information.**

    IRQ, which stands for *interrupt request,* is used by the different hardware pieces to signal the main CPU that some data needs to be processed.

    No two devices can have the same IRQ. Copying the information in these columns for all 16 IRQs (0–15) is important for later sanity.

18. **Press Enter to return to the main screen and then press F3 to end the msd program.**

Leave a Trail of Bread Crumbs

 This next step is very important: Back up your system! Follow your system's directions for making a backup disk that includes your master boot record, or MBR. If you're concerned about how to back up your entire system, at least copy your most valuable files to a floppy diskette, network server, or someplace out of reach of the OpenLinux installation program. The Installation program is smart, but you don't want to be overly trusting when everything on your system is at stake.

Chapter 4

Making Room for OpenLinux

In This Chapter
▶ Creating your Install and Modules disks
▶ Squeezing OpenLinux onto your disk
▶ Finding out what you need to install from a CD-ROM

*N*ow's the time to open your copy of OpenLinux — unless you're the impatient type and have already ripped it from its packaging. If you have a boxed copy of Caldera Systems OpenLinux or are using the copy on the *Caldera OpenLinux For Dummies* CD-ROM, the installation should work almost exactly as described here.

To install OpenLinux you must take care of two things:

✔ Make room for the OpenLinux operating system
✔ Launch the OpenLinux installation program

This chapter gently guides you through both processes.

Move Over and Make Room for OpenLinux

Before you can install OpenLinux on your system, you need to make room for it. Some people find space by getting rid of Microsoft Windows altogether. Others don't want to make such drastic changes and prefer to have both OpenLinux and their other operating system peacefully coexist. If having both systems fits the bill for you, your easiest way to have both systems is to add a new hard disk — either IDE or SCSI — to your system and then install OpenLinux on the new hard disk.

If you don't want to get rid of your current operating system and can't add another hard disk to your system, you need to make some free space on the hard disk containing Microsoft Windows so that the hard disk can also contain OpenLinux. Freeing space on your hard disk takes a few extra steps up front but is commonly done and doesn't cause any problems with either operating system.

The basic idea process that you use to free space on your hard disk is to

 ✓ Defragment your hard disk so that all the free space is collected at the end of the disk.

 ✓ Cut off the free space so that the free space can be used for OpenLinux.

 ✓ Mark the free space as a Linux file system.

You can alter the space allocated to each operating system on your hard disk by using standard tools in Windows or OpenLinux. But under normal circumstances, changing the space allocation, or partitions, on your hard disk erases everything on the hard disk. This is called *destructive repartitioning*. We assume that you don't want to use this method, because it requires you to back up and later restore your entire Windows system. So, we describe two methods of *nondestructive repartitioning* that let you rearrange how the space on your hard disk is used for different operating systems without wiping out all the data on the hard disk.

You can choose from two methods of nondestructive repartitioning of your hard disk:

 ✓ Using commercial disk repartitioning software, such as the PartitionMagic CE utility that we discuss in the next section. Unfortunately, PartitionMagic is available only if you've purchased a commercial (boxed) copy of OpenLinux.

 ✓ Manually repartitioning the hard disk. This method (the one we both use regularly) relies on the free utilities that come with the *Caldera OpenLinux For Dummies* CD. (See "Manual repartitioning" later in this chapter.)

Before performing any major work on restructuring your disk — as you're about to do — backing up your system in case something goes wrong is always wise. You don't want to lose any data or programs that you worked hard to install. Please refer to your system's owners' manual to find out how to back up your system (and how to restore the data if necessary). We can't stress this point strongly enough. Unfortunately, deciding to back up data after a catastrophic problem has occurred is too late.

Use some magic on your hard disk

Rearranging all the data on your hard disk can be an intimidating task. You start with a working system but you're never quite sure if you're going to end up with a working system, especially the first time you try these antics.

To make things a little easier on everyone, Caldera Systems worked with a world-class disk-utility company called PowerQuest. PowerQuest produces a disk-partitioning tool called PartitionMagic. Together PowerQuest and Caldera Systems created a special version of PartitionMagic called CE (Caldera Edition). By using this utility you can squeeze an existing Microsoft Windows partition and make everything ready to install OpenLinux without even breaking a sweat.

Unfortunately, the PartitionMagic CE utility is a commercial package that's only included in the boxed version of OpenLinux. If you have the boxed version of OpenLinux, you can follow these steps to use PartitionMagic CE.

1. **Start Microsoft Windows and insert the commercial OpenLinux CD in your drive.**

   A menu appears, as shown in Figure 4-1.

2. **Choose Install Products.**

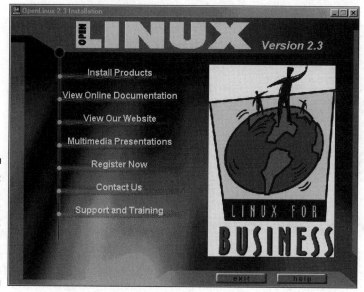

Figure 4-1:
You can
start the
OpenLinux
installation
from within
Windows.

3. **Choose Install PartitionMagic CE.**

   The PartitionMagic CE utility is installed on your Windows partition. This process works just like any other Windows program that you've installed.

4. **Choose Programs⇨OpenLinux⇨Launch PartitionMagic CE from the Windows Start menu.**

5. **Follow the on-screen instructions to prepare your system for a reboot. Then let PartitionMagic CE reboot your system.**

   The PartitionMagic CE screen, shown in Figure 4-2, appears as the system reboots.

6. **Choose a partition size on the right side of the screen.**

7. **Choose OK to repartition your Windows system so that OpenLinux can be installed.**

   After your system reboots, you have a Linux-formatted partition that's ready to use for the installation. Skip ahead to "Launching the Installation" to do just that.

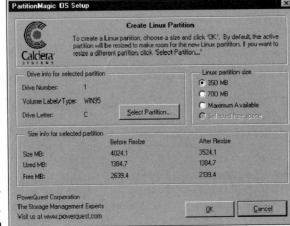

Figure 4-2: PartitionMagic CE provides a graphical interface to repartition your hard disk for OpenLinux.

Manual repartitioning

You can use the tools on your *Caldera OpenLinux For Dummies* CD to set up a separate partition for OpenLinux on your Microsoft Windows PC. To set up a separate partition for OpenLinux, first defragment your Windows partition, and then use a utility called FIPS to make some free space for OpenLinux.

Although FIPS is supposed to be nondestructive, make sure that you always back up your system and defragment your hard disk before using FIPS.

The FIPS utility works by dividing the drive into two partitions. The first partition is the DOS partition that the existing Microsoft Windows operating system will continue to use. The second partition, beginning at the end of the space used by Windows software and encompassing the rest of the drive space, is the non-DOS partition where OpenLinux will be installed.

Defragmenting

Follow these steps in Windows 95 or Windows 98 to defragment the hard disk on which you want to install OpenLinux. (This process is sometimes called optimizing the hard disk.)

1. **Close all programs and windows on your system, leaving only the desktop and icon bar.**

2. **Double-click the My Computer icon on the desktop.**

3. **Click C disk.**

4. **Choose File⇨Properties.**

   The Properties dialog box appears.

5. **Choose the Tools tab in the dialog box.**

6. **Click Defragment Now.**

   You may get a message telling you it's not necessary to defragment because your disk is not very fragmented. Under normal circumstances this may be true, but in this case it's necessary to defragment your disk because you're going to move the end of the file system and make it smaller. Any data outside that barrier is lost, so you have to move the barrier closer to the front.

7. **Click Start.**

   The defragmentation window appears.

8. **Click Show Details.**

   The defragmentation takes some time to finish. As the defragmentation continues, you can scroll up and down the large window watching the progress (represented by different colored blocks). You can expect to see white space appearing toward the bottom of the window, which represents the end of your disk and shows that the data is being moved forward on the disk. At the end of the defragmentation process, no colored blocks should appear at the bottom of the window, instead all the blocks should be compressed toward the top of the window. The colored blocks represent programs and data, and the white space is free space in your file system that you now may allocate to the OpenLinux file system.

FIPS

After you move the data in your Microsoft Windows partition as far as possible to the front of the partition, you can use the FIPS program to shrink the Windows partition.

Because FIPS works with low-level hard-drive operations, you can't run FIPS directly in Microsoft Windows. Instead, copy the FIPS program onto your Windows hard disk so that the FIPS program is accessible without using the CD. Assuming that your CD-ROM drive is D:, use standard copy procedures in Windows to copy the file D:\col\tools\fips\fips.exe to the root of your Windows partition (C:\). You can use your Microsoft Windows Explorer windows to drag and drop the file or use a DOS command like this:

```
copy D:\col\tools\fips\fips.exe C:\
```

After you've made FIPS available on the Windows partition, the next step is to shut down your Windows system so that you're in MS-DOS mode. The easiest way to change to MS-DOS mode is as follows:

1. **Click the Start button.**

2. **Click Shut Down.**

3. **Select the Restart the Computer in MS-DOS Mode option.**

4. **Click the Yes button.**

   As soon as the computer restarts, your system's in MS-DOS mode.

Next, you begin the process of starting the FIPS program and shrinking the Windows partition. This process involves quite a few steps, but each step is simple:

1. **Type** cd \ **and press Enter.**

2. **Type** FIPS **and press Enter.**

   Some messages appear, but you can ignore them — well, ignore all but the following message.

3. **As soon as you get the message to press any key, then press any key.**

   You see all the existing partitions on the disk.

4. **After you get another message to press any key, then again press any key.**

   You're getting pretty good at this. You see a description of the disk and a series of messages. Then FIPS finds the free space in the first partition.

5. **After you're asked whether you want to make a backup copy of sectors, type** y **for yes.**

   The screen asks whether a floppy disk is in drive A.

6. **Place a formatted floppy disk into drive A and then press y.**

   A message similar to "Writing file a:\rootboot.000" appears, followed by other messages, and then the message "Use cursor key to choose the cylinder, enter to continue" appears.

   Three columns appear on the screen: Old Partition, Cylinder, and New Partition. The Old Partition number is the number of megabytes in the main partition of your disk. The Cylinder number indicates the position on the hard disk marking the division of the two partitions that you're creating. The New Partition number is the number of megabytes in the new partition that you're making for the OpenLinux operating system.

7. **Use the left and right arrow keys to change the numbers in the Old Partition and New Partition fields to give you the space you need for both the Microsoft operating system and OpenLinux.**

   A minimum OpenLinux installation — without X Window System (the graphical environment) — requires about 200MB of disk space. A standard installation requires about 580MB of disk space. The full distribution (along with all the programs and compilers on the disk) requires about 1,400MB of disk space. (Whew!) Add to the amount of disk space that you need for OpenLinux, the amount of data space that you need for your own files and additional applications. The amount of data space that you leave for the OpenLinux and Microsoft Windows operating systems is up to you.

8. **After you have the correct amount of disk space in each field, press Enter.**

   FIPS displays the partition table again, showing you the new partition that has been created for the OpenLinux operating system. This partition will probably be partition 2; your Windows C: drive is probably partition 1.

   You also see a message at the bottom of the screen asking whether you want to continue or to reedit.

9. **If you are *not* satisfied with the size of your OpenLinux and Microsoft Windows partitions, type r, which takes you back to Step 7. Otherwise, type c to continue.**

   You see a lot more messages about your disk. Then a message appears stating that the system is ready to write the new partition scheme to disk and asking whether you want to proceed.

10. **Type y, and FIPS writes the new partition information to the disk.**

    If you type **n**, FIPS exits without changing anything on your disk. Your disk is exactly the way the disk was after you defragmented it.

11. **To test that the nondestructive partitioning worked properly, reboot your system by pressing Ctrl+Alt+Delete.**

12. **Allow Windows to start, and then run Scandisk, checking all your folders and files.**

    Scandisk indicates whether you have all the files and folders you started with and whether anything was lost.

Remember those backup files of your important Windows information that you created before using FIPS? Although everything may appear to have gone perfectly, keep those backup files around for a while.

Now you're ready to launch the OpenLinux installation.

Launching the Installation

You can launch the OpenLinux installation in several ways. You can

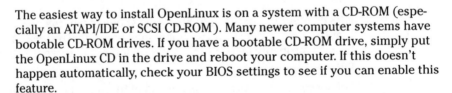

✔ Boot the *Caldera OpenLinux For Dummies* CD-ROM directly by restarting your computer (this only works if you have a bootable CD-ROM drive).

✔ Use the "Boot from Windows" feature on the OpenLinux CD-ROM.

   You can't use the above method if you're running Windows NT.

✔ Create an Install disk and a Modules disk and boot your computer from these disks.

The easiest way to install OpenLinux is on a system with a CD-ROM (especially an ATAPI/IDE or SCSI CD-ROM). Many newer computer systems have bootable CD-ROM drives. If you have a bootable CD-ROM drive, simply put the OpenLinux CD in the drive and reboot your computer. If this doesn't happen automatically, check your BIOS settings to see if you can enable this feature.

If you don't have a bootable CD-ROM drive, you can start the installation from Windows or you must create an Install floppy and a Modules floppy from the CD files.

Boot the installation from Windows

If you want to install both Microsoft Windows and OpenLinux on the same computer, then this method to start the installation works great. Just follow these steps:

1. **While running Microsoft Windows, insert the *Caldera OpenLinux For Dummies* CD (or another copy of OpenLinux that you've purchased).**

   After a moment a menu window appears on your Windows screen (refer to Figure 4-1).

2. **Select Install Products from the menu.**

   Another menu appears.

3. **Choose Launch Linux Install (loadlin).**

4. **Follow the instructions on screen to reboot your computer.**

   The OpenLinux installation that's described in Chapter 5 starts automatically.

Boot the installation from a floppy disk

You almost always can boot a computer from a floppy disk, so this method is the last resort. This method takes more effort but is sure to work. In addition, if you want to prepare disks to install OpenLinux on a system that's not loaded with Windows and doesn't have a bootable CD-ROM drive, then this option is your only option.

If you bought a commercial (boxed) copy of OpenLinux, you probably have the disks already in hand.

Creating the Install and Modules disks in Windows

You can make the Install and Modules disks in Windows or in another Linux system that's already running. To make the Install and Modules disks in Windows, be sure to have two formatted 3½-inch disks and then follow these instructions:

1. **Start Microsoft Windows.**

2. **Insert the *Caldera OpenLinux For Dummies* CD in your CD-ROM drive.**

   After a moment, a menu screen automatically appears.

3. **Choose Install Products from the menu.**

   Another menu appears.

4. **Choose Create Floppy Install Diskettes.**

   Yet another menu appears, as shown in Figure 4-3.

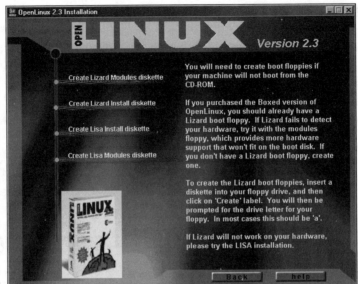

Figure 4-3:
Make Install
and
Modules
diskettes in
Microsoft
Windows by
using this
menu from
the *Caldera
OpenLinux
For
Dummies*
CD.

5. **Insert one of your 3½-inch disks into the floppy drive.**

6. **Choose Create Lizard Install diskette.**

   Another window opens asking you for the destination drive. Normally this drive is "a" for drive A:.

7. **Type a and press Enter.**

   OpenLinux creates the Install disk for you. (This process takes several minutes.)

8. **Insert your other 3½-inch disk into the floppy drive and return to Steps 6 and 7, this time selecting Create Lizard Modules diskette.**

   After you've created both disks, choose Exit on the menu to close the OpenLinux program in Windows.

The menu items in the preceding procedure use a DOS program called RAWRITE.EXE. You can use this program directly in DOS or in an MS-DOS box in Windows if you prefer. The RAWRITE.EXE command is located in the \col\launch\floppy subdirectory on the *Caldera OpenLinux For Dummies* CD.

After you've got your floppy disks, you're ready to turn to Chapter 5 and install the OpenLinux operating system.

Creating the Install and Modules disks in Linux

If you don't have access to Windows but do have access to another Linux system, create the Install and Modules disks in Linux instead. To make the Install and Modules disks in Linux, you must be logged in as a user with permissions to write to the 3½-inch drive, which Linux refers to as /dev/fd0.

To make the Install disk, follow these steps:

1. **Put a blank, formatted floppy in the floppy drive.**

2. **Place the *Caldera OpenLinux For Dummies* CD-ROM into your CD-ROM drive and then mount the Linux CD (connecting it to the rest of the file system).**

   You can do this by typing a command, such as the following (the exact command depends on how the Linux system is configured — this command works on an OpenLinux system):

   ```
   mount /mnt/cdrom
   ```

3. **Change to the location of the floppy information on the CD by typing**

   ```
   cd /mnt/cdrom/col/launch/floppy
   ```

4. **Type the following command to copy the disk image from the CD to the floppy disk.**

   ```
   dd if=install.144 of=/dev/fd0
   ```

   After the floppy-disk-drive light goes out, you're ready to make the Modules disk.

5. **Place the second blank disk in the floppy drive and then type this command:**

   ```
   dd if=modules.144 of=/dev/fd0s
   ```

6. **After you're finished making the floppies, dismount the CD-ROM so that it can be ejected by typing these commands:**

   ```
   cd /
   umount /mnt/cdrom
   ```

Wait until the floppy-disk-drive light goes out before removing the floppy disk. Now you're ready to install the OpenLinux operating system, so turn to Chapter 5 and get started!

Chapter 5

Installation: Down to the Final Stretch

· ·

In This Chapter

▶ Starting the actual installation

▶ Setting up your mouse and keyboard

▶ Making your video card work

▶ Partitioning and formatting your disk

▶ Selecting packages to install

▶ Networking or not

▶ Setting the clock

▶ What's my password?

· ·

Sit down, grab your favorite drink, and contemplate the excitement about to unfold. If you have a commercial OpenLinux CD or are using the *Caldera OpenLinux For Dummies* CD-ROM, the installation should work almost exactly as described in this chapter.

Getting Ready to Install

The OpenLinux installation is arguably the easiest Linux installation available. Of course, being the easiest to install doesn't mean that the installation always goes off without a hitch. Most of us aren't used to installing operating systems. We simply buy PCs that have the operating systems installed for us (you can do precisely that with OpenLinux if you prefer — visit www.varesearch.com). But with OpenLinux, you have everything going for you to complete a flawless installation in about 30 minutes (depending on how fast you read and how fast your system is).

Keep a few things about this installation interface in mind:

✔ On most systems, the mouse pointer works automatically as soon as you move your mouse. If the mouse pointer doesn't work, use the arrow keys to select items, then tab to different buttons and press Enter to *push* the button.

✔ The Back and Next buttons can be used in most parts of the installation to return to a previous step and make a change. In one or two places doing this isn't possible, but we warn you (as does an on-screen message). For example, after you choose a language, you can't back up and pick a different one. Sorry.

✔ On each screen of the installation you can use the Help button to open a separate dialog box with instructions for that screen. Basic information is provided on the right side of each screen; the help window tells you even more.

Beginning the Installation

To begin installing OpenLinux, follow these steps:

1. **Start the installation program by using one of the methods outlined in Chapter 4:**

   • Insert your *Caldera OpenLinux For Dummies* CD and reboot your computer.

   • Insert the Install disk that you made from the CD and reboot your computer.

   • Insert your *Caldera OpenLinux For Dummies* CD and launch the OpenLinux installation from Microsoft Windows.

   No matter what you do to perform the installation, the installation begins. First you see a text screen with the name Caldera written in big letters, then you get a graphical image with messages scrolling down the screen, and then you're charmed by a cute little animation. Finally, you get the first screen that you need to do anything with. If you turned on your computer, walked away, and then came back after five minutes, you'd be greeted by the Language Selection screen.

2. **On the Language Selection screen, choose which language you want to use for OpenLinux.**

   We stick with English for now, but you also can choose German, French, or Italian if you prefer. All the help messages and dialog boxes are in your chosen language.

3. **Choose Next to move to the next screen, shown in Figure 5-1, on which you can refine your mouse's configuration.**

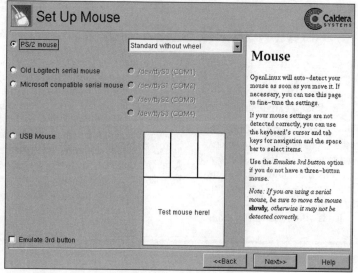

Figure 5-1:
You can
refine the
configura-
tion of your
mouse on
this installa-
tion screen.

Normally the installation program correctly auto-detects your mouse as soon as you move it around. Thus, you may be able to click Next and go on. Checking the following features first, however, may be a good idea:

- The Emulate 3rd button checkbox lets you pretend you have a three-button mouse when you really have only two buttons. To use 3-button emulation within OpenLinux, you press both mouse buttons at the same time. Some programs like to use the middle button, so selecting the Emulate 3rd button checkbox is a good idea.

- The PS/2 mouse probably was auto-detected if you have a laptop. If you prefer to use a serial mouse attached to the back of your laptop instead of the built-in PS/2 mouse, you can select a serial mouse now.

- A mouse with a wheel won't be auto-detected. You can select a mouse with a wheel from the drop-down list.

- The mouse's buttons can be tested to see whether they're recognized by moving to the outline of a mouse and clicking away.

Remember, if your mouse isn't auto-detected, you can use arrow and Tab keys on your keyboard to select the items that are needed to configure your mouse manually.

4. **After you've completed your mouse configuration, choose Next to move to the next screen, on which you select your keyboard type.**

For most users, a standard United States keyboard is an easy choice. But OpenLinux supports many keyboards. (See the sidebar "It's a small, small world.") You can click in the Test here field to try out any special characters on your keyboard.

It's a small, small world

Different countries have different keyboards. OpenLinux, like many UNIX systems, has a keyboard-mapping feature that enables you to use the system with different keyboards.

The Select Keyboard screen in the OpenLinux installation lists the keyboard maps available for the system. If you're in the United States, you'll probably choose the U.S. option. Even then, however, you may have a different keyboard than the U.S. keyboard, so browsing through the list to see what else is offered is worthwhile.

If you're not in the United States, you'll probably choose something other than the U.S. keyboard (unless you bought your system in the United States). If you don't see an obvious choice, choose a keyboard that looks close and test the one you've selected in the Test here field. If that keyboard seems to work, finish the installation. After the installation, you can change the keyboard mapping if necessary with the `/usr/sbin/kbdconfig` command.

5. **After you've selected a model and a layout for your keyboard, choose Next to move to the Select Video Card screen.**

Setting Up Your Graphics Hardware

The Select Video Card screen is one of the most impressive features of the OpenLinux installation. But if you're new to the world of Linux, you don't know how rough we used to have things trying to configure our video cards. Suffice it to say that in the old days (say, 18 months ago), getting video hardware to work correctly with any version of Linux was often exceedingly difficult. Now, you don't even know the troubles you've missed.

Follow along through the next few screens of the installation to get your graphics in optimal shape:

1. **After the Select Video Card screen (shown in Figure 5-2) appears, check and — if necessary — correct the entry in the Card Type field at the top of the screen.**

   The entry you see in the Card Type field at the top of the screen is a first-guess identification about your video card. If the card indicated isn't correct, you can choose the right card from the hundreds of cards in the drop-down list, or better still, choose the Probe button on the lower-left side of the screen. The Probe button spends a little more time looking at your graphics hardware and generally does an excellent job of identifying what you've installed, especially on newer computers.

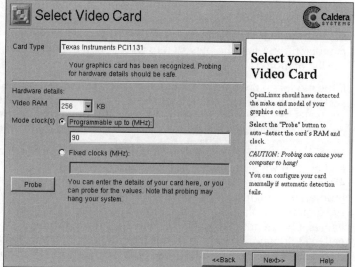

Figure 5-2:
The Select
Video Card
screen
determines
what
graphics
hardware
your com-
puter uses.

2. **Click the Probe button and, after you see a dialog box asking you to confirm that you want to probe the hardware and warning that the process takes a few seconds, go ahead and press Probe to begin.**

   After a moment of blackness the screen returns, and you get a message stating that "Probing is complete and apparently successful." Not overly optimistic, but probing actually has an excellent track record.

3. **Click OK to close the message box, then choose Next to move to the next screen (shown in Figure 5-3) and then select a monitor.**

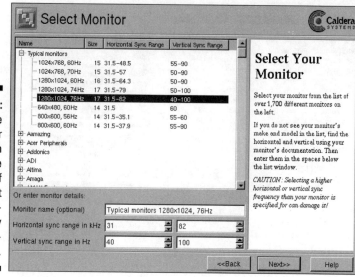

Figure 5-3:
You choose
a monitor
from an
extensive
list of
options that
are orga-
nized by
manufac-
turer.

On this screen you select the monitor model that you're using. The computer can't probe to discover the model, so you need to select the model yourself. The list includes several thousand models divided by manufacturer. Click the plus sign to the left of a manufacturer to open the list of models.

If the model you're using isn't listed, choose from the Typical Monitors section at the top of the list. If you have a newer computer, the line 1024x768, 70Hz should be safe to choose. But don't take our word for it; check your monitor's manual.

Older monitors can't handle resolution rates and scan frequencies higher than what they were designed for. A monitor designed for a 640 x 480 resolution (and a low scan frequency) can't display 1600 x 1200 resolution (and a high scan frequency). More important, if you try to make the monitor display that high a frequency, the monitor may burst into flames. (We're not joking. We've seen the smoke.) Modern monitors, called Multisync, can match themselves automatically to a series of scan frequencies and resolutions. Some of these monitors are even smart enough to turn themselves off if the frequencies become too high, rather than burst into flames. What's best (particularly with older monitors) is to find the documentation and properly match your vertical and horizontal frequencies. Lacking the correct documentation for your monitor, you can try a lower resolution (VGA or SVGA) first, just to get the graphics running.

4. **After you've selected a monitor, choose Next to move to the Select Video Mode screen, as shown in Figure 5-4.**

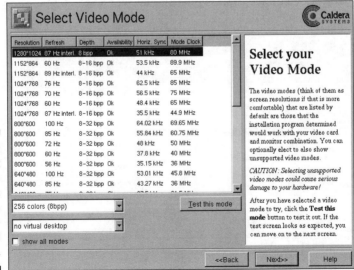

Figure 5-4:
The Select Video Mode screen lets you choose your resolution and color depth.

Based on the video card and monitor settings, this screen displays all the video modes that can be supported by your hardware. In this screen you make three selections:

- Click a resolution line in the list of modes. Several lines often have the same resolution but different refresh or scan rates. Different rates may cause a flicker on different monitors, so you can try different modes to find the right mode (we explain how in a moment).

- Choose a color depth, from 256 colors to 16 million colors. The resolution that you select and the video card and monitor determine what options are available in the drop-down list below the mode list.

- Choose a virtual desktop size. If you want a screen that's larger than the actual screen resolution, choose a virtual desktop size (no virtual desktop is the default). Using a virtual desktop means that you can move around a *larger* screen by moving your mouse to the edges of your screen. Some people find doing this very disconcerting; others like the flexibility.

5. **After you've set up these three things, select the Test this mode button, and when a message box warns you about what's going to happen, click OK to continue.**

The screen goes black; after a moment a desktop interface appears with a color pattern in the middle of the desktop. You can click your mouse button anywhere in the desktop to end the test, or just wait and the test view of the desktop disappears on its own.

- If you don't see this test display of a desktop, or if the display is strange or flickers, you need to select another mode and press Test this mode again.

- If you *do* see this test display of a desktop, then you're finished with the graphics configuration. Click Next to go on.

If you can't find a mode that works for you, continue with the installation by choosing Next. Chapter 6 is all about troubleshooting graphics hardware. If you're installing OpenLinux on a laptop, try visiting www.cs.utexas.edu/users/kharker/linux-laptop/, as laptops can be a particular headache at times.

Preparing Your Hard Disk

With the video-card-setup features of OpenLinux going for you, the hardest thing left about installing a Linux system is getting the hard-disk partitions right. The next screen that appears lets you select an Installation Target. That means you need to specify where on your system OpenLinux will be installed.

Note carefully these installation options:

- **Entire Harddisk:** Assumes that you want to use an entire hard disk for OpenLinux, saving nothing on the disk for another operating system (such as a shared Microsoft Windows hard disk). If you choose this option, the installation program sets up the partitions on the hard disk for you. But watch out! Everything on the hard disk that you select will be erased as the installation proceeds (not quite yet, but in a screen or two).

  If you select Entire Harddisk, choose Next to go to the next screen, in which you can select which hard disk you want if your system contains multiple hard disks.

- **Prepared partitions:** Assumes that you used the PartitionMagic CE program to set up a Linux partition for OpenLinux on a shared Microsoft Windows/OpenLinux system. If you used the PartitionMagic CE, everything is great. Choose Next and go to the next section. If you *didn't* use PartitionMagic CE but you have partition set up for Linux, you can use the Custom option to set up the exact location where OpenLinux will be installed.

- **Custom:** Assumes that you want to specify the exact hard-disk partitions on which OpenLinux will be installed. This option also assumes that you're an expert. Well, we just have to make you one. Read on.

If you select the Custom option, the Next button takes you to the screen shown in Figure 5-5. On this screen you must define the partition on which OpenLinux will be installed.

Figure 5-5:
The Custom option lets you select exactly where OpenLinux will be installed by using the Partition Hard Disk(s) screen.

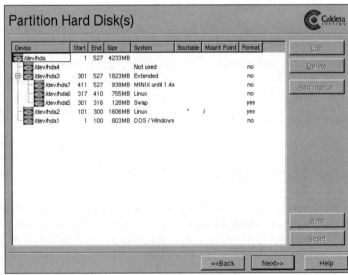

All about files

OpenLinux, like UNIX, refers to everything as a *file*. In other words, the name for a device, such as a hard drive, is the *file address* of its driver. For example, /dev/hda is the name of the first IDE hard drive and /dev/sdb is the name of the second SCSI hard drive.

OpenLinux refers to disks and disk partitions by using a system of letters and numbers, which may seem confusing to the DOS or Windows user. Following is a short description of the naming conventions for hard drives and partitions.

Letters refers to the device on which the partition is located. IDE hard drives, for example, are named *hda, hdb, hdc,* and so on. SCSI drives are referred to as *sda, sdb,*

sdc, and so on. (The *hd* stands for hard drive, and the *sd* stands for SCSI drive.)

Numbers designates the partitions. The BIOS that controls PC hardware supports only four partitions, but one partition may be an extended partition, that is, subdivided into more *logical* partitions. The numbers 1, 2, 3, and 4 denote primary partitions; the logical partitions start at 5. For example, /dev/hdb3 is the name for the third primary partition on the second IDE hard drive. In an SCSI world, /dev/sdc6 is the name for the second logical partition on the third SCSI hard drive.

Your task in this screen is to set up two partitions on your hard disk. One partition is for the Linux Swap partition, which is used for virtual memory storage (like extra RAM stored on the hard disk). The swap partition should be between 32 and 128 MB, depending on how much space you can spare on your hard disk and how much RAM you have.

The second partition is for OpenLinux itself. Make this partition as large as it needs to be, based on the type of system that you want to install (we cover that shortly). We recommend having at least 500 MB for the Linux partition.

To set up these partitions, select the Add logical button if you have empty space from which to create the partitions or select an existing partition and choose Edit. In either case you open a dialog box and specify the following:

- ✔ **The Partition Size:** Change the Start and End cylinder numbers as needed to make the size (shown to the right of the End field) match what you want the size to be.

- ✔ **The System Type:** You need one Linux Swap and one Linux partition. The system type is shown in the System field on the main part of the Partition Hard Disk(s) screen.

- ✔ **The Mount Point:** This feature is the access point for the partition within OpenLinux. The Linux Swap partition doesn't have a mount point; the Linux partition should have a mount point of /. Choose this from the drop-down list.

🖛 **The Bootable Checkbox:** We recommend making the Linux partition bootable by selecting this feature, which allows you to start either OpenLinux or Windows each time you start your system.

🖛 **The Format Checkbox:** For the Linux partition, this checkbox is automatically checked. The partition on which you install OpenLinux must be formatted first.

After you've set up the two needed partitions, choose Next to continue. Nothing's happening to your hard disk quite yet.

The Partition Information screen shows you which partitions will be used for the root partition (the core of OpenLinux) and the swap partition.

After you're satisfied that these are the correct partitions, select the Format chosen partitions button. The Next button isn't active until the formatting operation is completed. You can choose the Back button to make changes in your partitioning plan before choosing Format chosen partitions if necessary.

During installation activities, you can press Ctrl+Alt+F5 or Ctrl+Alt+F6 to watch the information from the background processes that the installation program's using. Press Alt+F8 to return to the installation screen.

Next you choose which packages to install from the Select Installation screen, as shown in Figure 5-6. The available options include:

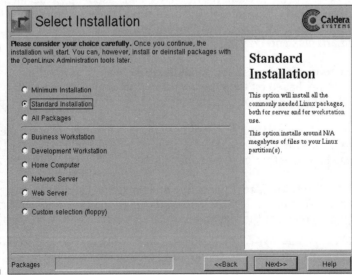

Figure 5-6:
The Select Installation screen lets you choose among several installation options depending on what you'll use OpenLinux for.

- ✔ **Minimum Installation:** No graphics support, requires only 170 MB, good for experimenting or creating a minimal OpenLinux system for testing.

- ✔ **Standard Installation:** A good choice, requires 650 MB of hard-disk space.

- ✔ **All Packages:** Requires about 1.4 GB of disk space. Installs everything on the CD.

- ✔ **Business Workstation:** Installs software determined by Caldera to be useful for business users running OpenLinux as their desktop operating system.

- ✔ **Development Workstation:** Installs tools useful for using OpenLinux as a software development platform.

- ✔ **Home Computer:** Installs programs useful to home users, including Internet connectivity tools.

- ✔ **Network Server:** Installs a collection of Internet services and networking utilities and protocols.

- ✔ **Web Server:** A small installation focused on the Apache Web server and supporting utilities.

- ✔ **Custom selection (floppy):** If you've set up a floppy disk with installation instructions (which we're not showing you how to do), then choose this option.

If you don't have enough hard-disk space for some options, those options won't be active on the list. Also, remember that you easily can add packages by using the graphical package manager after you finish the installation, so don't feel as if your package selections on this screen are set in stone.

Most users who are figuring out OpenLinux should choose Standard Installation. If you have a specific purpose in mind, such as an Internet server or a development workstation, feel free to choose the matching installation option.

After you select Next to continue, the packages that you select are installed immediately as you make other configuration choices. You cannot use the Back button to return to this screen and make a different selection.

Finishing the Configuration

As OpenLinux goes merrily about installing itself, you can continue to select a few more configuration options. The next screen lets you select a root password for OpenLinux, as shown in Figure 5-7.

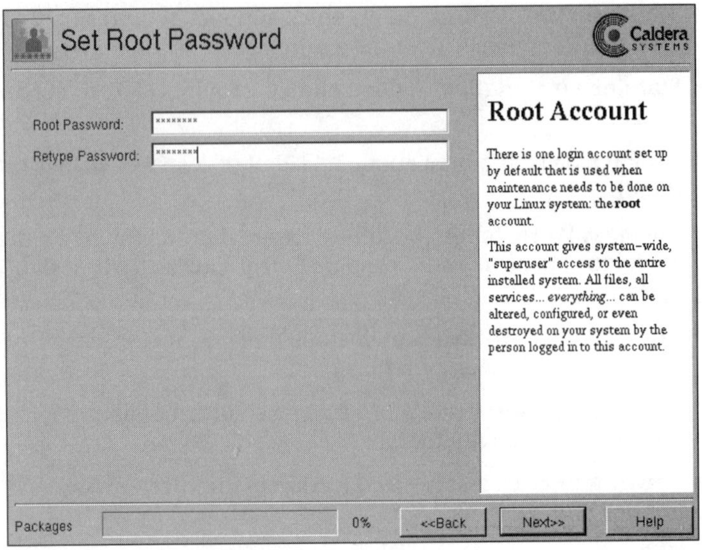

![Set Root Password screen showing Root Password and Retype Password fields with Caldera Systems logo and Root Account description panel.]

Set Root Password   Caldera
                                                                 SYSTEMS

Root Password: ********
Retype Password: ********|

Root Account

There is one login account set up
by default that is used when
maintenance needs to be done on
your Linux system: the **root**
account.

This account gives system-wide,
"superuser" access to the entire
installed system. All files, all
services... *everything*... can be
altered, configured, or even
destroyed on your system by the
person logged in to this account.

Packages   [   ]   0%   <<Back   Next>>   Help

Figure 5-7:
Enter a root
password to
protect the
superuser
account on
your
OpenLinux
system.

The root user is the superuser in OpenLinux. After you log in with the username root and the password that you define here, you can do anything to the
system, including destroying it with a few false moves. Log in as root only
when you need to do system administration work (reconfiguring OpenLinux)
and guard the root password carefully!

Enter the root password that you have selected in the Root Password field.
Enter the same password a second time in the Retype Password field. As
soon as the two passwords match, the Next field becomes active.

Your computer's response time may be a little slow as the packages are
installed in the background. Be patient (read, move slower), and everything
will work just fine.

Next, you need to set up a regular user account. The root user account is too
powerful to use all the time, so in the Set Login Name(s) screen you define a
regular user account that you can use for day-to-day work. Before the Next
button becomes active, you must set up at least one user in this screen, as
shown in Figure 5-8. You can set up others if you choose.

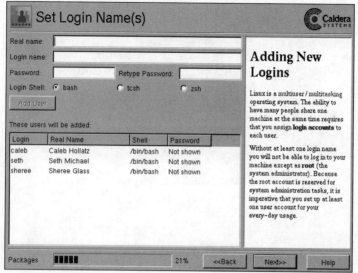

Set Login Name(s)

Caldera
SYSTEMS

Real name:

Login name:

Password: Retype Password:

Login Shell: ⦿ bash   ○ tcsh   ○ zsh

Add User

These users will be added:

Login	Real Name	Shell	Password
caleb	Caleb Hollatz	/bin/bash	Not shown
seth	Seth Michael	/bin/bash	Not shown
sheree	Sheree Glass	/bin/bash	Not shown

Adding New Logins

Linux is a multiuser / multitasking operating system. The ability to have many people share one machine at the same time requires that you assign **login accounts** to each user.

Without at least one login name you will not be able to log in to your machine except as **root** (the system administrator). Because the root account is reserved for system administration tasks, it is imperative that you set up at least one user account for your every-day usage.

Packages ▮▮▮▮▮   21%   <<Back   Next>>   Help

Figure 5-8:
At least one regular user account must be created for OpenLinux.

To set up a user account, follow these steps:

1. **Enter the name of the person who will use the first regular user account (that's probably your name) in the Real Name field.**

2. **Enter a login name for the account in the Login Name field.**

   Common practice is to use something like the first name, or last name, or first initial and last name, and so on. The login name should not be longer than eight letters.

3. **Enter a password for the regular user account, then enter the same password again in the Retype Password field.**

4. **Choose a login shell (that's the command line environment that this user will use).**

   The standard login shell for all Linux systems is bash (see Chapter 10). Don't choose something different unless you're coming from another type of UNIX system and want to use your favorite shell in OpenLinux.

5. **Choose the Add User button.**

   This button won't be active until the two password fields match.

6. **After you've added all the regular users that you want, choose Next to go on.**

In the Set Up Networking screen you configure how your system functions on your local area network (LAN). This screen is actually pretty easy. Either you don't have networking or your system administrator gave you a list of numbers to enter in this screen. The screen appears similar to the screen in Figure 5-9.

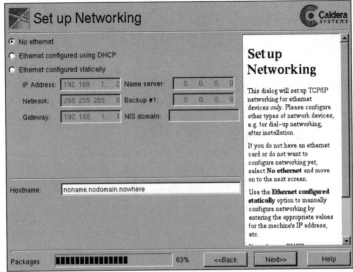

Figure 5-9:
Networking
configura-
tion is part
of the
OpenLinux
installation.

Networking can be done by using DHCP (automatically assigns you networking numbers as you work) or by using a set of static networking numbers (IP addresses).

- ✔ If your system administrator tells you to use DHCP, then select the Ethernet configured using DHCP button and skip to the next step to enter a Hostname.

- ✔ If you need to set up static IP addresses, then select the Ethernet configured statically button and enter the numbers that your system administrator assigned to you. Don't simply guess which numbers to use or other users on your network may be very unhappy with you — their systems will start acting strangely if you choose the numbers that are assigned to them.

The OpenLinux installation program attempts to determine the numbers for networking by reading information on your network, but you should check the results before assuming that any of the numbers are correct.

Having set up the network-address information, enter a Hostname for your computer. The system administrator probably gave you a domain name (something like yahoo.com or nasa.gov). But we think you should get to choose your own computer name. Combine the computer name (anything you choose, but not too long, please) with the domain name and enter that name in the Hostname field. Then choose Next to move on.

We're almost done now! The Linux Loader screen, shown in Figure 5-10, sets up a boot loader that lets you choose between OpenLinux and any other operating systems installed on your computer. OpenLinux chooses the best location for this program in the Where to install LILO section of the screen.

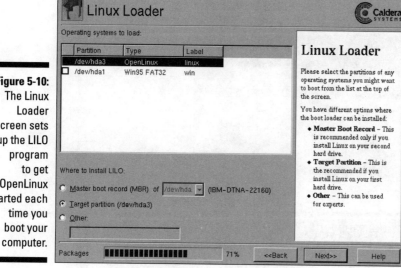

Figure 5-10:
The Linux Loader screen sets up the LILO program to get OpenLinux started each time you boot your computer.

If you have other partitions on your system (such as a Microsoft Windows partition), each partition is listed in the box at the top of the screen. Click the checkbox to the left of any partition that you want to be able to boot after you start your system.

If you're using a commercial copy of OpenLinux, use the BootMagic program instead of LILO. The BootMagic program provides a few additional features. The documentation for OpenLinux explains how to get BootMagic started from your Windows system.

In the next screen, shown in Figure 5-11, select your time zone by either clicking on the map (very cool) or selecting an item from the drop-down list (more precise). Then choose whether to use GMT (universal time) or local time for your computer's clock. OpenLinux prefers GMT, but if you're sharing your system with Windows, choose Local Time to avoid confusing the Windows system. Choose Next to go on.

You're done! And to prove that you're done, the OpenLinux installation provides the nice game, shown in Figure 5-12, for you to play as the package installation finishes in the background.

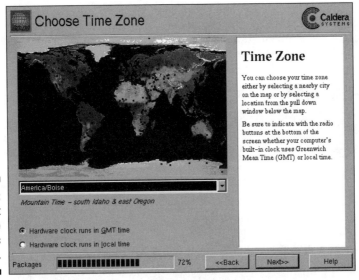

Figure 5-11:
You select
your time
zone in this
map screen.

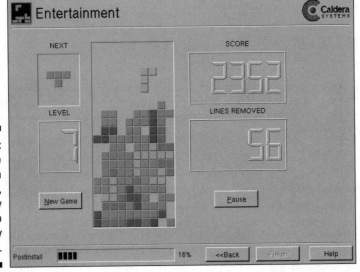

Figure 5-12:
As the
installation
proceeds,
you can play
a game to
while away
the time.

A progress bar at the bottom of the screen shows you how the installation is coming along. The bar is labeled Packages and must reach 100% for the installation. Then the label changes to Postinstall and must climb to 100% again. During this phase the installation is configuring all the packages that were installed. The Finish button isn't active until the Package installation and Postinstall phases are completed. After the Finish button becomes active and you press the Finish button, your system reboots; and you're immediately ready to log in and begin using your new OpenLinux system!

Chapter 6

Solving Problems with the Graphical System

● ●

In This Chapter

▶ Uncovering details about your video controller, monitor, and mouse

▶ Trying the Lizard again

▶ Configuring the X Window System with other tools

▶ Finding some help if nothing seems to work

▶ Paying attention to shutting-down etiquette

● ●

Did you have trouble during the configuration of your video hardware during the installation of OpenLinux? If so, this chapter is for you. Take solace in the fact that the graphical hardware is probably the most difficult part of an OpenLinux system to get working properly. But graphics also are among the most important parts of your OpenLinux system — unless you prefer working at a command line all the time.

The graphical interface that OpenLinux uses — the KDE desktop — is built on the X Window System (also called simply "X"). If X is not correctly configured to use your video hardware, then KDE can't provide a nice graphical interface or access to all the graphical programs that are described elsewhere in this book (see Chapter 12).

Discovering Your Hardware's True Identity

Before you can start the X Window System with KDE on top of it, your configuration files must contain correct information about your video controller card, monitor, mouse, and keyboard. Normally the OpenLinux installation process automatically determines all the information, but if that doesn't happen, you still can get things working correctly.

For your video controller card, you need to know

- ✔ The model number (and perhaps the video chip used)
- ✔ The amount of video RAM on the card

You can find this information in your system's documentation or — if you're using a dual-boot system — by using the Microsoft Windows Control Panel (described in Chapter 3). But now that you have OpenLinux up and running, you also can try the Lizard X and XF86Setup configuration tools that we describe later in this chapter.

Next, you need to know the following about your mouse:

- ✔ The model number and manufacturer
- ✔ Whether the mouse is a PS/2 bus mouse or a serial mouse

Again, your system's documentation should have this information, and the bottom of the mouse often has some basic information, too.

A PS/2 mouse usually has a round connector on the end of its wire, or tail. A serial mouse has an oblong connector with nine holes. All varieties of PS/2 bus mice look the same to OpenLinux. Different serial mice, however, have different characteristics. If you have a serial mouse, you have to know its model number and manufacturer, or whether your mouse emulates some other well-known mouse. Also, not many OpenLinux programs support the scrolling wheel available on many mice.

Three-button mice work best with OpenLinux, but you can get by with a two-button mouse. To X, simultaneously holding down both buttons on a two-button mouse feels the same as holding down the middle button on a three-button mouse (but only if the system is configured correctly by using the Emulate 3 Button option, as discussed in Chapter 5).

Finally, you need to know about your monitor. Most monitor manuals have a table at the back with information, such as:

- ✔ Horizontal sync range
- ✔ Vertical sync range
- ✔ Resolution
- ✔ Whether the monitor is *multisync,* which means that your monitor can run at several resolution rates

Older monitors, particularly VGA monitors that came with older systems, often aren't multisync. These monitors can be damaged if you try to use them at a resolution higher than VGA, which is 640 x 480.

Horizontal and vertical sync range numbers help X determine the different ways in which X can place the dots on the screen. The resolution number tells X how many dots can be horizontally and vertically on the screen. A 640-x-480 resolution is usually considered the worst, and a 1280-x-1024 resolution is usually considered the best for normal use. Strive for 800 x 600 as a minimum resolution and 1024 x 768 as an ideal resolution for most systems.

Higher video resolution uses more video memory (which is on the video card and, therefore, separate from the system memory), allows fewer simultaneous colors on the screen (for a given amount of video memory), and typically shrinks text on the screen, making the text more difficult to see. On the other hand, using a higher resolution means that more information can be visible at one time on the screen for the same-size monitor (even though the writing may be so small that you can't read the writing without a new prescription for your glasses). Some video cards can be upgraded to add more video memory, and some cannot.

Most newer monitors have built-in protection mechanisms to keep them from burning up in what is known as *overdriving*, but older monitors don't have such protection. Older monitors literally can catch on fire. Try to find your monitor's specifications in the manual, from a dealer, or from the Web pages of the monitor's manufacturer.

If you hear noise from your monitor, smell burning components, or think that the screen doesn't look right, press Ctrl+Alt+Backspace right away to exit X and try a lower resolution. Otherwise, you easily can damage the monitor.

Probing the System

If your system has booted and is in command-line mode, you still may not have all the information that you need to configure X. A final chance to gather this information is to ask X itself to probe the hardware. To do this, you need to have an X Server program installed, which the OpenLinux installation should have done even if the configuration couldn't be completed. The default X Servers in OpenLinux are from the XFree86 Project. All the software-package names for these X Servers begin with XF86, as in XF86_SVGA. (If you see a "No such file or directory" message when you try this procedure, then you don't have an X Server installed. Go back to your manuals to get the information you need.)

To have the X Server probe your hardware, run this command:

```
X -probeonly
```

You see a lot of text scroll down your screen, and then the screen goes blank. After a moment, the command-line screen reappears. Hopefully, among all the text that appears, you'll see the information about your video chipset. X can't determine much about your monitor — it relies on you for that information. But the video chipset and possibly the amount of video memory can be a helpful start.

The following lines show the result of this command if run on a Toshiba 2595 laptop. Note that the X-server program probed the lines with (–).

```
XF86Config: /etc/XF86Config
(**) stands for supplied, (–) stands for probed/default
        values
(**) XKB: rules: "xfree86"
(**) XKB: model: "pc101"
(**) XKB: layout: "us"
(**) Mouse: type: microsoft, device: /dev/ttyS0, baudrate:
        1200
(**) Mouse: buttons: 3, 3 button emulation (timeout: 50ms)
(**) SVGA: Graphics device ID: "Primary Card"
(**) SVGA: Monitor ID: "Primary Monitor"
(**) FontPath set to
        "/usr/X11R6/lib/X11/fonts/Type1,/usr/X11R6/lib/X11
        /fonts/Speedo,/usr/X11R6/lib/X11/fonts/misc,/usr/X
        11R6/lib/X11/fonts/75dpi"
(–) SVGA: PCI: Trident Cyber 9525 DVD rev 73, Memory @
        0xff800000, 0xff000000, MMIO @ 0xff7e0000
(–) Trident chipset version: 0xf3 (Cyber9525)
(–) SVGA: BIOS reports Clock Control Bits 0x3
(–) SVGA: Detected a Trident Cyber 9525 DVD.
(–) SVGA: Detected an STN 800x600 Display
(–) SVGA: Revision 65.
(–) SVGA: Using Trident programmable clocks
(–) SVGA: chipset: cyber9525
(**) SVGA: videoram: 2048k
(**) SVGA: Using 16 bpp, Depth 16, Color weight: 565
(–) SVGA: Maximum allowed dot-clock: 230.000 MHz
(**) SVGA: Mode "800x600/60Hz": mode clock = 40.000
(**) SVGA: Virtual resolution set to 800x600
(–) SVGA: SpeedUp code selection modified because virtualX !=
        1024
(–) SVGA: Using Linear Frame Buffer at 0x0ff800000, Size 2MB
```

As you can see, the probe command provides lots of useful information, including that the computer has a Trident 9525 video card, a PCI bus, and 2 MB of memory.

Configuration Conflagration

Now that you know all the information about your video hardware, start configuring the X Window System. We assume you don't have your graphical system up and running already. If the graphical system is up and running, what are you doing here? Go on to another chapter.

Several tools are provided with OpenLinux to help you get the X Window System configured and running. The three we look at here are

- Lizard X configuration tool
- XF86Setup
- xf86config

Note: You see in the figures for this chapter that we already had the X Window System running in order to take the screen captures and show you how things work. Rest assured that the programs we describe work from a character-cell command line as well.

A running Lizard

The Linux Wizard (or Lizard X) installation program that we discuss in Chapter 5 is just about the best tool for configuring X that we've ever seen.

You can use the same tool (after you've installed the rest of OpenLinux, rebooted, and logged in) to adjust the graphical settings or get things working the first time.

You can start the program two ways:

- If you don't have X working at all yet, enter the command `lizardx` to start this utility.
- If you have the graphical environment running and want to adjust it by using this utility, choose COAS⇨X server on the main menu (click the K icon in the lower left corner of the screen to open the main menu).

After you've started Lizard X, follow these steps:

1. **Configure your mouse in the first Lizard X screen (shown in Figure 6-1), and then select Next to continue.**

   Follow the same instructions that are provided in Chapter 5.

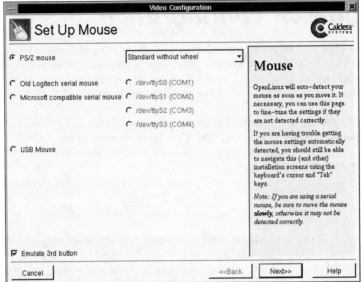

Figure 6-1:
The Lizard
video con-
figuration
utility begins
with a
mouse con-
figuration
screen.

2. **Next select your keyboard model and layout from the list shown. Select the Next button to continue.**

3. **On the Select Video Card screen, shown in Figure 6-2, choose the Probe button and confirm the autoprobing of your video hardware. Then select Next to continue.**

   The real power of the Lizard X utility lies here. Lizard X probes your video hardware and determines everything it needs to set up a correct video configuration. All you have to do is click Probe and watch it work.

4. **Select a monitor based on the information that you've gathered about your monitor capabilities. Again, select Next to continue.**

5. **Select a video mode in the Select Video Mode screen, shown in Figure 6-3, and then test the mode by clicking the Test this mode button.**

   The ability to test video modes is another powerful feature of Lizard X. If the mode you select at first doesn't display correctly, use the Back button to return to the Select Video Card screen and try again. Keep trying modes until you find a mode that works, as shown in Figure 6-3.

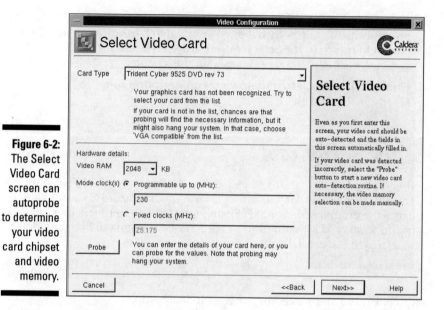

Figure 6-2: The Select Video Card screen can autoprobe to determine your video card chipset and video memory.

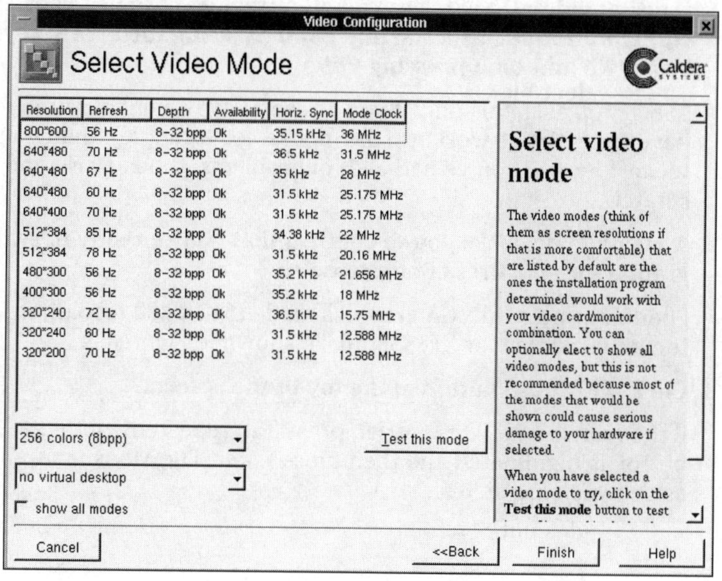

Figure 6-3: In the Select Video Mode screen you can test video modes until you find one that works correctly.

Note: If you can't find a mode that displays correctly, the Lizard X utility probably hasn't correctly detected your video hardware. Use the Back button to return to the Select Video Card screen and try again, or try one of the other methods discussed in this chapter.

6. **Finally, click Finish to update your configuration file** (`/etc/XF86Config`).

Try the setup tool

Another OpenLinux tool that you can use to configure X is the XF86Setup utility. This utility is not as easy to use as Lizard X, but if Lizard X wasn't able to configure the graphics for you, XF86Setup may have better luck. Use this command to start XF86Setup from a character-cell command line (and don't forget to match the capitalization!).

```
XF86Setup
```

Now follow these steps to configure X with XF86Setup:

1. **If prompted, tell XF86Setup whether you want to use your existing configuration file as a starting point by using the arrow keys to select Yes or No and then pressing Enter.**

   XF86Setup asks this only if you already have a configuration file. If you have some things working (the mouse, for example), then you may want to start here. If you've had a lot of problems, then say No and start from scratch.

2. **A message box asks you to confirm that you're ready to switch to graphics mode. Press Enter to do so.**

   Suddenly you're in VGA graphics mode (640-x-480 resolution), looking at the initial screen for XF86Setup, as shown in Figure 6-4.

3. **Click the Mouse button at the top of the screen.**

   If the mouse isn't working yet, press Tab repeatedly until the Mouse button is highlighted and then press Enter. The Mouse screen appears, as shown in Figure 6-5.

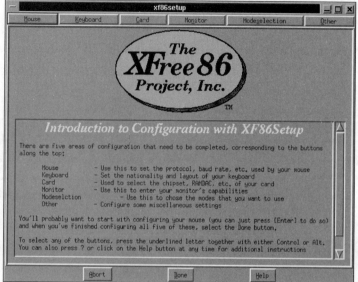

Figure 6-4:
XF86Setup
begins with
an informa-
tional
screen
about the
utility.

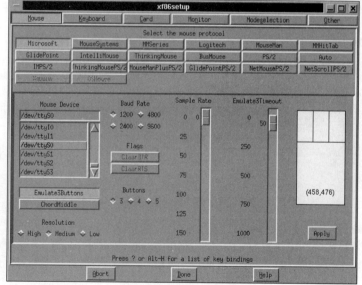

Figure 6-5:
The mouse
is config-
ured in
XF86Setup
using this
window.

4. **Choose the protocol and device name used by your mouse.**

Don't worry about the other settings until you get the mouse to work.

5. **Click the Apply button (on the lower right side of the screen) to activate your selections.**

Again, use Tab and Enter if the mouse still isn't working.

6. **If you're using a standard U.S. keyboard, you can skip the Keyboard button; otherwise, click the Keyboard button at the top of the screen, then select a keyboard model and layout from the Keyboard screen.**

7. **Choose the Card button from the row of buttons across the top of the screen.**

A window appears in which you define for XF86Setup which video card you're using, as shown in Figure 6-6.

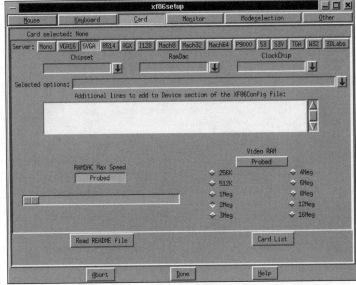

Figure 6-6:
In this
window you
select your
video card
for
XF86Setup
to configure.

8. **Select which X Server you want to use, based on the chipset on your video card. For the other fields you can choose Probed. (If Probed doesn't work you can return to this screen and choose a specific option.)**

You may be able to locate your specific video card in a list of manufacturers and models, which saves you from manually entering all these video settings. (If you can't see your video card in the list provided by XF86Setup, you have to use the regular card screen.) (Refer to Figure 6-6).

9. **Choose the Card List button to view the card list, shown in Figure 6-7, to see whether your video card is listed.**

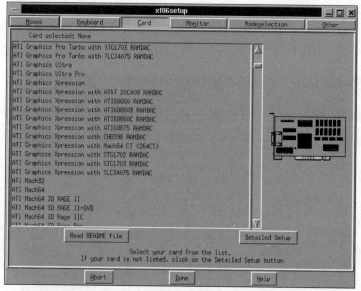

Figure 6-7:
Hundreds of
video cards
are listed in
the Card List
screen.

10. **Choose the Monitor button. Select the line that best suits your monitor capabilities.**

    If you're unsure about your monitor but have a newer monitor, choose the Super VGA, 800x600 line, shown in Figure 6-8, as a starting point.

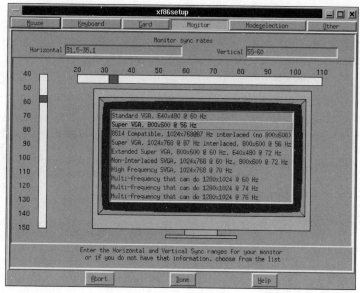

Figure 6-8:
Carefully
choose a
monitor
description
in this
screen
within
XF86Setup.

11. **Choose the Modeselection button, as shown in Figure 6-9.**

In this screen choose the resolution that you want to use. Most users will want 800x600 or 1024x768.

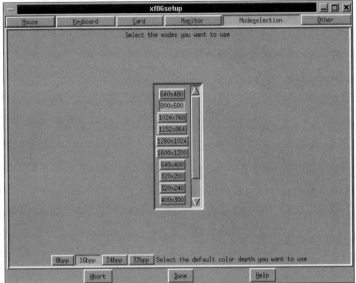

Figure 6-9:
The resolution and color depth are selected on the Modeselection screen.

12. **Choose the color depth from the buttons at the bottom of the screen.**

The 8bpp button is for 256 colors; 16bbp is for 32 thousand colors; 24bbp or 32bbp is for millions of colors. The greater number of colors require more video memory.

Very few video cards need to set any options on the Other screen. Feel free to look at those options if you wish.

13. **Choose Done, followed by Okay in the pop-up window.**

The graphical system starts up (or attempts to). If things work correctly, you see a graphical screen with a small X mouse pointer. You then can save the configuration and use the kde command to start the standard OpenLinux desktop interface.

The really hard way

If the Lizard X and XF86Setup utilities haven't worked, chances are you're going to need some help from a real-life OpenLinux wizard. You can try, however, one other tool — xf86config (all lowercase), an old-fashioned character-mode utility. Although `xf86config` is rarely used, OpenLinux includes `xf86config` (which uses a different internal process that may result in a successful configuration).

Enter this command to begin:

```
xf86config
```

A full screen of text appears (see Figure 6-10). Keep the information that you gathered about your video hardware nearby and carefully read all the information on each screen, following the directions.

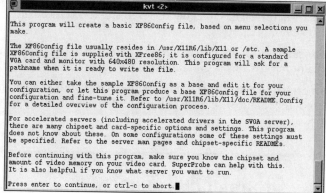

Figure 6-10: The xf86config utility is a character-based program for setting up X.

```
kvt <2>

This program will create a basic XF86Config file, based on menu selections you
make.

The XF86Config file usually resides in /usr/X11R6/lib/X11 or /etc. A sample
XF86Config file is supplied with XFree86; it is configured for a standard
VGA card and monitor with 640x480 resolution. This program will ask for a
pathname when it is ready to write the file.

You can either take the sample XF86Config as a base and edit it for your
configuration, or let this program produce a base XF86Config file for your
configuration and fine-tune it. Refer to /usr/X11R6/lib/X11/doc/README.Config
for a detailed overview of the configuration process.

For accelerated servers (including accelerated drivers in the SVGA server),
there are many chipset and card-specific options and settings. This program
does not know about these. On some configurations these settings must
be specified. Refer to the server man pages and chipset-specific READMEs.

Before continuing with this program, make sure you know the chipset and
amount of video memory on your video card. SuperProbe can help with this.
It is also helpful if you know what server you want to run.

Press enter to continue, or ctrl-c to abort.
```

The `xf86config` program is effective but requires that you read a lot more than XF86Setup, for instance, before you know what to choose from the numbered menus that appear. Still, `xf86config` provides another option that has worked well for thousands of people before shiny new utilities (such as Lizard X) were available.

After you've answered all the questions posed by `xf86config`, the `xf86config` program creates a configuration file for you. As soon as `xf86config` exits, you can try immediately to run the graphical desktop in OpenLinux by using the command `kde`.

Start Your Engines

After you've successfully configured X for your video hardware, it's time to try out the graphical system with the KDE desktop. To do this, simply type the following:

```
kde
```

The screen goes black, flashes, displays a background color (probably with an X mouse pointer in the middle of the screen), and — if all goes well — begins by displaying the KDE Panel, desktop icons, and maybe a dialog box or two.

Or maybe not. (Sigh.) If the screen reverts to a character-cell interface, you will see all sorts of messages about what may have gone wrong. You may have specified the video card incorrectly or incorrectly answered some other question. If that's the case, you can do several things:

- ✔ Find out more detailed information about your video card by using Windows 98 (if available), as described in Chapter 3.

- ✔ Find a newer version of the X server (XFree86) by contacting Caldera, looking on the Caldera FTP site (`ftp.calderasystems.com`) under the update directories, or checking the Web site for XFree86 at `www.xfree86.org`.

- ✔ Find a seasoned OpenLinux person to help you. (The users' mailing list that Caldera provides is great for this sort of help.)

- ✔ Take a cruise to Fiji — at the University of the South Pacific, they have a really good computer-science department in which everyone uses Linux. (Hi folks!)

Origin of this species

Your X Window System programs come from code that was contributed to the X Window System project, which was first connected with Project Athena at the Massachusetts Institute of Technology. Later, the project became the main focus of the X Consortium, a nonprofit group established to develop the X Window System technology.

Because the source code was freely distributable, a group of programmers from all over the world formed to give support to X Window code on low-end PC systems. These programmers called themselves XFree86 because their code was free and was directed toward PCs, which were largely based on Intel x86-compatible processors.

Over time, the programmers ported their code to freely distributable operating systems on other architectures. They did this — and continue to do this — for the love of programming.

The XFree86 team of programmers tries to give support to new video controllers as they come out. Unfortunately, doing so is often difficult for several reasons:

- ✔ The XFree86 developers have no relationship with the video controller manufacturer.

- ✔ The video controller manufacturer thinks that keeping programming interfaces secret gives the manufacturer an edge against its competitors.

- ✔ The video board is built into a larger system board.

- ✔ The video controller is simply too new for the development team to have had time to develop support for it yet.

Until support is available, most people rely on SVGA compatibility mode to get the card to work.

If you try these solutions and still don't have the X Window System running, look around for a Linux users' group at a local college or high school. Or perhaps a group of computer professionals in your area may help. If you call the folks at a local college computer-science department, they probably can help you find a student or staff member who uses Linux, has installed Linux on several types of machines, and can help you figure out why your graphics system isn't working or help you get a newer version of XFree86 that may support your video card.

If you feel strange going to these people to ask them to help, remember that they, too, once were new to Linux and probably had to struggle through an even more difficult installation. If you do contact them, remember to take with you *all* the accumulated information that you've detected about your system. Doing so will save both them and you time and energy.

Finally, if your hardware is too new or too proprietary, or if you have a notebook computer, you may want to buy a commercial X Server from Metrolink (www.metrolink.com) or Xi Graphics (www.xigraphics.com). Sometimes Metrolink's or Xi Graphics' codes work when XFree86 doesn't. Plus, if you buy an X Server, you can call the company's technical support line if you can't get the X server installed.

It Worked!

We congratulate you for getting the X Window System working. If you knew all the issues involved in working with PC video hardware, you would think it fantastic that the XFree86 developers can get graphics working at all. Even though XFree86 is freely distributable, you may want to make a donation to its development fund, listed at www.XFree86.org.

If you want to shut down the graphical system (or at least go back to the graphical login prompt, depending on your system's configuration), right-click the background of the desktop and choose Logout.

A configuration dialog box warns you about any open application windows that you may want to close before exiting. Choose OK to exit the graphical environment.

If you're having trouble exiting from the graphical environment, try pressing Ctrl+Alt+Backspace. Doing so should take you immediately back to character-cell mode. Of course, if you have open any application windows, you'll lose any unsaved data. Also, the KDE graphical environment won't be able to save your status to restore open windows the next time you work in the graphical environment (see Chapter 11). In general, use Ctrl+Alt+Backspace only if the regular method (the Logout menu item) isn't working for you.

Shutting Down OpenLinux

If you're accustomed to an older Microsoft Windows system, then having a section on shutting down the system may seem strange. After all, shouldn't you just turn off the power switch? No! All modern operating systems require that you "officially" shut down the system, effectively telling the system to get ready for the power to go off. OpenLinux requires a systematic process to shut down the operating system, after which you can turn off the power switch.

If you've just finished installing the system, you're logged in as a system administrator called root. Follow these steps to shut down the system:

1. **If the graphical environment (KDE) is running, choose Logout from the main menu (or right-click the desktop background and choose Logout).**

   The system returns either to character-cell mode with a # prompt, or to the graphical login screen. If you're in character-cell mode, type **shutdown -h** at the prompt. Doing so tells OpenLinux to halt the operating system now rather than first waiting a while. Otherwise, continue to Step 2.

2. **If you're at the graphical login screen, choose Shutdown.**

   A small dialog box appears where you can choose to shut down the system or shut down and restart the system (along with a couple of other options).

3. **Choose the option you need and press OK.**

shutdown is a command to OpenLinux. Some commands have options, or flags, that provide additional information about what the command should do. -h means to halt the system after it shuts down, rather than rebooting. -r means to start rebooting after shutdown. now means to start the process of shutting down immediately. Without the now, the shutdown command hesitates and sends warning messages to people still working on the system, telling them that the system is about to be turned off.

Another method of rebooting the system is the infamous three-finger salute that all Microsoft users know: Ctrl+Alt+Delete. The three-finger salute simply sends a shutdown -r now command to OpenLinux, and the result is the same as if you had typed this command.

As an OpenLinux user, rebooting the system should be an infrequent occurrence. Because the login procedure provides an OpenLinux system with the necessary security, you don't need to shut down the system between sessions. OpenLinux is stable, so it doesn't freeze up or crash often, as do some other PC-based operating systems. If you have multiple operating systems on the same machine, however, rebooting takes you back to the LILO prompt (or Boot Magic, or System Commander, or some other booting program) to allow you to boot another operating system.

Chapter 7

Using OpenLinux for the First Time

*A*fter you've loaded OpenLinux on your computer system (see Chapters 4 and 5), the software eagerly awaits its first chance to show off for you. But wait! Logging in to OpenLinux the first time is a little more complicated than you think. And after you're in OpenLinux, you face all sorts of questions about how you want the graphical interface to appear.

Granted, the graphical interface questions are easy ones. This chapter leads you through them nonetheless, and explains how you can add accounts for different users and change passwords. And when you're ready to quit OpenLinux, we show you how to stop gracefully but completely.

Giving OpenLinux the Boot

Are you ready to boot OpenLinux? Here goes:

1. **Make sure everything is turned off.**

2. **Turn on all peripheral devices, such as a printer and a scanner.**

3. **Turn on the power to the monitor (if separate from the main system box).**

4. **Turn on the main power switch.**

   After a short time, LILO boot: appears on the OpenLinux logo screen.

5. **Press the Tab key to see the operating systems that are available to boot.**

   You may see something like the following, depending on what options you selected during the OpenLinux installation. The boot prompt waits for you to select an operating system to launch. Pressing <TAB> shows all the available operating systems (linux and dos are the labels in this example). The boot prompt then appears so that you can enter your choice:

   ```
   boot:
   linux  dos
   boot:
   ```

6. **Type the name of one of the listed operating systems and then press Enter.**

   The operating system boots. You then must be fast enough to type **linux** after the boot prompt.

   If you do nothing — that is, you ignore these wonderful instructions — after a short time (usually 5 to 20 seconds), the first-listed operating system (known as the *default system*) boots.

For OpenLinux to boot, then

✔ OpenLinux must be the only operating system installed; or

✔ OpenLinux must be the first operating system listed so that it boots as the default system

Otherwise, you may have to wait for the other operating system to finish booting, shut that system down, reboot, and then make sure you're fast enough to type **linux** after the prompt.

As the OpenLinux operating system boots, you see all sorts of messages scrolling by on the screen as lots of technical things happen. You can ignore these messages, unless you need to call Caldera Technical Support. After the scrolling stops, the screen flashes a few times, and a graphical login screen appears, as shown in Figure 7-1.

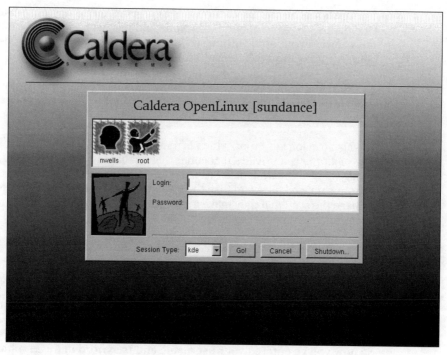

Figure 7-1:
The graphi-
cal login
screen for
OpenLinux.

Now you're ready to log in to the system and begin using it. How fortunate
that we cover this topic in the next section!

The Root of All Power

If you want to use OpenLinux, then you must log in as a particular user with a
distinct username. Why? Because OpenLinux is a multiuser system that uses
different accounts to keep people from looking at other people's secret files,
erasing necessary files from the system, and otherwise doing bad things.
Having a unique identity also helps to keep the actions of one person from
affecting the actions of another, because many people may be using the same
computer system at the same time.

The upshot of all this protection is that no one can do anything in an OpenLinux system without a username and password. The benefit is that no one can ruin your stuff without *your* username and password (unless, of course, that person has the superuser password).

As a first step, you log in by using the regular user account that you created during the installation. The name of this account probably matches your own name.

You also can log in as root, which is the username for the OpenLinux superuser. The *superuser* is a privileged account that enables a person to go anywhere and do anything in the system. Superusers can add disk drives, create backups, restore damaged files, and turn the system off and on. Superusers also can damage the system if they make a mistake. Because superusers are all-powerful, their mistakes can be all-bad.

You can log in as root anytime, because you know the root password for the system that you installed (and you had best not forget it). But logging in as root is dangerous, because you can destroy things very easily as you figure out OpenLinux. For that reason, you're better off to log in by using your regular account and then switch temporarily to the root account to complete any administrative tasks that require superuser privileges.

So now you've entered your username and password in the graphical login screen.

You don't see the password as you type it in the dialog box on screen. This secrecy ensures you that your coworkers, who may be watching over your shoulder, won't see the password and later try to log in as you. (So much for trust in the workplace.) If you enter the wrong password, then the graphical login screen returns so that you can try entering your password again.

Starting Your KDE Desktop

After you enter your username and password, the KDE Desktop appears, as shown in Figure 7-2. The KDE Desktop is the main working environment for OpenLinux.

KDE includes a main menu that you open by clicking on the K icon (shown in Figure 7-3), a desktop background where you can store frequently used programs, and a complete set of graphical configuration tools.

Figure 7-2:
The main
KDE
Desktop
window.

The first thing you want to do is set up KDE to match your personal preferences. The KDE Setup Wizard appears automatically the first time you log in to OpenLinux. Follow the steps below to configure your desktop so that the desktop looks the way you want it.

1. **Select a Desktop Theme from the four options shown (KDE, Windows, Macintosh, or BEOS).**

   After you click one of the buttons, the screen changes immediately to the setting that you select. For example, if you choose a Macintosh interface, then the menu bar appears at the top of the screen. The screen figures we show are based on the KDE theme, but you can choose any one you want.

2. **Select Next to continue.**

   A list of device icons appears.

3. **Click any of these devices that you want to access from your desktop.**

   Most newer computers include a 3½-inch diskette drive and a CD-ROM drive. When you click one of the icons, that icon appears immediately on your desktop to the left of the KDE Wizard window.

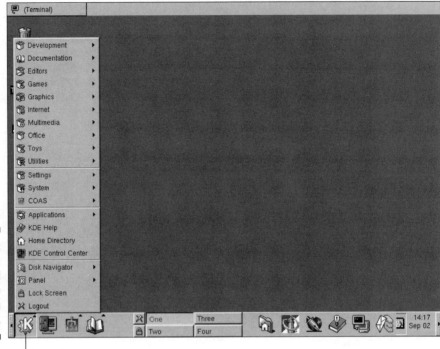

Figure 7-3:
The K icon
on the Panel
opens the
main menu
in KDE.

K icon

4. **Select Next to continue.**

   A printer icon appears.

5. **Click printer if you want to access a local printer from your desktop (so you can drag and drop files on the printer, for example).**

   The printer icon immediately appears on your desktop.

6. **Select Next to continue.**

   You get a list of Internet sites (see Figure 7-4).

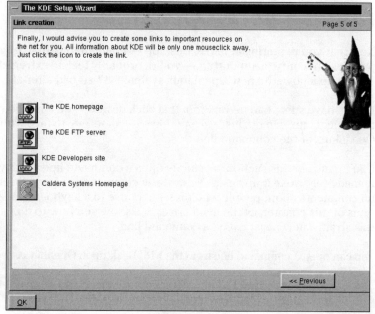

The KDE Setup Wizard

Link creation   Page 5 of 5

Finally, I would advise you to create some links to important resources on
the net for you. All information about KDE will be only one mouseclick away.
Just click the icon to create the link.

The KDE homepage

The KDE FTP server

KDE Developers site

Caldera Systems Homepage

<< Previous

OK

Figure 7-4:
Links to
Internet
sites can be
added easily
to your KDE
desktop.

7. **Select the icon for each of the Internet sites that you want to access
   instantly from your desktop.**

   After you click an icon in the Wizard window, an icon named for the corresponding site immediately appears on your KDE Desktop to the left of
   the Wizard window.

   If you're connected to the Internet (which you will be after reading
   Chapter 15), clicking one of these desktop icons takes you directly to the
   Internet site that is named on the icon.

8. **Choose File⇨Exit to close the KDE Setup Wizard.**

   Your KDE Desktop configuration is finished!

KDE has hundreds of other configuration options, such as setting up a wallpaper graphic, choosing a color scheme, setting display fonts, and choosing a
screen saver (see Chapter 11 for details). In this chapter we explore some
topics you're likely to need even before you start tinkering with the screen-
saver settings.

Face-to-Face with OpenLinux

Now that you're staring at a KDE Desktop — configured with a drag-n-drop printer and a nifty menu button — you're probably feeling extremely relieved. Setting up a powerful new OpenLinux system isn't so bad after all.

But we have some bad news: From this slick desktop you can't do *everything* that OpenLinux can do. Instead, you have to come face-to-face with OpenLinux at the command line.

Don't panic. In this section we simply open a command-line window and then immediately close it up again. No esoteric commands, no cryptic editors, and no comments about people who prefer a mouse to a keyboard. In later sections of this chapter, as the need arises, we show you how to do more with this strange new beast called a command line.

You can open a command line from the KDE Desktop in OpenLinux two ways:

> ✔ **Click the Terminal Emulator icon on the Panel.** A command-line window (also called a terminal-emulator window) appears, as shown in Figure 7-5.

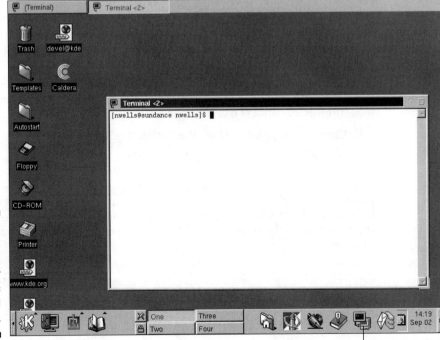

Figure 7-5:
The Terminal Emulator icon opens a command line window.

Terminal Emulator icon

A command line by another name

If you're coming from the world of DOS or Windows, you've probably seen the command-line prompt, which looks something like this:

`C:\>`

The OpenLinux command-line prompt looks similar, but it works a little differently. The command line in OpenLinux is actually a program called a *shell*. A shell in OpenLinux is like COMMAND.COM in DOS, only a lot better, of course. Never mind how for now. The particular shell used in OpenLinux (and many other Linux and UNIX systems, actually) is called *bash*. (Chapter 10 goes on about bash in detail.)

The shell, or command line, in OpenLinux also is called at various times a *terminal emulator* (because it's as if you have a dumb terminal connected to your OpenLinux system), or an Xterm window (because that's the name of the graphical program that opens a window that's running bash).

So when you see any of these terms, just remember, they're all talking about a place where you can enter commands at the keyboard and have the OpenLinux system process them. (For more than that, see Chapter 10.)

✔ Or, go to the main menu and choose Utilities➪Terminal, as shown in Figure 7-6.

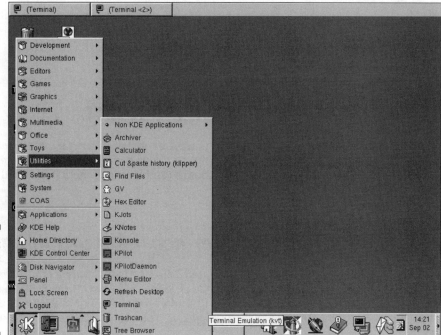

Figure 7-6: The Utilities menu includes the Terminal item.

A command-line window appears, as shown in Figure 7-7. You can change the size and colors in this window by using options in the menu bar. (See Chapter 11 for more details about working with windows.)

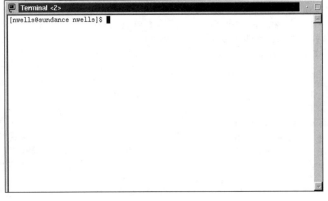

Figure 7-7:
A Terminal
Emulator
window
provides a
command-
line
interface.

To close the command-line window, do any one of the following:

✔ Type the logout command at the command line.

✔ Press Ctrl+D as soon as the command-line window is active (the title bar lights up).

✔ Click the Close Window icon on the title bar of the command-line window.

✔ Choose File⇨Exit.

Creating a New User Account

As you work with OpenLinux, you probably need to set up additional user accounts for other people who want to use your OpenLinux system. Each user needs a separate login account (and each user gets a personal home directory in the bargain).

Creating new user accounts graphically

New user accounts can be created either by using graphical utilities or from a command line. The main graphical-system-administration utility included with OpenLinux is called COAS (Caldera Open Administration System — no, we don't know who picked the name). You must be logged in as root to create a new user account.

1. **At the KDE desktop, open the COAS user configuration tool by choosing COAS⇨System⇨Accounts.**

   An introductory dialog box appears.

2. **Choose OK to close the introductory dialog box.**

   The COAS User Accounts window appears, as shown in Figure 7-8.

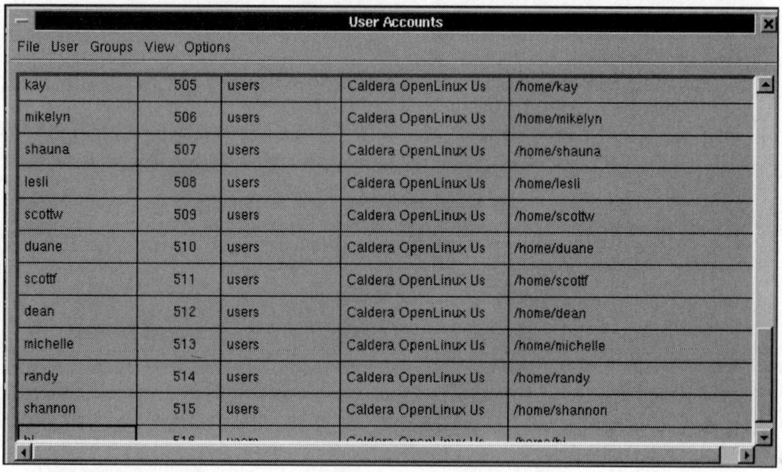

Figure 7-8:
New user
accounts
can be cre-
ated graphi-
cally by
using COAS.

3. **Choose User⇨Create User to open the Create User Account window.**

4. **Enter the login name for the new user account and click OK.**

   A dialog box appears where you enter the information for new user accounts, as shown in Figure 7-9.

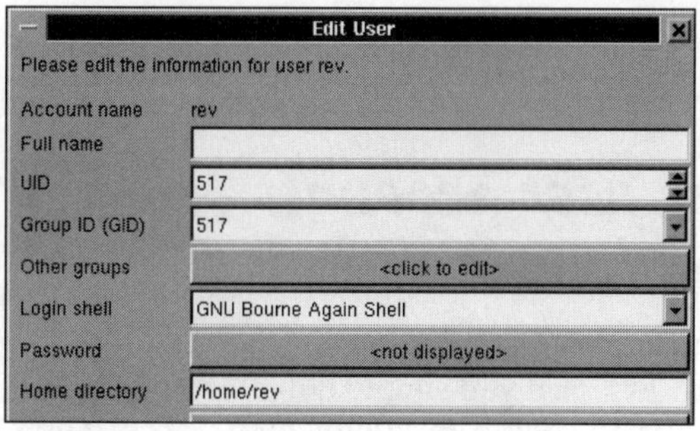

Figure 7-9:
The dialog
box for
entering
new user
information.

5. **Fill in the information about the new account you want to create, such as the person's full name.**

Most of this information is self-explanatory, but here are a few hints:

- Make the username short and all lowercase.

- Make a password difficult to guess by using a long password in a combination of uppercase, lowercase, and special characters. Don't use common words, nicknames, or other words that people can guess. Remember, everything in OpenLinux is case sensitive!

- Make /bin/bash your default shell, which is a good choice among your many choices. (For more on shells, see Chapter 10.)

6. **Click the OK button to add the new user to your OpenLinux system.**

   The new user is added to the list of user accounts on your system (it then appears in the COAS User Management window).

7. **Choose File⇨Exit to close the COAS dialog box.**

   Your changes to the user account information for OpenLinux are saved to the hard disk.

Did you make a mistake? If so, changing your account is easy. Just follow these steps:

1. **Open the COAS User Accounts window using the steps from the previous procedure.**

2. **Click the account name you want to view or change.**

3. **Choose User⇨Edit User.**

   The Edit User dialog box appears.

4. **Make your changes.**

5. **Click the OK button.**

6. **Choose File⇨Exit.**

   Your changes are saved automatically.

Creating new user accounts via command line

If you don't have the KDE Desktop running (you see later how to do that if you prefer things that way), or if you simply don't like the COAS tool previously described, then use the following command to create a new user account in OpenLinux.

```
useradd <name>
```

where <name> is the account name (username) for the new regular account that you want to create.

Pick meaningful account names

The name you choose for your account name (username) is also the name you use to send and receive e-mail, so choose the name carefully. A name that seems cute or appropriate now may not seem so later on. Also, avoid choosing a name that's too long, because you may have to type that name several times a day. You also may have to give someone your e-mail address over the telephone, so a username like *phool* will result in mis-sent messages, leaving you feeling very phoolish.

Years ago, a former student named Tom Chmielewski came to work at my company. Our

corporate standards mandated that login names be the person's last name. As I created his account, I knew that people would have little chance of spelling Tom's name correctly, so I created his account as TomC. Tom Chmielewski became known as TomC throughout the group, the department, and the entire company of 130,000 people. After Tom recently left the company, his new company had the same policy as ours. But before his first day was over, he was TomC again.

What's the password?

Changing your password regularly is a great way to improve the security of your OpenLinux system, and the act is something that you can do with a simple command. If you are logged in as root, just use the following code, remembering to replace *<name>* with your username:

```
passwd <name>
```

Whenever you enter a command like this, you are prompted for the new password for the account *<name>*.

```
New Unix password:
Retype new UNIX password:
passwd: all authentication tokens updated successfully
```

In the preceding example, the password was typed correctly twice. You can't tell that, however, because the program doesn't let you — or anyone else — see the passwords as they're typed. Marker dots don't even appear on the screen.

By the way, if you're logged in as root, you can change any user's password by using the command shown in this section. If you're logged in with your regular old username, you can change only your own password. The command is similar but doesn't include a username (yours is assumed):

```
passwd
```

To use this command to change your own password, you have to enter your current password before entering a new password. Doing so helps prevent a friend from changing your password while you're at the drinking fountain.

Be careful when you use the `passwd` command. If you're logged in as root and forget to include the username whose password you want to change with the `passwd` command, you end up changing the root password. Then you have a big surprise the next time you try to log in as root and the password doesn't work — because you changed it!

Ending Your First Session

OpenLinux, like all modern operating systems, requires that you complete a *graceful* shutdown, rather than simply pulling the plug. This prevents any information that is momentarily stored in the computer's memory from being lost. A graceful shut down records everything to hard disk and closes all programs in an orderly way.

Logging off the system is simplicity itself. Just follow these steps:

1. **Choose the Logout item from the main menu by clicking the K icon on the Panel, as shown in Figure 7-10.**

   A dialog box appears. Any programs that you have running are listed in this dialog box. KDE attempts to restart these programs the next time you log in. Look over the list before you log out to see whether anything in the programs needs to be saved before closing down the desktop. (If so, choose Cancel.)

   You can also choose the Logout option by right-clicking anywhere on the KDE desktop background and choosing Logout from the pop-up menu. The Panel also includes a small icon containing an X to the left of the virtual desktop buttons (labeled one, two, etc.). Clicking on the X icon initiates a logout sequence.

2. **Click Logout to confirm that you want to log out.**

   After a moment, the graphical login screen appears. At this point you can log in again (with your regular username or root, if needed). You can also choose to shut down your computer from this point.

To shut down the computer, continue with the following steps:

3. **Click the Shutdown button.**

   A small dialog box with shutdown options appears.

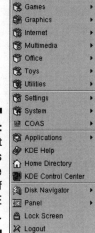

Figure 7-10:
The Logout command is at the bottom of the KDE main menu.

4. **Select the appropriate shutdown option (such as _restart_ or _halt the system_).**

   After your screen reads "System halted" or begins to reboot, then you can turn off the power.

We probably shouldn't tell you this, but you can skip this entire logout procedure if you're logged in as root with an open command-line window. Just type the command, **reboot**. This command results in a graceful shutdown, but it closes all open programs without prompting you to save any unsaved files, so use this command very carefully.

Part III
Using OpenLinux

The 5th Wave   By Rich Tennant

BRAD WAS BEGINNING TO FEEL PRESSURED TO FIND A WAY HIS
CALDERA OPENLINUX USERS COULD TALK OVER A PEER-TO-PEER NETWORK

In this part . . .

In Part III you find out about the basics: Files and commands, editors and shells, and windows. Chapter 8 takes you on a journey through the OpenLinux system, and along the way you meet file types, subdirectories, and the root directory. Then you use commands to navigate through the OpenLinux file system — changing, moving, creating, and deleting files as you go.

In Chapter 9, your journey takes you through the maze of text editing: Searching, moving, adding, and deleting text. Being the ever-conscientious tour guides, we present a few text editors to ease your tasks.

On occasion, any far-flung traveler has used an interpreter. In OpenLinux, you use a command interpreter, or shell. In Chapter 10 you get a short history lesson in shells. And, to give you one less decision to make, we offer a suggestion for which shell to use (don't worry, our suggested shell is the default anyway).

The KDE Desktop provides the graphical interface for OpenLinux. In Chapter 11, we show you how to use KDE to move, resize, hide, and close windows. Lots of programs run under KDE, and in Chapter 12, we show you a few.

Chapter 8

Working with Files and Commands

· ·

In This Chapter

▶ The ins and outs of files and directories

▶ Finding your way through the OpenLinux file system

▶ Changing where you are in the OpenLinux file system

▶ Creating, moving, copying, and destroying directories and files

▶ Giving permissions and taking them away

▶ Puzzling out command syntax

▶ Discovering a few OpenLinux commands

▶ Modifying commands to suit your fancy

· ·

*I*n this chapter, you take your first steps through the directory. We introduce you to file types, subdirectories, and the root directory, and we show you the way home — to your home directory, that is.

Next, you discover that you don't need a map to find your way through the OpenLinux file system; a few commands do the trick. Now that you're oriented with the file system, you're ready to make some changes. You find out how to copy and move files and directories, as well as how to create and destroy them.

Then we take you through the process of changing a file's ownership and permissions. And you get to practice your OpenLinux command syntax by tweaking a few OpenLinux commands.

OpenLinux File Facts

Files stored in the OpenLinux file system are similar to DOS, Windows, and Macintosh files — and a lot like UNIX files. Follow the bouncing prompt as we make short work of long files.

Files 101

A *file* is a collection of information with a distinct identification made up of a filename and a location (called a *directory path*) that houses the file. OpenLinux can store many files in the same directory — as long as the files have different names. OpenLinux also can store files with the same name in different directories.

Confused? An example may help. Suppose you get a grand idea and decide to keep your idea in a file named *idea* in your directory called /wonderful. Now suppose you're having a very fertile day and come up with another idea. If you want to keep your second idea file in the /wonderful directory, then you use a different name, such as /wonderful/idea2. (We hope your ideas are more original than our filenames.) You also, however, can keep the file in another location — called, perhaps, the /bizarre directory. If you decide to keep your second idea in /bizarre, you can call it idea, and the filename then becomes /bizarre/idea. OpenLinux sees this file and the /wonderful/idea file as different files. Remember, though, that each directory may contain only one file with the same name.

OpenLinux filenames can be as long as 256 characters. They can contain uppercase and lowercase letters (also known as mixed case), numbers, and special characters, such as the underscore (_), the dot (.), and the hyphen (-). Because OpenLinux filenames can be made up of mixed case names — and each name is distinct — we call these names *case sensitive*. For example, the names *FILENAME, filename,* and *FiLeNaMe* are unique filenames of different files; on some systems (such as Compaq's OpenVMS), however, they're read as the same filename.

Although filenames technically can contain wildcard characters, such as the asterisk (*) and the question mark (?), using wildcard characters isn't a good idea. Various command interpreters, or shells, use wildcards to match several filenames at one time. If your filenames contain wildcard characters, you'll have trouble specifying only those files. We recommend that you create filenames that don't contain spaces or other characters that have meaning to shells.

The File Manager

The easiest way to work with files in OpenLinux is by using the KDE File Manager, which also is called kfm (for KDE File Manager). You can open a File Manager window by choosing Home Directory from the KDE main menu or by clicking the home directory icon on the Panel (yes, the home directory icon is the one with a little house on it). Figure 8-1 shows a simple home directory window.

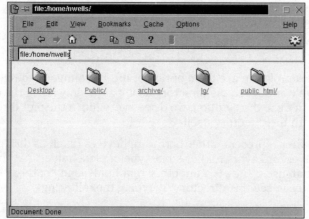

Figure 8-1:
A File
Manager
window
showing a
user's home
directory.

As you find out about working with files and directories in this chapter, you see how to complete many tasks both from the command line and within a File Manager window. You can take your pick any time you've got a job to do.

File types

OpenLinux files can contain all sorts of information. Five categories of files will become the most familiar to you: User data files, system data files, directory files, special files, and executable files.

- ✔ **User data files** contain information that you create. User data files, sometimes known as *flat files,* usually contain the simplest data, consisting of plain text and numbers. More complex user data files, such as graphics or spreadsheet files, must be interpreted and used by a special program. These files are mostly illegible if you look at them with a text editor because the contents of these files are not always ASCII text. Changing these files generally affects only the user who owns the files.

- ✔ **System data files** are used by the system to keep track of users on the system, logins, passwords, and so on. As system administrator, you may be required to view or edit these files. As a regular user, you don't need to be concerned with system data files except, perhaps, the ones you use as examples for your own private startup files.

- ✔ **Directory files** hold the names of files — and other directories — that belong to them. These files and directories are called *children.* Directories in OpenLinux are just another type of file. If you're in a directory, the directory above you is called the *parent.* Isn't this homey?

If you list files with the `ls -l` command, then lines containing directory files begin with the letter *d*. For example:

```
ls -ld plot
drwxr-xr-x 2 nwells nwells 1024 Jul 111997 plot
```

In this example, we use the `d` option of the `ls` command to tell the command we want to see the directory as if it's the only file in the directory. If we didn't use the `d` option, we'd see every file in the plot directory, along with the directory itself.

✔ **Special files** represent either hardware devices (such as disk drives, tape drives, or keyboards) or some type of placeholder that the operating system uses. `/dev` is a directory that holds many of these special files. You can see this directory by typing the following:

```
ls -l /dev
```

✔ **Executable files** contain instructions (usually called *programs,* or *shell scripts*) for your computer. If you type one of these filenames, you're telling the operating system to *execute* the instructions. Some executable files look like gibberish, and others look like long lists of computer commands. OpenLinux has standard directories in which most of these executable files are located: `/bin`, `/usr/bin`, `/sbin`, and `/usr/sbin`. By placing executable files in a predefined directory, OpenLinux can find the files when you want to run them.

Files and directories

You can think of the OpenLinux file system as one huge file folder that contains files and other file folders, which in turn contain files and other file folders, which in turn contain files and other file folders, and so on. In fact, the OpenLinux file system is generally organized this way. One big directory contains files and other directories, and all the other directories in turn contain files and directories.

Directories and subdirectories

A directory contained, or *nested,* in another directory is called a *subdirectory.* For example, the directory called `/mother` may contain a subdirectory called `/child`. The relationship between the two is referred to as parent and child. The full name of the subdirectory is `/mother/child`, which would make a good place to keep a file containing information about a family reunion. It could be called `/mother/child/reunion`.

The root directory

In the tree directory structure of OpenLinux, DOS, and UNIX, the big directory at the bottom of the tree that is the parent for all the other directories is called the *root* directory and is represented by a single / (pronounced "slash"). From the root directory, the whole directory structure grows like a tree, with directories and subdirectories branching off like limbs.

If you turn the tree over so that the trunk is in the air and the branches are toward the ground, you have an *inverted tree* — which is the way the OpenLinux file system is normally drawn and represented (with the root at the top). If we were talking about Mother Nature, you'd soon have a dead tree. Because this is computer technology, however, you have something that looks like an ever-growing, upside-down tree.

What's in a name?

You name directories in the same way that you name files, following the same rules. Almost the only way that you can tell whether a name is a filename or a directory name is the way that the slash character (/) is used to show directories nested in other directories. For example, usr/local means that local is found in the usr directory. You know that usr/ is a directory because the trailing slash character tells you so, but you don't know whether local is a file or a directory.

If you issue the ls command with the -F option, then directories are listed with a slash character at the end, as in local/, and you then know that local is a directory.

The simplest way to tell whether the slash character indicates the root directory or separates directories, or directories and files, is to see whether anything appears before the slash character in the directory-path specification. If nothing appears before the slash, then you have the root directory. For example, you know that /usr is a subdirectory or a file in the root directory because it has only a single slash character before it.

Home again

OpenLinux systems have a directory called /home, which contains the user's home directory, where he or she can

- Store files
- Create more subdirectories
- Move, delete, and modify subdirectories and files

OpenLinux system files — as well as files belonging to other users — are never in a user's /home directory. OpenLinux decides where the /home directory is placed, and that location can be changed only by a superuser, not by general users. OpenLinux is dictatorial because it has to maintain order and keep a handle on security.

Your /home directory is not safe from prying eyes. To be sure that your privacy is maintained, you need to lock your directory. (We tell you how in the "May I Please . . . " section.) Anyone logging in to your system as root (superuser), however, can see what's in your /home directory, even if you do lock it up.

Getting Around with pwd and cd

You can navigate the OpenLinux file system without a map or a GPS. All you need to know are two commands: pwd and cd.

Where are we?

To find out where you are in the OpenLinux file system, simply type **pwd** at the command prompt as follows:

```
pwd
/home/nwells
```

This command indicates that we're logged in as nwells and the current working directory is /home/nwells directory. Of course, *you* should be logged in as *yourself* and be in the /home/yourself directory, where *yourself* is your login name.

The pwd command stands for *print working directory*. Your *working directory* is the default directory where OpenLinux commands perform their actions. After you type the ls(1) command, for example, OpenLinux shows you the files in your working directory. Any file actions on your part occur in your working directory.

Conventions without Shriners

You see a lot of commands, so you may benefit by reviewing the syntax of OpenLinux commands:

✔ Text *not* surrounded by [ ], { }, or < > must be typed exactly as shown.

✔ Text inside brackets [ ] is optional.

✔ Text inside angle brackets < > must be replaced with appropriate text.

✔ Text inside braces { } indicates that you must choose one of the values that is inside the braces separated by the | sign.

✔ An ellipsis (. . .) means *and so on* or to repeat the preceding command line as needed.

Type this command:

```
ls -la
```

You see only the files in your working directory. If you want to specify a file that isn't in your working directory, you have to identify the directory that contains the file, as well as the name of the file. For example, the following command lists the passwd file in the /etc directory:

```
ls -la /etc/passwd
```

Another method for determining your current working directory is to look at the top of the File Manager window that you're working in, just below the toolbar. The path shown there indicates which directory you're viewing in that window.

Every directory has a parent and lots of relatives

If the file you want to read is in a subdirectory of the directory you're in, you can reach the file by typing a relative filename. *Relative filenames* specify the location of files relative to where you are.

In addition to what we tell you earlier about specifying directory paths, you need to know these three additional rules:

- ✔ One dot (.) always stands for your current directory.
- ✔ Two dots (..) specify the parent directory of the directory you're currently in.
- ✔ All directory paths that include (.) or (..) are relative directory paths.

You can see these files by using the -a option of the ls(1) command. Without the -a option, the ls(1) command doesn't bother to list the . or .. files, nor does the command list any filename that begins with a period. This may seem strange, but the creators of UNIX thought that having some files that were normally hidden kept the directory structure cleaner. Therefore, filenames that are always there (. and ..) and special-purpose files are hidden. The types of files that should be hidden are those that the user normally doesn't need to see in every listing of the directory structure (files used to tailor applications to the user's preferences, for example).

Now specify a pathname relative to where you are. For example:

```
pwd
/home/nwells
ls -la ../../etc/passwd
```

This pathname indicates that to find the passwd file, we go up two directory levels (../../), then down to /etc.

If you want to see the login accounts on your system, you can issue the following command from your home directory:

```
ls -la ..
```

This command lists the parent directory. Because the parent directory (/home) has all the login directories of the people on your system, this command shows you the names of their login directories.

In pathnames, there are absolutes

You've been looking at relative pathnames, which are relative to where you are in the file system. Filenames that are valid from anywhere in the file system are called *absolute filenames*. These filenames always begin with the slash character (/), which signifies root.

```
ls -la /etc/passwd
```

In the View menu of each File Manager window, you can choose Show Hidden Files to include dot files in the window. If you're viewing hidden files, you can click on the dot-dot (..) directory to change to the parent directory of your current working directory. You also can click the up arrow icon on the toolbar, which is usually the easier way to change to a view of the parent directory.

Changing your working directory

Sometimes, you may want to change your working directory because doing so allows you to work with shorter relative pathnames. To do so, you simply use the cd (for *change directory*) command.

To change from your current working directory to the /usr directory, for example, type the following:

```
cd /usr
```

In a File Manager window you can click the location field below the toolbar and enter a pathname to change the window's contents to view files and directories at that path. You also can click (just once) any directory that you see in the File Manager window to change to that directory.

Going home

If you type **cd** by itself, without any directory name, you return to your home directory. Just knowing that you can get back easily to familiar territory is comforting. There's no place like home.

You also can use cd with a *relative* specification. For example:

```
cd ..
```

If you're in the directory /usr/bin and type the preceding command, you're taken to the parent directory called /usr, as follows:

```
cd /usr/bin
cd ..
```

Here's a trick: If you type **cd ~<*username*>**, you can go to that user's home directory. On very large systems, this command is useful because it eliminates the need for you to remember — and type — large directory specifications.

Remember that each File Manager window includes an icon on the toolbar for the home directory. Just click the icon containing a little picture of a house to return immediately to your home directory.

Using cat to Create and Add to Files

The cat command is simple, easy to use, and one of the most useful OpenLinux commands. The cat name stands for *concatenate,* meaning *to add to the end of.* The cat command takes all the input it gets (mostly from the keyboard) and outputs it to the screen.

Make sure you're *not* logged in as root (see Chapter 7) when you go through this section and the sections that follow. Wait until you're thoroughly familiar with this chapter before you log in as root and try the examples. OpenLinux (for the most part) doesn't have an *undo* function, although a change is on the horizon.

To find out what the `cat` command is all about, follow these steps:

1. **Make sure you're in the /home directory.**

   To go home, click your heels . . . no, that's another book. Type **cd** at the prompt, and then type **pwd**.

2. **Type cat at the command line, as in this example:**

   ```
   cat
   ```

   The cursor moves to the next line, but nothing else happens because `cat` is waiting for you to input something.

3. **Type your input and then press Enter, then type a few more lines.**

   Here's what we typed followed by what appears on the screen:

   ```
   Hi
   Hi
   What?
   What?
   Hey! How do I get out of this?
   Hey! How do I get out of this?
   ```

   Everything you type is repeated on the screen after you press Enter. Big deal, you say? We explain why this is useful in a moment.

4. **To get out of the cat command, press Ctrl+D. If you're not at the beginning of a line, press Ctrl+D twice.**

   Most UNIX and OpenLinux people write Ctrl+D as ^D, which means *end of file* (EOF) to OpenLinux. When the `cat` command sees ^D, the command assumes that it's finished with that line and moves to the next line. If ^D is on a line by itself, the `cat` command has no other input to move to and thus exits.

We promised that we'd explain the usefulness of the `cat` command. We always try to keep our promises, so here goes. The `cat` command is the perfect way to use the contents of files within other commands, or to copy information that you enter on the keyboard to a file. To do these things, you need to know three symbols:

- ✔ > is known as *redirection of standard output*. When you use >, you tell the computer "Capture the information that normally goes to the screen, create a file, and put the information in it."

- ✔ >> is known as *appending standard output*. When you use this symbol, you tell the computer "Capture the information that would normally go to the screen and append the information to an existing file. If the file doesn't exist, then create it."

- ✔ < is used to tell the computer "Take the information from the specified file and feed it to *standard in* (also known as *standard input*), acting as though the information is coming from the keyboard."

Follow these steps to use the `cat` command to create a file by redirecting the output of the `cat` command from the screen to the filename that you want:

1. **At the command line, type** `cat >` **followed by the name of your file, then type your little heart out.**

   Here's what we typed:

   ```
   cat > dogfile
   Hi again
   Dogfish. Dogleg. Dog days.
   Doghouse. Dogfight. Doggone.
   ```

   Everything is repeated to the file called `dogfile`, not to the screen. OpenLinux created dogfile for us because the filename didn't already exist.

2. **After you finish typing, just press ^D (Ctrl+D) on an empty line.**

   You're right back at the OpenLinux prompt.

Are you wondering whether the `cat` command did what you wanted? You can check by using the `cat` command and the filename again:

```
cat dogfile
Hi again
Dogfish. Dogleg. Dog days.
Doghouse. Dogfight. Doggone.
```

This time the `cat` command took the file off the disk and put the output to *standard out* (also known as *standard output*), which in this case is your computer screen.

If you think of something else that you want to add to the file, you can use the append symbol (>>) with the filename. OpenLinux adds whatever you type to the end of the filename. Returning to dogfile:

```
cat >> dogfile
Dog-eared. Doggerel.
```

Are we confusing you? You use the `cat` command to concatenate files or concatenate input to either the beginning or the end of the file. The `cat` command is the only command created to do this. You also can use the >> symbol to add data to the *end* of a file.

The >> symbol can be used with many OpenLinux commands. For example:

```
cat file1 file2 file3 file4 >>fileout
```

joins file1, file2, file3, and file4, putting the results in fileout. In the following:

```
sort file1 >>file2
```

the `sort` command sorts the contents of `file1` and appends it to a (perhaps already existing) `file2`. If `file2` doesn't exist, then the system creates `file2` and puts the sorted output into it.

After you finish, be sure to end the session with ^D.

Manipulation at Its Best

OpenLinux has many ways to create, move, copy, and delete files and directories. Some of these features are so easy to use that you need to be careful: Unlike other operating systems, OpenLinux won't tell you that you are about to overwrite a file — it just follows your orders and overwrites!

We said it once but we'll say it again: Make sure that you're *not* logged in as root while you go through these sections.

Creating directories

To create a new directory in OpenLinux, use the `mkdir` command (just like in DOS). The command looks like this:

```
mkdir newdirectory
```

This command creates a subdirectory under your current or working directory. If you want the subdirectory under another directory, change to that directory first and then create the new subdirectory.

Create a new directory called `santa_cruz`. Go ahead, do it:

```
mkdir santa_cruz
```

Now create another directory called `work`:

```
mkdir work
```

and then change the directory to put yourself in the `santa_cruz` directory:

```
cd santa_cruz
```

Now create a file under `santa_cruz` called `radman`, by using the `cat` command (see "Using cat to Create and Add to Files" earlier in this chapter):

```
cat >radman
Once upon a time there lived a handsome prince.
^D
```

Now create another file:

```
cat >jewels
Once upon a time there lived a beautiful princess.
^D
```

And one more:

```
cat >moody
The handsome prince and beautiful princess had a dog named
          Moody.
^D
```

Now you have some files to work with.

For those of you following this exercise in a File Manager window, you can choose New from the File menu and then choose Directory to create a new subdirectory in your current working directory. You can't, however, use the cat command as described from within a File Manager window because this exercise requires you to enter text at a command line.

Moving and copying files and directories

OpenLinux allows you to move and copy files and directories two ways — by using commands or by using the File Manager.

Using commands to move and copy

The commands for moving and copying directories and files are mv for move and cp for copy. If you want to rename a file, you can use the move command. No, you're not really moving the file, but in OpenLinux the developers realized that renaming something was a lot like moving it. The format of the move command is

```
mv <source> <destination>
```

With your example files from the preceding section, you can move the file named radman to a file named bryant by executing the following command:

```
mv radman bryant
```

This command leaves the file in the santa_cruz directory, but changes its name to bryant. So you see the file was not really moved, but just renamed.

Now try moving the bryant file to the work directory. To do that, first you have to move the file up and then into the work directory. You can do that with one command:

```
mv bryant ../work
```

Note that the destination file uses the .. (or parent directory) designation. This command tells OpenLinux to go up one directory level and look for a directory called work, and then put the file into that directory with the name bryant, because you didn't specify any other name. If you instead typed this:

```
mv bryant ../work/supersalesman
```

the bryant file would move to the work directory named supersalesman. Note that in both cases (with the file maintaining its name of bryant or taking the new name supersalesman), your current directory is still santa_cruz, and all your filenames are relative to that directory.

Strictly speaking, the file still has not really moved. The data bits are still on the same part of the disk where they were originally. The *file specification* (the directory path plus the filename) that you use to talk about the file is different, so it appears to have moved.

In early versions of UNIX, you were not allowed to use mv to move a file from one disk partition to another; you could only copy a file by using the cp(1) command. OpenLinux allows you to use the mv command to move a file anywhere. Normally, mv leaves the data in place and just changes the file's name or the directory where the name is placed. But when the file is moved across disk partitions (for example, from /usr to /home in a lot of OpenLinux systems), the data is copied to the new disk partition, the new name is put in place in that partition's directory structure, and the name and file's data are removed from the old disk partition.

Copying a file does move some data. The syntax is

```
cp <source> <destination>
```

Look familiar? This is the same syntax you use for the move command.

Now, make two copies of the jewels file. Because you can't have two files with the same name in the same directory, you have to think of a new name, such as jewels2.

```
cp jewels jewels2
```

If you want a copy of a file but in a different directory, you can use the same filename. For example, suppose you want to copy a file called moody to the ../work directory. You can keep the name moody because its full pathname has work in it instead of in santa_cruz:

```
cp moody ../work
```

As you can see, the pathname specifications for files are similar from command to command, even though the file contents and commands are different.

Using File Manager to move and copy

Moving and copying files in the graphical File Manager is easy. Just follow these steps:

1. **Open two File Manager windows (click the house icon on the Panel a second time).**

   Make sure that one window contains the directory with the file you want to move or copy and that the other window contains the directory you want to move or copy the file to.

2. **Next, click and drag the file from one window to the other, releasing the mouse button over the destination directory.**

   You see a pop-up menu in which you can choose to Move, Copy, or Link the file that you dragged, as shown in Figure 8-2. (Choosing Link creates a pointer from the new location to the file, which remains in the original location.)

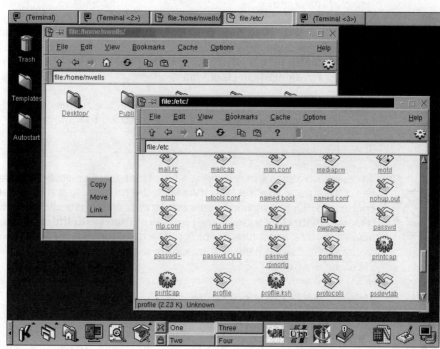

Figure 8-2: Open multiple File Manager windows to copy or move files using drag and drop.

Removing files

Like the flexibility you have by being able to move and copy with commands or the File Manager? Then you're in luck: OpenLinux gives you the same options for removing files.

Using commands to remove files

The command for removing, or deleting, a file is `rm`. If you followed our little story in the "Using commands to move and copy" section, the handsome prince now has two beautiful princesses (`jewels` and `jewels2`) in the `santa_cruz` directory. Most people know that this is probably one too many princesses, so get rid of the second princess:

```
rm jewels2
```

You've removed the extra file from the current directory. To remove a file from another directory, you provide a relative filename or absolute filename. For example, if you want to expunge `moody` from the `work` directory, you would type the following:

```
rm ../work/moody
```

You're allowed to use wildcards with `rm`, but please be careful if you do! When files are removed in OpenLinux, they're gone forever — kaput, vanished — and they can't be recovered. Check out Chapter 10 to learn more about using wildcards in OpenLinux.

The following command removes *everything* in the current directory and all the directories under it that you have permission to remove:

```
rm -r *
```

To lessen the danger of removing a lot of files inadvertently when using wildcards, be sure to use the `-i` option with the `rm`, `cp`, `mv`, and various other commands. The `-i` option means *interactive,* and it lists each filename to be removed (with the `rm` command) or overwritten (with the `mv` or `cp` command). If you answer either y or Y to the question, the file is removed or overwritten, respectively. If you answer anything else, OpenLinux leaves the file alone.

Using File Manager to remove files

Because moving files in OpenLinux (or any Linux or UNIX system, for that matter) is so dangerous — so final — we recommend using the KDE features to protect yourself from costly errors in judgment. To delete any file from a File Manager window, use one of these methods:

✔ Right click the file's icon and choose Move to Trash.

✔ Click and drag the file's icon, dropping it on the Trash can icon on your KDE desktop.

In either case, the file is moved to a desktop directory called Trash. The file still is there if you decide discarding it is a bad idea. If you decide that discarding the file is a wise move, you can right-click the desktop Trash-can icon and choose Empty Trash from the pop-up menu. Or, you can click the Trash-can icon to view all the files in the Trash, dragging one back to your home directory (or any other location) if you decide to keep the file after all.

Some brave souls may think that Trash cans are only for novices. You also can right click an icon in a File Manager window and then choose Delete. But remember that we warned you.

Removing directories

You can remove not only files but also directories. If you're still following our story about the handsome prince and his princess, you now have two directories in your home directory that are taking up a small amount of space. Because you're finished with these directories, you can delete them and recover that space for other tasks. As you may have guessed by now, you can remove directories either from the command line or within a File Manager window.

Using commands to remove directories

First, return to your `home` directory:

```
cd
```

Now remove the `santa_cruz` directory:

```
rm -rf santa_cruz
```

This command removes the `santa_cruz` directory and all files and directories under it. Note that this is just the `rm` command with *recursively* and *forcefully* options. (*Recursively* means to keep going down in the directory structure and remove files and directories as you find them. *Forcefully* means that the file should be removed if at all possible; ignore cases where `rm` may prompt the user for further information.)

Another command specifically for removing empty directories is called `rmdir`. With `rmdir`, the directory must be empty to be removed. If you attempt to remove the `work` directory without first deleting its files, the system displays the following message:

```
rmdir: work: Directory not empty
```

Using File Manager to remove directories

Once again, we recommend using the KDE features to protect yourself from costly errors in judgment as you delete directories. To delete a diretory from a File Manager window, use one of these methods:

- ✔ Right-click the directory's icon and choose Move to Trash.
- ✔ Click and drag the directory's icon, dropping it on the Trash-can icon on your KDE Desktop.

In either case, the directory is moved to a desktop directory called Trash. The contents of the directory are still in the Trash directory, waiting for you to rescue them should the need arise. Just click the Trash-can icon to view the contents of the Trash.

May I Please . . .

Files and directories in OpenLinux have owners and are assigned a list of permissions. This system of ownership and permissions forms the basis for restricting and allowing access to files. File permissions also can be used to decide whether a file is executable as a command and to determine who can use the file or command. Knowing how file permissions operate is important because even if you're the only one who uses your system, commands and databases are owned by other users, including root (the superuser). Permissions on these files either allow or disallow you — the general user — from updating these files.

Using the ls command with the -l option allows you to see the permissions of the files, along with other relevant information, such as who owns the file, what group of people have permission to access or modify the file, the size of the file or directory, the last time the file was modified, and the name of the file.

To take a look at a few simple file permissions, start by creating a new file with the touch command. The touch command is used for many things inside the UNIX and OpenLinux communities and is great for easily creating a little zero-length file:

```
touch tee time
ls -l tee time
-rw-r--r-- owner group 0 Oct 31 16:00 tee time
```

The `-rw-r--r--` are the permissions for the `tee time` file: The owner is you, and the group is probably you but could be someone or something else, depending on how your system is set up and administered (see Chapter 7 for more on setup and administration).

You may be wondering how you can become an owner of a file. Well, you're automatically the owner of any file you create, which makes sense. As the owner, you can change the default file permissions. If you're logged in as root, you can also change the ownership of any file.

To change the ownership of a file or a directory, use the `chown` command. (Get it? *chown* — *ch*ange *own*ership.) The syntax is

```
chown <new owner> <filename>
```

Suppose you've decided to settle down and lead a more contemplative life, one more in line with a new profession of haiku writing. Someone else will have to plan the weekend get-togethers. So you log in as root and change the ownership of the `tee time` file:

```
chown dtaylor tee time
```

This command changes the ownership of `tee time` to `dtaylor`. If you want to change the ownership back to its original owner, you can use the `chown` command again.

Files and users all belong to *groups*. In the `tee time` example, the group is users. Having groups enables you to give large numbers of users — but not all users — access to files. Group permissions and ownership are handy for making sure that the members of a special project or workgroup have access to files needed by the entire group.

To see which groups are available to you on your system, look at the `/etc/group` file. To do so, use the `more` command. You see a file that looks somewhat like this:

```
root::0:root
bin::1:1:root,bin,daemon
...
nobody::99:
users::100:your-user-name, maddog, nwells
floppy:x:19:
.....
your-user-name::500:your-user-name
```

where *your-user-name* is the login name you use for your account. Please remember that the file won't look exactly like this, just similar. The names at the beginning of the line are the group names. The names at the end of the line (such as `root`, `bin`, and `daemon`) are user-group names that can belong to the user-group list.

To change the group that the file belongs to, you use the `chgrp` command (while logged in as root) (its syntax is the same as that of the `chown` command). For example, to change the group that `tee time` belongs to, you issue the following:

```
chgrp newgroupname tee time
```

Making Your Own Rules

You, as the owner of a file, can specify permissions for reading, writing to, or executing a file. You also can determine who (yourself, a group of people, or everyone in general) can do these actions on a file. What do these permissions mean? Read on (you have our permission):

- **Read permission** for a file enables you to read the file. For a directory, read permission allows the `ls` command to list the names of the files in the directory. You also must have execute permission for the directory name to use the `-l` option of the `ls` command or to change to that directory.

- **Write permission** for a file means you can modify the file. For a directory, you can create or delete files inside that directory.

- **Execute permission** for a file means you can type the name of the file and execute it. You can't view or copy the file unless you also have read permission. This permission means that files containing executable OpenLinux commands, called *shell scripts,* must be both executable and readable by the person executing them. Programs written in a compiled language, such as C, however, must have only executable permissions to protect them from being copied where they shouldn't be copied.

   For a directory, execute permission means that you can change to that directory (with `cd`). Unless you also have read permission for the directory, `ls -l` won't work. You can list directories and files in that directory, but you can't see additional information about the files or directories just by doing an `ls -l` command. The requirement to have Execute permission to see file information may seem strange, but it's useful for security.

The first character of a file permission is a hyphen (-) if it's a file or `d` if the file's a directory. The nine other characters are read, write, and execute positions for each of the three categories of file permissions:

- Owner (also known as the user)
- Group
- Others

The `tee time` file from the previous section, for example, may show the following permissions if listed with the `ls -l tee time` command:

```
-rw-r--r--
```

The hyphen (-) in the first position indicates that it's a regular file (not a directory or other special file). The next three characters (`rw-`) are the owner's permissions. The owner can read and write to the file but can't execute it. The next three characters (`r--`) are the group's permissions. The group has read-only access to the file. The last three characters (`r--`) are the others' permissions, which are also read-only.

`[-][rw-][r--][r--]` illustrates the four parts of the permissions: the file type followed by three sets of triplets indicating the read, write, and execute permissions for the owner, group, and *other* users of the file (meaning *everyone else* who has logged in to OpenLinux).

Specifying most file permissions by using only six letters is easy — three letters define who gets permission; three different letters define the permission being granted:

- ✔ **ugo,** which stands for — no, not a car — user (or owner), group, and other
- ✔ **rwx,** which stands for read, write, and execute

These six letters and some symbols, such as = and commas, are put together into a specification of how you want to set the permissions of the file.

The command for changing permissions is `chmod`. The syntax for the command is

```
chmod <specification> filename
```

You can change the mode of `tee time` to give the user the ability to read, write, and execute the file with the following:

```
chmod u=rwx tee time
```

That was easy enough, wasn't it? What if you want to give the group permission to only read and execute the file? You can execute the following command:

```
chmod g=rx tee time
```

Note that this last command doesn't affect the permissions for owner or other, just the group's permissions.

Now set all the permissions at once. Separate each group of characters with a comma:

```
chmod u=r,g=rw,o=rwx tee time
```

This command sets the user's permissions just to read, the group's permissions to read and write, and the other's permissions to read, write, and execute.

If you want to change permissions assigned to a file or a directory, there's an easier way than using the chmod command that we've just shown you. While working in a File Manager window, right-click any icon, choose Properties from the pop-up menu, and then choose the Permissions tab from the Properties dialog box that appears. A sample is shown in Figure 8-3.

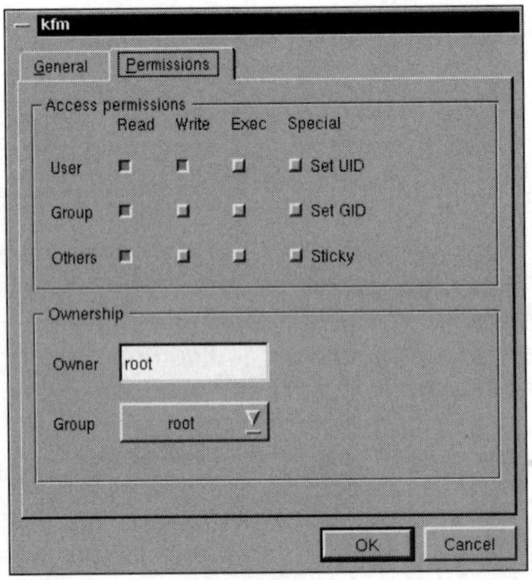

Figure 8-3: File permissions can be set in a File Manager window by using the Properties dialog box.

Within the Permissions tab you can select which permissions you want to grant for which users, and even change the ownership of the file. (Of course, you can do these things only if you're the owner of the file or you're logged in as root.)

Have Things Your Way

Most commands for your OpenLinux system are flexible and can be modified to perform special tasks. You can use two devices to alter a command: Command options and standard input and standard output redirection. You find out about command options first.

You can use *command options* to fine-tune the actions of an OpenLinux command. We introduce the ls command earlier in this chapter so that you can see the results of actions taken on the file system. To see how options work, in the next example you try out the ls command several times, with different options.

Use the mkdir command to make a new directory called gregger, and then use the cd command to change your working directory to that new directory:

```
mkdir gregger
cd gregger
```

At the OpenLinux prompt, type **ls** as follows:

```
ls
```

That didn't do much, did it? The account seems to have no files. You may need an option. Try the -a option and see what happens:

```
ls -a
. ..
```

Remember to type the commands and options exactly as shown. For example, the ls -a command has a space between the command and the option with no space between the hyphen and the letter *a*.

Notice the two files (they're actually directories, but in OpenLinux all directories are just files) that the ls command displayed. What? All you see are dots? Well, the single dot represents the directory you're in; the double dot represents the parent directory, which is typically the one above the directory you're in. (OpenLinux creates these filenames and puts them into the directory for you. If you just installed your directory, all you have are files that begin with a period.)

Now create a few additional files in the gregger directory by using the touch command:

```
touch file1
touch .dotfile
```

Now if you do the same ls command (without the -a option), you see the following:

```
ls
file1
```

And if you redo the ls command with the -a option, you get this:

```
ls -a
. .. .dotfile  file1
```

The ls command by default doesn't list files that begin with a period. By adding the -a option, you modified the action taken by ls to print every filename whether or not the filename begins with a dot.

The ls command has many options, and you can use more than one at a time. Want to see how? Modify the -a option by adding l to the option. The command line becomes

```
ls -al
  total 5
drwxr-xr-x 3(username)(groupname)(filesize) Jan 10 14:33 ./
drwxr-xr-x 6 root  root  (filesize) Jan 04 22:15 ../
-rw-r--r-- 1(username)(groupname)(filesize) Jun 18 11:30
          .dotfile
-rw-r--r-- 1 username)(groupname)(filesize) Apr 13 17:40 file1
```

As you can see, instead of just listing the filenames, the l option shows a more detailed listing of files. If long listings don't fit on a single line, OpenLinux simply wraps them to the next line.

Most of the time, OpenLinux doesn't care what order you type the options and therefore considers ls -al and ls -la to be the same. Multiple option choices aren't available with all commands, however, and work only with commands that have single letters to specify their options.

The ls command lists files in alphabetical order as the default, but you can tailor the output. For example, ls -alt displays the files in order by date and time, with the most recent first; ls -altr reverses that order.

Plumbing the Depths

Many OpenLinux commands generate a lot of output, and if the output all went to standard output as output to the screen, without some type of control, you wouldn't be able to see what the command generated because it would scroll past so quickly. For example, type the following:

```
ls -al /etc
```

This command lists all the files in your /etc directory. Because this directory holds a truckload of files, the information scrolls down your screen faster than you — or any Evelyn Wood graduate — can read it. You can, however, correct this.

With a process called *piping*, OpenLinux uses the output from one command as the input for another. Piping information isn't as confusing as it sounds. In the last example, you had too much information — or *output* — to fit on one lonely screen. You can take that information and put — or *input* — it into a program that divides the information into screen-sized pieces and then displays them.

To do this, you use the more command, which is an appropriate name for this tool. You *pipe* the list command's output to the more command. But how do you pipe? You use the | character on your keyboard. We just bet you were wondering what the heck that key was for. Type the command as follows:

```
ls -al /etc | more
```

OpenLinux doesn't care if spaces surround the | character, but you may want to use the spaces for clarity and to get in the habit of including spaces because they are important at other times.

After you press Enter, the information appears one screen at a time with the word *More* appearing at the bottom of each screen except the last one. To move to the next screen, press the spacebar. After you finish the last screen, the more command takes you back to the OpenLinux prompt. The more command can do even more. As soon as the screen halts with the word *More* appearing at the bottom, you can type some commands to the more program:

- ✔ q gets you out of the more command without wading through all those screens
- ✔ h shows you a list of all commands available in the more command

Note that some commands to the more program (such as the b command) don't work when you're piping input to the program, as opposed to using more with a file.

Everyone makes mistakes. Everyone changes his or her mind from time to time. For those reasons, you need to know how to delete text from the OpenLinux command line. If you want to start over, then press Ctrl+U to remove everything you've typed on the command line — if you haven't yet pressed Enter. The Backspace key erases one character at a time. The left and right arrow keys move the cursor along the line of characters without erasing them; after you get to the place you want to change, use the Backspace key to erase mistakes and retype changes. In most cases, the up-and-down arrow keys jump the cursor back and forth through the last few commands.

OpenLinux sometimes uses a command called less, which duplicates the functionality of the more command. Originally, the less command was designed to be more robust than the more command, but the more command caught up and now they're almost the same. Some OpenLinux systems display text with the less command instead of the more command, which most UNIX programs use.

The less and more commands have two apparent differences. One, the less command requires a q command to get back to the Linux prompt, even if you're at the end of the last page. Two, the more command always says *More* at the bottom of a screen, whereas less just has a : character at the bottom of the screen to indicate that it's waiting for you to input the next command. The *Caldera OpenLinux For Dummies* CD-ROM, which installs OpenLinux 2.3, includes both the more and the less commands.

Chapter 9

Working with Editors

*E*veryone who writes OpenLinux books needs a good editor. But the kinds of editors we talk about in this chapter are text editors, not the tweedy, frazzled, publishing professionals who struggle mightily with books. Text editors work with text files to give you the ability to add, delete, search, and move text — everything from thousands of lines of text right down to a single character.

Nowadays, text files are usually updated with word processors, but every once in a while you may have to update a file by using a text editor. In addition, text editors create small, compact files of characters, which are still the cheapest way to send e-mail and store character data on disk.

Take the time to play around with these editors, getting down the basics, because sometimes these editors are the only thing available. If all else fails, you use the ed text editor to boot. Other editors, such as emacs and word processors, are too big to fit on a recovery floppy. (For more on text editors, see Chapter 2.)

Your favorite editor for general work may be the graphical kedit program described later in this chapter. But because a graphical environment may not always be available, you can also learn about at least one other character-cell editor.

Remember, if you need to edit a system configuration file, such as /etc/passwd (which contains user account information), make a backup copy of the file first. If something goes wrong as you edit, you can revert to the backup and restore the previous configuration.

Text Editor Basics

A text editor is an essential tool for OpenLinux that enables you to create and modify an array of text files, including the following:

- User files, such as the `login` file
- System configuration files, such as `/etc/fstab`, `/etc/inittab`, and `/etc/lilo.conf`
- C and C++ programs
- Shell programs
- Mail messages

Graphical utilities are available to set up many of the text configuration files in OpenLinux, but graphical utilities won't always do everything you need. To take care of the details yourself, you have to use a text editor.

OpenLinux comes with a handful of text editors, including ed, vi(1), and two graphical text editors. The ed editor is a line-oriented text editor, less than 70 Kb, and one of the first editors for UNIX systems. Traditionally, the ed editor is included with every UNIX and Linux system. The second editor included with OpenLinux is vi(1), which is a powerful and popular full-screen editor. A third major text editor for OpenLinux is emacs(1), which some people prefer to use for most of their work. Finally, the KDE Desktop includes two editors: A simple editor called Kedit, and a more powerful editor (intended for programmers) called kwrite.

Although these editors have different interfaces and capabilities, all the editors support the following standard features: Reading and writing files, searching text, inserting and deleting text, and copying and moving text. In this chapter we focus on two editors: Kedit, because it's graphical and easy to use without much practice, and vi(1), because it's the most well-known editor in the Linux world and is always available from a command line.

Need help? Ask the program!

We can't possibly detail *all* the options these editors offer. So before you get involved in some monstrous editing project, read the manual page or online help file for the editor you want to use. You may be surprised to find some handy shortcuts. Where *editorname* is ed, vi, or emacs,

you can find the manual page on the editor by typing the following at a command prompt:

```
man editorname
```

Or, choose Help⇨Contents from the menubar within a graphical editor.

Two for one

Some editors use Control keys or Meta keys, which are indicated by Ctrl+ or Meta+, respectively, in this book and are sometimes shortened to C+ and M+. The Ctrl key is usually marked on your keyboard, but the Meta key often hides under an assumed alias, usually as the Alt key.

When you see Ctrl+Z, for example, press and hold the Ctrl key while pressing the Z key. (Don't press Ctrl+Shift+Z.) Likewise, Meta+H means to hold down the Meta key (in most cases Alt) while pressing the H key. Doing this really *is* much easier than rubbing your stomach and patting your head at the same time.

Most UNIX books show Meta keys without the + sign. For example, Ctrl+Z in this book becomes Ctrlz, ctl-z, or ^z. Another frequent occurrence in UNIX texts is ^d as the symbol for ending a file, which is the same as pressing the Ctrl key and the D key at the same time.

Saving yourself

When you work with the text of a file, the text is kept in a *buffer* (a place in memory), and no changes are made to the file until you save and exit the file. Our advice is to save your text early and often. Although OpenLinux systems are stable, a power failure after you've spent five hours typing a large, unsaved text file could be just your luck.

Saving your file is particularly useful when you're going to execute some large, complex command that will transform your text file dramatically. Yes, most editors have an undo command that backs out the last one or two (or more) commands and the text you've given the text editor. Writing the buffer to disk, however, is foolproof.

If you make a mistake and want your file back the way it was when you last saved it, you must quit — rather than exit — the editor. *Quitting* means leaving the editor without doing one last save of the file. *Exiting* means saving the changes that exist in the buffer and then leaving the editor. We show you how to use both functions for vi(1) and Kedit.

Some editors have autosave, which is a nice feature for people who are forgetful about saving their files. *Autosave* counts how many commands or changes you make to a file and then automatically saves the buffer to the file after a certain number of changes. Autosave does have its problems, however. One, the autosave feature causes some editors to freeze while autosaving, which is annoying. Two, autosave can happen at the worst time. For example, if you execute a complex command that erases your buffer and then autosave kicks in, the undo command may not be able to undo your complex command. Neither vi(1) nor Kedit use autosave by default (though it can be turned on within vi(1) if you really want it).

If you use autosave, we recommend that you consciously execute a manual save (which resets the autosave counter) right before you complete a complex command. Then you can recover the file, if necessary, by quitting the editor without saving the buffer, and then going back to the command prompt and restarting the editor on the file again.

Going Graphical with Kedit

Kedit isn't the most powerful editor that comes with OpenLinux, but Kedit is very easy to use. Because Kedit is always available in KDE, you may find yourself regularly using Kedit for simple editing tasks. Kedit includes a menu and dialog boxes, so if you're new to OpenLinux, you can start editing files immediately.

Kedit includes the ability to print your text file, e-mail it to another user, or even upload your file to an FTP or Web site, if your network connections and permissions are set up correctly.

Starting Kedit

You can start Kedit from the KDE Desktop by choosing Applications⇨Text Editor on the KDE main menu. If you're working at a command line, you also can start Kedit directly by using this command:

```
kedit
```

And if you want to start editing a specific file, then include the filename, as in

```
kedit kim.ch1
```

where kim.ch1 is the name of either an existing file that you want to edit or a new file that you want to create. Whichever method you use, the editor opens with a blank screen, as shown in Figure 9-1.

If you open a file manager window and a copy of Kedit, then you can start editing a file by dragging and dropping the file's icon on the Kedit window.

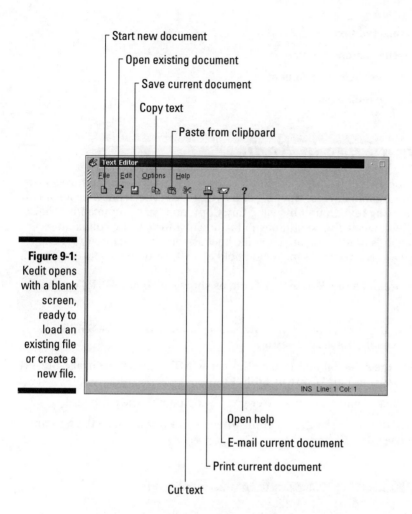

Start new document

Open existing document

Save current document

Copy text

Paste from clipboard

Figure 9-1:
Kedit opens
with a blank
screen,
ready to
load an
existing file
or create a
new file.

Open help

E-mail current document

Print current document

Cut text

The Kedit toolbar is located below the menu bar. You can hide the toolbar if you want to by using the Options menu. The icons on the toolbar map to features on the File and Edit menus, including the following:

- Start a new document
- Open an existing document
- Save the current document
- Copy selected text
- Paste from the clipboard

- ✔ Cut selected text
- ✔ Print the current document
- ✔ E-mail the current document
- ✔ Open the online help

Editing Files in Kedit

Kedit is somewhat like using a mini word processor, because Kedit uses many of the same commands for opening and saving files (check out the File menu) and for moving text around by using Cut, Copy, and Paste commands (check out the Edit menu). But Kedit doesn't include text formatting commands — the commands don't apply in a text file because only the characters themselves are saved. You can't make text bold or italic or define a font size for it.

To move around a block of text in Kedit, as shown in Figure 9-2, follow these steps:

1. **Select the text by using your mouse or holding down the Shift key while using the arrow keys.**

2. **Copy the selected text to the clipboard (KDE's internal storage buffer) by choosing Edit⇨Copy or Edit⇨Cut.**

   The text remains selected after you've copied it to the clipboard.

3. **Move the cursor to the location where you want to place the text and choose Edit⇨Paste.**

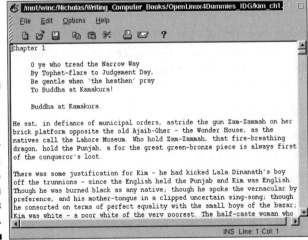

Figure 9-2:
Selected
text can be
moved or
copied
using simple
menu
commands
in Kedit.

When editing a file, you can insert the current date and time by choosing Edit⇨Insert Date. Or you can insert another text file by choosing Edit⇨ Insert File and then choosing the filename from the dialog box that appears.

Kedit is a simple editor, but it includes a spell checker! To start the spell checker, choose Edit⇨Spellcheck. The Spellcheck dialog box appears, shown in Figure 9-3, in which you can check each unknown word and then correct or skip it. The spell checker can be configured to use different spelling rules and to use different dictionaries by choosing Options⇨Spellchecker.

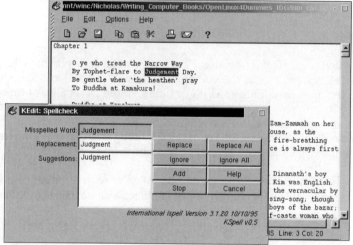

Figure 9-3: Kedit includes a spell checking dialog box.

Under the Options menu you also can choose the colors and the font in which you want your files to appear. Remember, these options are only for setting up the display of the file on screen. The color and font information isn't saved in the file. Someone else looking at the file won't see the font and color you select here.

By choosing Options⇨Font you can select a larger or smaller font, or a more decorative font, if you prefer that your display be hard to read.

More Kedit options can be set by choosing Options⇨Kedit Options and then selecting items in the dialog box that appears, as shown in Figure 9-4.

To close Kedit choose File⇨Exit. If the file has been changed since the last time it was saved, you see a message asking if you want to save changes to disk. If you don't, choose No to exit without saving (quit the editing session).

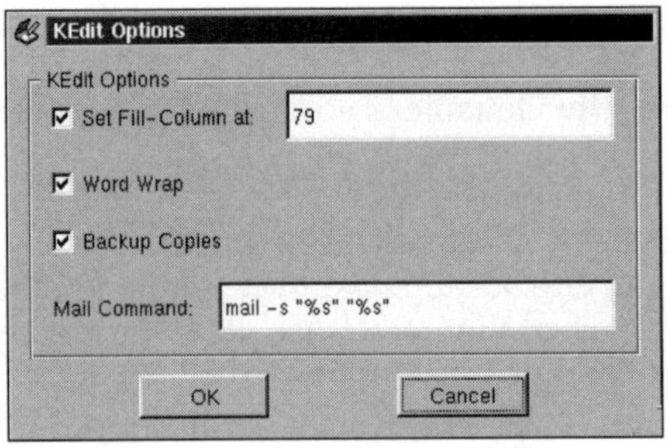

KEdit Options

KEdit Options

☑ Set Fill-Column at: 79

☑ Word Wrap

☑ Backup Copies

Mail Command: mail -s "%s" "%s"

[OK]   [Cancel]

Figure 9-4:
Kedit
options
can be
configured
using this
dialog box.

Here's vi

The vi editor is useful because it's always available. If you have to rescue a crashed system, edit at the command line (without KDE running), or work with text files on a buddy's UNIX or Linux system, vi is always there. The vi editor has two modes of operation and uses many single-letter commands. To start vi, you type **vi** at the command line. The screen clears, and the leftmost column displays tildes (~). You're now looking at an empty, unnamed buffer in memory in which you can enter text until you save the text to a named file.

You can start the vi editor in a number of ways with different options, but the most common way is to start vi with only a filename as the argument, like this:

```
vi kim.ch1
```

where kim.ch1 is the name of either an existing file that you want to edit or a new file that you want to create.

You can execute vi(1) by typing **vim**, but most distributions have a link to vim as vi and ex. A *link* is a way to give two names to the same program. Although the same program is being executed, the system is smart and looks at what the user types when starting the program. That way, vi users can continue to type **vi** and see what they're used to seeing with vi(1), and likewise vim(1) users can type **vim**.

The vi editor has three modes of operation:

✓ **Visual command mode:** Your keystrokes are immediately applied to the document as commands rather than being entered in the document. Pressing Enter is not required.

✓ **Colon command mode:** Complex commands similar to what you would enter at an OpenLinux command line use this mode. To execute these commands you press Enter.

> ✔ **Text mode:** In this mode the information that you type becomes part of the document itself.

After you invoke vi with a filename, the editor screen appears. At the bottom left corner is the following line:

```
"filename" [New File]
```

This status line tells you what the editor is doing. In this case, the editor has opened a buffer and the save and quit option saves the contents of the buffer to the filename file. If you do indeed invoke vi with the following command,

```
vi kim.ch1
```

then the bottom left corner displays the following line:

```
"kim.ch1" [New File]
```

When you first invoke vi, you are in visual command mode, which is the default. You can use four special commands to either locate text or transition to more complex commands:

/	Forward search
?	Backward search
n	Continue the search in whichever direction you were currently going
:	ex command (ex is the line editor included in vi)

In either visual or colon-command mode, the characters you type are used as commands, not as input into the file. To use commands, type the character on the command line. For the first two search commands (/ and ?), the cursor moves to the bottom of the screen, where you then type the string for which you are searching. As soon as you press Enter, the search begins. If you want to search for an additional string, then you can just press N to reexecute the search.

When you type the : command to enter colon-command mode, the cursor moves to the bottom of the screen and waits for you to enter a command or a command string. You must press the Enter key to execute the command.

Given that the characters you type are interpreted as commands in command mode, how do you get from command mode to text mode? Simple. Enter a command to do something in text mode, and vi will take you there. Here are some commands that can be used to illustrate how to switch from command mode to text mode:

i	Insert text before the cursor
a	Insert text after the cursor
I	Insert text at the beginning of the current line
A	Insert text at the end of the current line

As soon as you type any of these commands, you are placed in text input mode. Do not press Enter after entering the command. Any text you type after you invoke the command is placed in a buffer and echoed to the screen.

You may be asking yourself (because the directions are skimpy or no one is around to ask) "How do I get out of text mode and back to command mode?" Again, the answer is simple. If you want out of text mode, then just press the Escape (Esc) key and you're immediately whisked back to command mode. That's pretty easy, isn't it?

If you don't know whether you're in visual or colon command mode, then just press Esc.

Moving around in a file

Now that you know how to open a file in vi, knowing how to move around the file may help. The commands in Table 9-1 move the cursor around. First, make sure that you are in command mode; otherwise these keys are placed in your file just like any other data.

Table 9-1	Moving Around in vi
Command	*What the Command Does*
j	Move one line down
k	Move one line up
h	Move one character to the left
l	Move one character to the right
Ctrl+f	Scroll down a full screen
Ctrl+b	Scroll up a full screen

If you want to go to a specific line number, then you use a colon command. Type a colon (:) and the colon appears at the bottom of the screen; then type the line number where you want to be. For example:

```
:12
```

Press Enter, and the cursor moves to the beginning of line 12. This command becomes more useful as your files become larger.

Deleting and moving text

The vi editor has several commands for deleting text. You can delete characters, words, or lines. The command for deleting a word is dw; this command deletes the word to the right of the cursor. More words can be deleted at once by prefacing the dw command with the number of words you want deleted from the cursor position. For example, the command 6dw deletes the next six words that follow the cursor. Table 9-2 lists additional deletion commands.

Table 9-2	Deleting in vi
Command	*What the Command Does*
D	Deletes up to the end of the current line
dd	Deletes the current line
x	Deletes the character under the cursor (4x, 5x, and so on)

A handy command to remember is u, which is the undo command that undoes edits immediately in the unlikely event that you make a mistake.

The business of moving text around in the file usually requires the following general steps:

1. **Position the cursor at the beginning of the first line that you want to move or copy.**

2. **Type ma, marking that position with the letter a.**

3. **Position the cursor at the beginning of the last line that you want to move or copy.**

4. **Type mb, marking that position with the letter b.**

5. **Position the cursor at the line where you want to insert the text.**

6. **Type 'a,bm.** if you want to move the text, or **'a,bt.** if you want to copy the text.

   Note that the single quotation marks and period are required.

Using common vi commands

Table 9-3 summarizes common vi commands. Some of these commands have already been described; other commands are new.

Table 9-3	Everyday vi Commands
Command	*What the Command Does*
a	Inserts text after the cursor
A	Inserts text at the end of the current line
I	Inserts text at the beginning of the current line
i	Inserts text before the cursor
o	Opens a line below the current line
O	Opens a line above the current line
C	Changes up to the end of the current line
cc	Changes the current line
cw	Changes the word
J	Joins the current line with the next one
r*x*	Replaces the character under the cursor with *x* (*x* is any character)
~	Changes the character under the cursor to the opposite case
$	Moves to the end of the current line
^	Moves to the beginning of the current line
mx	Marks the current location with the letter *x*
Ctrl+l	Redraws the screen
:e filename	Edits the file
:N	Moves to line *N* (*N* is a number)
:q	Quits the editor
:q!	Quits the editor without saving any changes
:r filename	Reads the file and inserts after the current line

Command	What the Command Does
`:w filename`	Writes the buffer to a file
`:wq`	Saves changes and exits the editor
`/string`	Searches forward for string
`?string`	Searches backward for string
`n`	Finds the next string
`u`	Undoes the last command
`Esc`	Ends input mode and enters visual command mode

Controlling the environment

You may control your editing environment in vi by setting options with the `:set` command. Table 9-4 lists some common `:set` command options.

Table 9-4	Everyday :set Options
Command	**What the Command Does**
`all`	Displays a list of all `:set` commands and their status
`errorbells`	Sounds the terminal bell when errors occur
`ignorecase`	Makes searches case insensitive
`number`	Displays line numbers in the leftmost column on the screen
`showmode`	Displays an indicator at the bottom right of the screen indicating which mode you are in: input mode, change mode, replace mode, and so on

Note: Set command options can be toggled off by prefixing the command with `no`, as in

`:set nonumber`

which toggles off the line numbering.

What about emacs?

Many OpenLinux hackers quickly would tell you that the best reason you may have for learning vi is that you may someday be unfortunate enough to sit down at an OpenLinux box that doesn't have emacs loaded.

The reason for GNU emacs's popularity is understandable. For starters, emacs can run under X Window System and almost every computer system around, including MS-DOS PCs and UNIX workstations. For programmers, emacs can be configured to format source code for several languages, including C, C++, and Lisp. While emacs is indeed a powerful editor, emacs is also a bear to use. (And you thought vi sounded challenging.) If you want to find out more about emacs, then you have many books to choose from, such as the *GNU Emacs Manual* by Richard Stallman (published by the Free Software Foundation, Cambridge, Massachusetts).

Chapter 10

Avoiding Shell Shock

• •

In This Chapter

▶ Discovering bash

▶ Experimenting with wildcards

▶ Using bash history to find files

▶ Banging around to find files

▶ Writing a simple shell program

▶ Writing a not-so-simple shell program

▶ Just a bit on multitasking

• •

*I*magine that you're in a foreign country and don't know the language, so you hire an interpreter to accompany you on your visits to customers. You tell the interpreter what you want to do and where you want to go. The interpreter then decides what steps to take (hire a taxi or take the subway, for example) and in what order. When the time comes for you to talk to customers, the interpreter takes the statements that you make in your language and changes them into the customer's native language.

Shells (also known as *command interpreters*) do much the same thing in Linux. Shells take the English-like commands that you type, gather resources (such as filenames and memory), and supply lower-level computer statements to do what you want.

Many shells have evolved throughout the history of UNIX and Linux. Their history and derivation is discussed in the sidebar titled "The Bourne-again shell," which appears later in this chapter. For now, we'd like to simplify the issue of which shell is best and suggest a shell for your use.

We recommend *bash* because bash is widely available and has more features than you'll ever need as a user. If you go on to become more of a programmer or if you really enjoy investigating shells, then you may want to try the popular zsh or the even-more-popular Tcl/Tk or Python scripting languages, both of which have graphical interfaces.

This chapter assumes understanding of common Linux commands. If your Linux syntax could use some brushing up, check out the Introduction and Chapter 8.

See Shells

The first thing you want to do before continuing with this chapter is to make sure that you're using the bash shell. If you're using Linux without a graphical desktop and you're logged in as a general user (rather than as the superuser, root), then you're probably at a *shell prompt*. If you're using the graphical desktop, then you must log in and use the KDE desktop to launch a Terminal-Emulator window, which probably contains a shell prompt. If you're not familiar with how to do this, check out Chapter 11.

Your shell prompt should look something like this:

```
[username@hostname loginname]$
```

The most important element is the $ at the end of the line. This element is the *prompt* and is the shell's method of saying, "Okay, I'm finished with the last thing so give me something else to do."

If you're logged in as root or have become a superuser through the use of the su(1) command, the $ is replaced with a # sign, which indicates that the user is root or otherwise has become a superuser.

To make sure you're using the bash shell versus one of the other shells, type **bash,** as follows:

```
[username@hostname loginname]$ bash
```

As soon as you press Enter, Linux comes back with one of two responses. If the person who installed your Linux system didn't install bash properly, then you see the following:

```
command not found
```

You can find the person who installed your Linux system and throttle him within an inch of . . . no, no. You can find the person who installed your Linux system and calmly ask her to kindly help you use the bash shell as your default shell.

If you're lucky, you see the following:

```
[username@hostname loginname]$
```

TIP

The Bourne Again Shell

When Ken Thompson and Dennis Ritchie, two programmers at AT&T Bell Labs, first created UNIX, they wanted to investigate lots of new ideas in using computers. One of the ideas they explored was making the human interface to the computer changeable and adaptable to the specific needs of the application.

This human interface (or more specifically, what humans interact with most) is typically called a *command interpreter,* because the interface looks at each command as the command is typed and converts the command into something that the computer can follow as an instruction. Most computer systems at that time had the command interpreter built into the operating system, which meant that the user couldn't change it. The UNIX developers wanted to separate the command interpreter from the rest of the operating system. Because the desired functionality was both a command interpreter and a complete environment, the function was called a *shell.* The first command interpreter for UNIX was called the Bourne shell, often abbreviated as sh.

Later, when UNIX escaped from Bell Labs and fled to the University of California, Berkeley, the developers decided to extend the shell. They made the shell more of a programming language and included some features found in the C language. The resulting shell was the C shell, abbreviated csh. So, now, whenever Suzie takes her OpenLinux laptop to the beach, she sits sifting C shells on the seashore.

Both the Bourne shell and the C shell existed for many years. The Bourne shell version was available on both System V and Berkeley-based systems. The C shell was used only on Berkeley systems — AT&T was paranoid about having a shell on its system that was created by long-haired college students. The researchers at Bell Labs fought to add the C shell, and eventually it was ported to System V, also.

Next, enter GNU, a collection of software based on UNIX and maintained by the Free Software Foundation. (GNU, by the way, stands for GNUs, not UNIX.) The GNU project decided that it needed a shell free of royalty restrictions. Unfortunately, at the time, the C shell was still under restrictions from AT&T. So the GNU folks decided to create their own royalty-free, GPL shell. Their new shell would be compatible with the Bourne shell, incorporate some of the C-shell idea, and have some interesting new features. GNU called its shell bash, for Bourne Again SHell.

Meanwhile, David Korn, an AT&T researcher, merged the best of the Bourne shell, C shell, and any other shells he could find, and made the resulting shell even better for programmers by implementing several programming features. The most notable addition was *functions* (which helps to divide large shell programs into smaller, easier-to-maintain ones). His shell was named the Korn shell (abbreviated ksh). Eventually, this shell also developed graphical features and was adopted by the Open Software Foundation folks as part of their Common Desktop Environment (dtksh).

As the price of computers dropped and freely distributable versions of UNIX (netBSD, FreeBSD, and Linux) made their way across the

(continued)

(continued)

Internet, new shells evolved from the old ones and other shells started to appear, such as:

- ✔ **tcsh:** A C shell with filename completion and command-line editing

- ✔ **ash:** A System V-like shell

- ✔ **zsh:** Like ksh, but with built-in spelling correction on the command-line completion, among other useful features

- ✔ **pdksk:** A public domain reimplementation of the Korn shell

- ✔ **Perl:** Practical Extraction and Report Language

- ✔ **Tcl/Tk:** A string-oriented language with a graphical interface toolkit

- ✔ **Python:** A powerful scripting language with a built-in graphical interface

So why do we have all these shells (and shell-like languages)? Shells are examples of how separating the command interface from the operating system can allow the language to grow and improve. The shells also are examples of how specialized languages can be combined with other shells and programs to do really powerful work. If only one shell existed, under the control of one person or organization, innovation would probably take much longer.

Geez. It doesn't look like Linux did much, but it did. You're definitely in the bash shell and ready to see its power.

If you're logged in as superuser or root (a # appears at the end of your shell prompt), change over to a regular user account (probably the one that looks like your own name) by using the su command with the regular username. No examples in this chapter require superuser privileges. And because you're experimenting with shells, limiting potential damage is the best thing to do. Remember, it's not called *superuser* for nothing.

OpenLinux at your command

OpenLinux commands usually consist of three major parts:

- ✔ The command name
- ✔ Options to the command (telling the command how to change its actions for a specific execution)
- ✔ Input or output files, which supply data or give the command a place to put output data, respectively

Commands can contain one, two, or three parts, but the first part — the command name — must always be present.

Regular expressions: Wildcards and one-eyed jacks

If you had to type every filename for every command, OpenLinux still would be useful. But something that makes OpenLinux more useful is its capability to use a few special characters — called *pattern-matching characters, wildcards,* or *regular expressions* — to supply filenames. Just as you can substitute a wildcard for any card of your choice in a poker game, OpenLinux pattern-matching characters can be substituted for filenames and directory names, much like DOS wildcards.

Three of these special pattern-matching characters are

- ✔ * (asterisk)
- ✔ ? (question mark)
- ✔ \ (backslash)

The asterisk matches at least one character in any filename. For example, * matches the following filenames:

```
a
acd
bce
moody
```

You'll probably use * most in commands where you want to list all the files in a directory, such as the command ls -l *.

The question mark matches any single character. The string of characters a?c, for example, match the following:

```
abc
adc
aac
afc
a9c
```

The question mark and the asterisk can be helpful for identifying a particular type of file, if you're careful in naming your files. For example, text editor files usually have the .txt extension, and Microsoft Word files have the .doc extension. OpenLinux doesn't care about the name of a file, but some programs work only with particular types of files.

Now suppose you follow the convention of naming all your text files with the .txt extension, and then you want to see all the text files in a directory. You can use the ls command like this:

```
ls -l *.txt
```

The screen displays all the files in this directory with the .txt extension. Notice we didn't say that the command shows you all text files or that it shows only text files. If you want to name a graphics file with a .txt extension, OpenLinux happily obliges you. For your own sanity, however, be diligent in naming files. Some programs (such as those that create audio files or picture files) strictly enforce a naming convention on files they create, but OpenLinux doesn't care.

What do you do if the * is part of the filename that you're trying to match? How do you tell the shell you want only the file that contains *, not all the other files? The backslash character *escapes* the meaning of the special character. In effect, the backslash says, "don't treat the next character as a special character, just treat it as a normal character." For example, hi*est matches a file named hightest, but hi*est matches only the hi*est filename.

Although more regular-expression characters are available, this list of characters gives you some to work with for a while.

We command you

Let's see how the three parts of a command work together. Suppose you type the following OpenLinux command at the shell prompt:

```
ls -l *
```

After bash looks at that line, it performs the following steps:

1. bash creates a new environment in which to execute the ls command and determines what is *standard input* and *standard output* to the command. Standard input is normally the keyboard, and standard output is normally the video screen. (You find out more about environments in a moment.)

2. bash expands * to match all the filenames in that particular directory. By *expanding* the filenames, we mean that certain special characters are used to indicate groups of filenames. When these characters are used, the computer sees what filenames match these special characters and supplies the filenames to the command, instead of the special characters.

   For example, suppose you have the files ert, wert, uity, and opgt in your current directory. If you type

```
ls -l *
```

to the ls command, then it looks as if you typed

```
ls -l ert opgt uity wert
```

Note that the shell puts the names in alphabetical order before giving the names to the command.

3. Next, bash searches the PATH environmental variable looking for a command called ls. The PATH variable holds the names of directories that contain commands you may want to execute. If the command you want is not in the list, then you explicitly have to tell the shell where it can find the command by typing either a complete or a relative pathname to the command.

4. bash executes the ls command in the new environment, passing to the command the -l argument and all the filenames it expanded, as a result of using the * character in the command.

5. After ls runs, bash returns to the current environment, throwing away all the side effects that occurred in the new environment, such as an environmental variable changing its value.

In Step 1, we mention the *environment*. A shell operates in an environment just as humans live and work in an environment. We humans expect to have and use certain things in our environment. Suppose, for example, you leave your office for a few days and someone else decides to use it in your absence. At first, this coworker uses your environment exactly as you left it. The individual actually appreciates the fact that the phone works and the desk is stocked with office supplies, so that person doesn't have to go out and find a phone and supplies. But after a while, this newcomer starts changing things, maybe even drinking decaffeinated coffee out of your coffee mug! When you return from your trip, everything in your office is different. You can't find anything easily, and green stuff is growing in the bottom of your coffee mug. Wouldn't it have been nice if that person had arranged your office (your environment) exactly as you left it?

Bash creates an environment in which commands operate. As soon as a new command is executed, bash creates a clean copy of the environment, executes the command in that environment, and then throws away that environment, returning to the environment it started with.

Now look at a more complex example than the one ls -l * command:

```
cd /usr/lib
ls -l * | more
```

In this case:

1. bash creates a new environment in which to execute the `ls` command and determines what is *standard input* and *standard output* to the command. You can call this new environment child 1; the old environment is child 1's parent.

2. bash creates another new environment in which to execute the `more` command, called child 2, and determines what is standard input and standard output to the `more` command. Because the | symbol is used between the `ls -1 *` command and the `more` command, the standard output of the `ls -1 *` command is attached to the standard input of the `more` command. The standard output of `more` is attached to the standard output of the parent bash shell. The parent shell is the one in which you type commands and information, and the standard output of that original bash shell is the screen.

3. bash expands * to match all the filenames in that particular directory, as before.

4. Next, in the child 1 environment, bash searches the PATH environmental variable looking for a command called `ls`. The same process occurs for the `more` command in child 2.

5. bash executes the `ls` command in the child 1 environment, passing to the command the `-1` argument and all the filenames it expanded, as a result of using the * character in the command.

6. `more` sees the output of `ls -1 *` as its input and puts its standard output to the screen.

7. After `ls` runs, bash returns to the parent environment, throwing away all the side effects that occurred in the child 1 environment.

8. `more` sees the end of its input from `ls`, puts the last of its data out to the screen, and terminates.

9. bash returns to its parent environment, throwing away all the changes that `more` may have made to the child 2 environment.

The original bash shell is called the *parent,* and the two new environments bash created are called *children,* or *child 1* and *child 2.*

Putting the standard output of one command into the standard input of the other, as was demonstrated with the command

```
ls -1 * | more
```

is called *piping.* The | symbol is called — you guessed it — the *pipe symbol.*

We did that already

One of the most useful features of bash is *command-line editing,* which is the capability to change parts of a command line without having to retype the entire command. Suppose you type the following line:

```
ls -l * | more
```

Your mind is wandering and you meant to use the less command, not the more command, but you press Enter anyway.

You groan. You press Ctrl+C to halt the command. You really want to reexecute the command, changing *more* to *less*, without having to retype the entire command. Easy. Just type the following:

```
^more^less
```

In the above command, enter the "^" character just as it's shown. This character doesn't refer to the Ctrl key or anything special like that.

This line resubmits the command to bash with more changed to less, as follows:

```
ls -l * | less
```

Output appears. If you have to stop the less command, then press Q.

Note that the shell redisplays the first command with the change, and then the command is reexecuted. How does the shell know about the first command? History. bash remembers all the commands you have typed (to a certain extent) and allows you to edit and resubmit the commands. Awesome.

We say "to a certain extent" because bash remembers only a certain number of commands, depending on a parameter in the environment. After bash holds a given number of previous commands, it throws away the oldest ones as you type in new ones. Normally, this given parameter is large (at least 100 commands), so bash probably will remember every command that you remember.

Bang-bang

The fact that the shell remembers the command lines you type is useful for reexecuting commands at a later time. Simple *reexecution commands* are represented by exclamation points. In computerese, an exclamation point is called a *bang* and two exclamation points are called — you guessed it — *bang-bang.*

Here are two key ways that you can use the exclamation point:

- !! reexecutes the last command
- !<*partial command line*> reexecutes the command line that started with <*partial command line*>

Here's an example of reexecuting a command. Type **!cat** on the command line as follows. (cat is the <*partial command line*> mentioned in the preceding list.)

```
!cat
```

bash searches backwards through the previously executed commands in this session, looking for the first occurrence of a command line that starts with cat. As soon as the program locates the command, the command is reexecuted.

A little timid about this? Perhaps your memory of which command you typed and when you typed it is a little faulty. Append :p to the command line to see what history finds. The command looks like this,

```
!cat:p
```

with the shell then printing the matching command with the appended information before executing the command:

```
cat /etc/passwd
```

To run the command that !:p finds, enter bang-bang, like this:

```
!!
```

While using history to find and reexecute command lines, you can also make additions to the command line. Starting from the beginning with our example, if you enter the following:

```
cat /etc/passwd
```

then the file /etc/passwd is output to standard output, which in this case is the screen.

When you reexecute the preceding command by typing **!!**, you also can send the output to the sort command by using the pipe symbol:

```
!! | sort
cat /etc/passwd |sort
[username@hostname loginname]$
```

OpenLinux pulls the /etc/passwd file from the disk, passes it to standard output, feeds it into the standard input of sort, and then outputs it to the screen in sorted fashion.

Several shells (such as csh, bash, tcsh, and zsh) have this type of simple editing, but bash also has more elaborate editing.

Back to the future

OpenLinux offers a handy tool for rerunning long commands that you've already entered. Press Ctrl+P, and the display scrolls through the history of the commands you've entered, one command at a time in reverse order, with the most recent command first. After the command you want appears on the screen, just press Enter to run the command.

Do what we want, not what we say

Suppose your mind has been out wandering, and although you do remember that the file in /etc contains passwords, you can't remember whether the file is in /etc/passwd, /etc/password, or whatever. You may want the command interpreter to choose the proper spelling of the filename for you, rather than your typing what you think it may be.

You first can list the files in the /etc directory, and then use more to view the specific file that you want to see (/etc/passwd):

```
ls /etc/pass*
/etc/passwd
more /etc/passwd
```

Or you can use a shortcut with bash by pressing the Tab key after you think you have a unique match:

```
more /etc/pass<TAB>
```

The shell automatically expands the name of the file to /etc/passwd, and then hesitates to see whether you want to accept the command:

```
more /etc/passwd
```

When the shell automatically expands a filename and then hesitates, waiting for you to confirm a command by pressing the Enter key, the action is known as *command completion*. Now you can press the Enter key to execute the command.

But wait! What happens if you have two files, one /etc/passwd and the other /etc/password? After you press the Tab key, the system rings the bell and the name doesn't expand. Press the Tab key a second time,

```
ls a<TAB><TAB>
```

and bash shows you all possible expansions of that argument. If a huge number of expansions results, bash warns you:

```
There are 255 possibilities. Do you really
wish to see them all? (y or n)
```

Pressing the <TAB> key repeatedly

```
lp<TAB><TAB>
```

is an interesting way to get a complete listing of every executable command available in your PATH because command completion works not only for the filename arguments, but also for the commands. For example:

```
lpq      lpr     lptest
lpqall.faces  lprm    lpunlock
```

Here's another example:

```
<TAB><TAB>
```

results in

```
There are 1455 possibilities. Do you really
want to see them all? (y or n) y
```

Stand back, because the shell now lists all 1,455 commands in your PATH!

Another useful command completion is the tilde (~), known to your business manager as the *squiggly thing*. When you use the tilde symbol in a command line, it represents your login (or home) directory.

Suppose you're in the /etc directory, and you want to put a copy of the passwd file (which normally resides in the /etc directory) into your home directory. You can type the entire pathname to your directory, or you can just type the following:

```
cp passwd ~
```

If you're root and want to put the passwd file into someone else's directory, then you can type the following, for example:

```
cp passwd ~maddog
```

A copy of `passwd` goes into the home directory of user `maddog`, assuming that `maddog` is a valid user account name with a valid home directory.

Your Wish Is Our Command

We've been showing you *interactive shell functions,* a fancy term that simply means that you type a command and the computer executes it immediately. After a while, you may notice that you're typing a certain series of commands over and over. Wouldn't it be nice to put the commands in a file and execute them all at once? Well, you can.

For the rest of this section you work on creating shell scripts, which contain a series of commands that are executed every time you type the name of the script as a command. First you create a simple shell script, and later you create a more complex one.

Suppose you want to generate a report from time to time showing all the user accounts on the OpenLinux system. You can simply print the `/etc/passwd` file, but that file has a lot more information in it than you need. Besides, you're an organized person who wants your report to be better formatted than the password file.

First, look at the following entry in the `passwd` file:

```
maddog:eyrtwuir:500:500:Caldera OpenLinux
          User:/home/maddog:/bin/bash
```

Each grouping of characters between the colons is called a *field.* For your report, you want only the first and fifth fields. The `cut` command is the way to go. The *man* page for the `cut` command shows that the command used to get the first and fifth fields is

```
cut -f 1,5 -d: /etc/passwd
```

The man pages (manual pages) are terse-but-complete online documentation for nearly all OpenLinux commands. To view the man page for the `cut` command, type **man cut** on the command line.

You use the `-f` option for the `cut` command to list the fields that you want printed, in this case the first and fifth fields. You use the `-d` option to specify the delimiter for the field, which in this case is a colon. The preceding command gives lines of output formatted like this:

```
maddog:Caldera OpenLinux User
```

Maybe you'd prefer to replace the colon with a hyphen, adding a space on each side to make the report easier to read. The stream editor, sed, is your ticket to formatting happiness. You can send the output of cut directly to sed by typing the following command line:

```
cut -f 1,5 -d: /etc/passwd | sed -e 's/:/ - /'
```

The pipe symbol, |, takes the output of the cut command and feeds it to the sed command. Look at the part of the command line to the right of the pipe symbol, and you can see that the -e option of the sed command tells the command to use the next string of characters (in this case, what appears between the two apostrophes, or single quotation marks) as a command for the sed stream editor. The command finds the string of characters between the first and second slash marks and replaces them with the characters between the second and third slash marks.

Note the single quotes around 's/:/ - /', which make the shell see the entire string of characters as one *thing* and present the string to the sed editor as the thing that -e works with. Without the single quotes, the shell would conclude from the blanks in the string that three different things exist in this string of characters: s/:/, -, and /. In shell statements, unquoted blank space (called *white space*) is considered a separator.

Continuing with your report, you want to have a header that states the subject of the report, and the date. You can use the echo command for the header and the date command for the date:

```
echo Report of user accounts and full names on the OpenLinux
          system
date
echo ==========================================
cut -f 1,5 -d: /etc/passwd | sed -e 's/:/ - /'
```

Although these four lines are not difficult to type, you have to remember them and retype them each time you run the report. Because we like to save time whenever we can, we use our favorite text editor to type the lines in a file.

Our favorite editor is vi. If you want to use another editor, then that's okay, too. But be sure to name your file quagmire so that the rest of the example will work.

In the following, we're using vi to edit a file named quagmire, entering the commands typed previously into that file:

```
  vi quagmire
a
echo Report of user accounts and full names on the OpenLinux
          system
date
echo =========================================
cut -f 1,5 -d: /etc/passwd | sed -e 's/:/ - /'
<ESC>
:wq
```

The last line, `:wq`, writes the file to the disk and quits the editor.

Now you must tell OpenLinux that executing the file is okay. To do this, you have to change the file permissions to execute:

```
chmod ugo+x,ugo+r quagmire
```

For more on permissions, check out Chapter 8.

When you create the file, it's probably created with the permissions of the owner (u), the group (g), and the rest of the world (o) as being at least read (r), if not read and write (rw). The owner (that's you), the people in the group, and the rest of the world should be able to read (r) and execute (x) the shell file, or *shell script*.

Just because a shell can be read doesn't mean it can be executed. You explicitly must tell the system that executing a shell is okay.

Now, type the following:

```
./quagmire
```

and right before your eyes, your report runs! Type

```
./quagmire | more
```

and you see that your quagmire program acts like any other program and allows piping to other programs, including the printer (if you have one available to your system):

```
./quagmire | lpr
```

But notice that for your program, you have to type `./` in front of the filename. If you don't include `./`, you get the following message:

```
bash: quagmire: command not found
```

The error message is generated by the shell because your current directory, where the `quagmire` shell script resides, is not in the list of directories contained in the PATH variable (nor should it be). Thus, the shell cannot locate the `quagmire` file. If you type the following,

```
echo $PATH
```

you probably see a line that looks something like this:

```
/usr/local/bin:/bin:/usr/bin:/usr/X11R6/bin:/usr/bin/mh:/home
            /maddog/bin
```

A colon separates each *path* of a directory, so the directories that are searched for valid commands are (in order) `/usr/local/bin`, `/bin`, `/usr/bin`, and so on. The path that is most interesting to you is probably at the end of the line and should be something like `/home/<your user name>/bin`. Likewise, you should have a `bin` directory in your `home` directory. If you don't, make one now, as follows:

```
mkdir ~/bin
```

Then move your quagmire file to the `bin` directory in your login account:

```
mv quagmire ~/bin
```

Now you can execute the quagmire program just as you can execute any other program:

```
quagmire
Report of user accounts and full names on the OpenLinux
            system
Sat Oct 9 08:57:01 EDT 1999
===============================================
root - root
bin - bin
daemon - daemon
adm - adm
lp - lp
sync - sync
shutdown - shutdown
halt - halt
mail - mail
news - news
uucp - uucp
operator - operator
games - games
gopher - gopher
ftp - FTP User
nobody - Nobody
maddog - Caldera OpenLinux User
. . .
```

Congratulations. You've just written a program — a simple program, but as far as OpenLinux is concerned, as much a program as any other.

What you have written is called a *shell program,* or a *shell script.* In many cases, shells are more efficient than writing many hundreds of lines in C or Java. Shell scripts are fairly easy to write, fairly easy to change, and even experienced C and Java programmers use shell scripts every day rather than write more complex programs using those other languages. Systems administrators can't survive without scripting languages, such as the one that is provided as part of the bash shell.

From the Simple to the Sublime

Although you have written a program, your program always works on the same file, which is hard-coded into the script. For the remainder of this chapter, we show you how to create more flexible shell scripts — ones that generate different filenames as needed and automatically adapt to being run on different dates.

Suppose you want to keep monthly copies of the passwd file and then see the differences between them. First, write a program that saves a copy of the passwd file and stores the file in a directory:

1. **Use the** cat **command to create a script in your ~/bin directory called genreport.**

   The genreport script is simple. The genreport script copies the file /etc/passwd to standard output using the cat command; the redirection symbol puts genreport script into a file.

2. **For a filename that the script will generate after it's executed, start with the name** passwd **but attach the appropriate year and the month to it.**

   For example, the passwd file for October 1999 would be passwd199910, and the passwd file for November 1999 would be passwd199911.

   To create these files, execute the date command inside the shell script line and use its output to append to the word *passwd.* If you use the backward single quote (called *accent grave*) around the date command, it generates the numbers *199910* to be appended to the string of characters *passwd,* if this is October 1999. The accent grave tells Linux to "execute what is between the accent grave symbols as a Linux command and use the results of that command as a string in the larger command." Therefore, the date command generates the string 199910, which is appended to the name *passwd* to create *passwd199910.*

If you're searching your keyboard for that accent grave character, you may find it under the tilde character.

3. **After you make this file in your** `bin` **directory, don't forget to change its permissions to make the file executable. (Chapter 8 discusses file permissions.)**

The following is the program that we've outlined, along with an example of the program being run:

```
cat ~/bin/genreport
cat /etc/passwd > passwd`date +%Y%m`
<CTRL+D>
chmod u+rx ~/bin/genreport
cd
mkdir reports ; cd reports;
genreport
ls
passwd199910
```

Note that on the second line, we've used two accent grave characters, not apostrophes.

Single commands that aren't separated by a pipe symbol — that is, their standard output won't be fed to the standard input of the next command — may be placed on the same line and separated with a semicolon (;). This shortcut is useful in interactive mode, because you don't have to press Enter and then wait for a response, but the shortcut seldom saves any time in scripts. In scripts, it's better to put commands on separate lines so that the commands are easier to change later, if necessary.

Suppose you run the program on the first day of the month over several months' time. You accumulate several copies of the passwd file, each with changes as user accounts are added and deleted.

Eventually the reports directory looks somewhat like this:

```
ls
passwd199907  passwd199909  passwd199911  passwd200001
passwd199908  passwd199910  passwd199912  passwd200002
```

To simulate running your genreport program over several months, follow these steps:

1. **Create a directory called** reports **and change to that directory (**cd**).**

2. **Execute the genreport program once.**

3. **Create seven copies of the report file for different months.**

   To do so, change the name of each new file to a different date. This creates eight files altogether (the original and seven copies). The files have the same contents, but that's okay for now.

   ```
   cp passwd199907 passwd199908
   cp passwd199907 passwd199909
   cp passwd199907 passwd199910
   cp passwd199907 passwd199911
   cp passwd199907 passwd199912
   cp passwd199907 passwd200001
   cp passwd199907 passwd200002
   ```

4. **Write a shell script that shows you the accounts that were added and deleted from month to month.**

   One way to do this is to create a program that allows you to supply the names of two of the files to see whether any accounts have been added or deleted. The second way is more automated; you have the program look through all the files to see whether any accounts have been added or deleted — exactly what you do as you follow along in this chapter.

Just a few good commands

Shell programming depends heavily on the many hundreds of specialized programs that come with most UNIX systems. Of these specialized programs, perhaps 20 or 30 of them are used in day-to-day scripting, but the other programs exist just in case. Most of these programs, if not all, are documented in Section One of the man pages.

Each of these commands typically does one thing very well, and you can put the commands together with pipes and shell-script glue to solve more complex problems. Becoming familiar with these specialized commands takes time and practice, but after you're familiar with them, your abilities expand a thousandfold.

I still remember the day I began to feel comfortable with UNIX (*long* before Linux was available). I was trying to do something with a shell script, utilizing the 20 to 30 commands I knew. Finally the thought occurred to me that although I was not sure UNIX had the command I needed, there was a strong probability that it did. So I started going through the manual pages looking for a command that might help. Sure enough, it was there. From that day on, I felt comfortable with UNIX, even though I keep learning about it every day. From time to time, I still go through the reference pages of the manual one by one, both to find out about new commands and to refresh my memory on old ones.

Passing information to your shell

The shell program can get several pieces of information from the arguments you use when you invoke the shell. To illustrate the presence of arguments on the command line and the capability of the shell to access the arguments, use a text editor to create a small, simple shell called stuff, and put it in the bin directory of your home directory (such as /home/maddog/bin). (Remember to change the shell's mode to be executable by you, the owner.)

```
cat > ~/bin/stuff
echo The zeroth argument $0
echo The first argument $1
echo The second argument $2
echo The third argument $3
echo The fourth argument $4
echo The number of expanded arguments $#
<CTRL+D>
chmod u+x ~/bin/stuff
```

That should be enough lines to put into the shell. Note that each line ends with either a number or the character #, preceded by a dollar sign. These are special names inside the shell that have values assigned to them according to what you type on the command line as a command name and the arguments you include when you invoke the shell.

You still should be in the reports directory, but just to make sure that you are, change directories to your reports directory. Then execute the stuff shell script that you just created:

```
cd ~/reports
stuff
The zeroth argument /home/maddog/bin/stuff
The first argument
The second argument
The third argument
The fourth argument
The number of expanded arguments 0
```

Note that the zeroth argument (called $0) is the full pathname for the executed shell command. When executing the command name by itself on the line with no additional arguments or options, the zeroth argument is the only argument that receives information.

Now supply a wildcard on the shell command line as follows:

```
stuff *
The zeroth argument /home/maddog/bin/stuff
The first argument passwd199707
The second argument passwd199708
The third argument passwd199709
The fourth argument passwd199710
The number of expanded arguments 8
```

The shell expands the wildcard to include all the filenames that match the *
wildcard, which in this case means all the files in the directory. The $# argu-
ment reports that eight arguments match the wildcard. Only four of the filenames are printed, however, because you requested only four arguments —
filenames in this case — in your shell script.

To see that eight arguments really are on the command line, type the following command:

```
echo *
```

The echo command echoes whatever appears to follow it on the line. If you
type echo Hi there and press the Enter key, then *Hi there* appears on the
next line. If you type the command line echo 5342 and press Enter, then *5342*
appears on the line.

But after you type echo * in your reports directory and press Enter, something different from * appears on the next line. What appears is the name of
every file or directory in the reports directory, because the bash shell sees
the * as a regular expression and expands it to match every filename or directory name in the directory that does not begin with a period. That expanded
line is then presented to the echo command.

The same thing happens to your stuff shell script or any other shell script
that has a regular expression passed to it as an argument. The shell — not
the command or shell script you invoke — expands the regular expression.
Because you created eight filenames in the reports directory, you know
eight arguments are on the line (for the eight names in your directory), and
not just the four you printed.

Now add the proper regular expansion to cover all the files called
passwd1999xx; there are six:

```
stuff *1999*
The zeroth argument /home/maddog/bin/stuff
The first argument passwd199907
The second argument passwd199908
The third argument passwd199909
The fourth argument passwd199910
The number of expanded arguments 6
```

Only four files are returned in your four arguments, $1 through $4, because the shell script asked for only four to be printed.

The final step causes wildcard expansion of the 2000 years:

```
stuff *2000*
The zeroth argument /home/maddog/bin/stuff
The first argument passwd200001
The second argument passwd200002
The third argument
The fourth argument
The number of expanded arguments 2
```

Only two of the four arguments are filled. Likewise, the $# argument reports that only two files were expanded and placed on the command line.

First, the conditions

One series of commands is typically not used on the command line, typed in one line at a time, but only in a shell script to make decisions. These commands are *flow control,* or *conditional,* statements, and are found in many computer languages in different forms. The simplest one in the bash shell language is if. The if statement is usually written as follows:

```
if list1
then
list2
[elif list3
then
list4]
[elif list5
then
list6]
[else list7]
fi
```

Seems ugly, doesn't it? But it isn't too bad. Note that overall it begins with if and ends with fi, which is the backward spelling of if. Who says computer programmers have no sense of humor?

The *list* statements represent other shell commands, statements, and so forth, that should be tested to see whether they are true or false (*list1, list3, and list5*) or executed (*list2, list4, list6, and list7*).

So what are some examples of *list* statements? You see one in the next example, which is a test to see whether a file exists. In this case, the built-in function test -e sees whether a filename exists; if it exists, echo says so. You can try this out on the command line without putting it in a shell. Make sure you have spaces in front of and behind each left bracket [and right bracket]. A small > appears after the first line, to show that the shell is expecting you to type some more:

```
if [ -e /etc/passwd ]
> then
> echo file exists
> else
> echo file does not exist
> fi
file exists
```

Now, to test to see whether the if statement can detect the passwd filename, type the name incorrectly:

```
if [ -e /etc/password ]
> then
> echo file exists
> else
> echo file does not exist
> fi
file does not exist
```

You can make other simple tests, such as:

- -f for whether a file exists and is a regular file, not a directory or device file
- -d for whether a file exists and is a directory
- -r for whether a file exists and is readable

You can read more in the manual about tests you can perform on filenames. You can even combine tests to check for many conditions at one time.

Putting your ideas together

Are you ready to put the concepts from the first shell script together with the concepts from the second shell script? The result is a program that selects two passwd files from different months and compares them. The program tests to make sure all the filenames are typed correctly on the command line, and then extracts the information from the files, compares them, and prints the differences, if any.

You should use a text editor to create a file called `passdiff` in your `~/bin` directory, putting the following lines in it:

```
# Shell comments start with a pound sign (#) on a line.
# Anything following a # is ignored by the shell and is
# used only by humans to understand what is going on
# in the script. Use comments liberally.
#
# if the number of arguments is not equal to 2
if [ $# != 2 ]
# then
then
# echo a usage message
echo Usage: passdiff file1 file2
# and exit with an error code of 9
exit 9
fi
# if the first argument is not a file
if [ ! -f $1 ]
# then echo message that the first argument is not a file
then
echo $1 is not a file
# and exit with an error code of 9
exit 9
#
fi
# test the second argument the same way
if [ ! -f $2 ]
then
echo $2 is not a file
exit 9
fi
# Now use the cut and sed statements, which we used
# before to create the user account-name/description. But
            this
# time, store the contents in files called
# /usr/tmp/quagmire.?.$$ where the ? matches any digit
# and the $$ assumes the process number of the shell to
# create a unique filename. Two files with unique
# filenames will therefore be generated temporarily in
# /usr/tmp: quagmire.1.<processnumber> and
# quagmire.2.<processnumber>
# There is a difference in OpenLinux (as in most programming
# systems) between a single quote (that symbol below the
# double quote on a U.S. keyboard) and accent grave`,
# that symbol below the tilde (the squiggly thing) on a
# U.S. keyboard. In the following lines, the ' symbol is
# a single quote, which turns off the shell's regular
# expression matching and allows the sed command to see
# the regular expression (if any).
cut -f 1,5 -d: $1 | sed -e 's/:/-/' \ >/usr/tmp/quagmire.1.$$
cut -f 1,5 -d: $2 | sed -e 's/:/-/' \ >/usr/tmp/quagmire.2.$$
# use the diff command to compare the two files generated.
```

```
# diff creates output lines with a < symbol pointing to
# extra lines from the first file and a > symbol pointing
# to extra lines from the second file. The results are
# placed in a third temporary file created
# using the process number as before.
diff /usr/tmp/quagmire.1.$$ /usr/tmp/quagmire.2.$$ \
        >/usr/tmp/quagmire.3.$$
# now we echo whether or not there were any extra
# logon names
echo password file $1 had these extra logon names:
# if there are any extra ones from the first file, print
# them to standard output
# We have to use single quote marks around the '^<'
# argument to tell the shell script this is an argument to
# the grep command, and not a redirection symbol telling it
# to take the file of /usr/tmp/quagmire.3.$$ and feed it
# through standard input
grep '^<' /usr/tmp/quagmire.3.$$
# now we echo whether or not there were any extra
# logon names
echo password file $2 had these extra logon names:
# if there are any extra ones from the second file, print
# them to standard output. (Note the use of single quotes
# in the line below.)
grep '^>' /usr/tmp/quagmire.3.$$
# remove all temporary files from /usr/tmp. The ? matches
# all three digits.
rm /usr/tmp/quagmire.?.$$
# exit with a successful error code.
exit 0
```

Remember to save the file. Change its mode to read and execute by typing the following:

```
chmod u+rx ~/bin/passdiff
```

Time to take the program on a test run. To do that, you need to make some of the files in the `reports` directory different. Add one more line to `passwd199908` as follows:

```
baddog::502:502:A BAD Caldera OpenLinux
        User:/home/baddog:/bin/bash
```

Then add one more line to file `passwd199910`:

```
bulldog::501:501:Yet Another Caldera OpenLinux
        User:/home/bulldog:/bin/bash
```

Now, cross your fingers and test the program! Oops. Uncross your fingers and type the following:

```
passdiff
Usage: passdiff file1 file2
 passdiff passwd199908 pass19910
pass19910 is not a file
 passdiff passwd199908 passwd199910
password file passwd199908 had these extra logon names:
< baddog - A BAD Caldera OpenLinux User
password file passwd199910 had these extra logon names:
> bulldog - Yet Another Caldera OpenLinux User
```

We Can Only Do 50 Things at Once

When executing programs on an OpenLinux system, taking advantage of its *multitasking* capabilities — that is, running multiple programs at the same time — is nice. This process is also called *job control*. Windows NT does multitasking, Windows 95 seems to do multitasking, and UNIX systems have been doing multitasking for almost 30 years. Most of this multitasking capability is due to the shell being able to launch background jobs and manage them.

For example, perhaps you have a task that will run a long time, with little or no human input needed. When you start that task, all you need do is put an & (ampersand) sign at the end of the line, and the job starts running in the background.

For example, if you start kCalc (a really nice graphical calculator that comes with the default KDE Desktop installation from the *Caldera OpenLinux For Dummies* CD-ROM), then you probably want it to run a long time, and yet you want to type other commands at the same time. (For more on the kCalc program, see Chapter 12.) To put kCalc into the background (assuming you have the KDE Desktop running), you can start kCalc by typing the following command into a terminal emulator:

```
kcalc &
[1] 2449
```

The number in brackets is the job number, followed by the process ID number. The *job number* is the number the shell gives the kCalc program to keep track of the ical job. The *process ID number* is the number the entire operating system uses to keep track of the kCalc program.

But wait, there's more

Linux is known for its *cryptic* command names, error messages, and documentation. We prefer to think of the command names as *terse* — a lot of meaning in a small space. The man page on bash, however, is more than 60 pages, with no examples and no cheery dialog to entertain you.

From that length, you can surmise that shell programming involves a lot more than we can tell you in these few pages. Entire books have been written just on shell programming. What we have shown here, however, can help you write a few short scripts to make your life easier.

To find all the programs running under the shell you're currently using, you can use the jobs shell command as follows:

```
jobs
[1]+ Running      kcalc &
```

This shell command tells you that kCalc is job #1, is running fine (thank you), isn't waiting for any input from the console, and is just having a great old time.

On the other hand, you can have another job (such as largejob) that you've put temporarily into the background simply by putting the & at the end of the line:

```
largejob &
```

After you type jobs as a command in this case, you see that largejob is stopped, waiting for input or some other reason:

```
jobs
[1]- Running      kcalc &
[2]+ Stopped (tty output) largejob
```

You can bring largejob into the foreground by typing fg %2 and giving it more input, and then put largejob back into the background by pressing Ctrl+Z and typing **bg.** Whew. Here's how it looks:

```
fg %2
largejob
MADDOG tries hard.
<CTRL+Z>
[2]+ Stopped      largejob
bg
[2]+ largejob &
```

You can have dozens or even hundreds of background processes. If all the background processes accept data from the keyboard at the same time, how do you know which program is receiving the data? Each program has to wait until you recognize it, bring the program into the foreground, enter the necessary data, and then put the program back into the background, where the program blissfully keeps running until it terminates or again needs input from the keyboard (or standard input, as you have come to know it). Now you know why `largejob` was waiting to accept such valuable and timely input.

Chapter 11

Windows on the World

● ●

In This Chapter

▶ The amazing KDE

▶ Moving windows

▶ Resizing windows

▶ Minimizing and maximizing windows

▶ Using virtual desktops

▶ Making your desktop look just so

▶ Exiting KDE

▶ Using other applications in KDE

● ●

*L*inux has used the X Window System almost from the beginning to provide a graphical environment for those who prefer a mouse to a keyboard. The X Window System has powerful features for remote access; X also has thousands of available applications. But X alone doesn't provide a full-featured desktop interface like a Microsoft Windows or a Macintosh computer.

Along about 1996, Matthias Ettrich founded a project called KDE, for the K Desktop Environment. KDE provides all the nifty windows and desktop tools that you're used to if you've used a Microsoft Windows system or something similar. KDE includes screen savers, color schemes, wallpaper images, and accessories (such as a calculator, calendar, and basic text editor). And Caldera OpenLinux includes them all.

In this chapter, you find out lots of ways to work in KDE, including how to work with individual windows, how to move between multiple applications, and how to set up the appearance of your desktop to fit your liking.

The Amazing KDE

After you log in to OpenLinux from the graphical login screen, you immediately start working in KDE. Figure 11-1 shows you the initial screen, which you may have seen already if you've read some of the other chapters in this part.

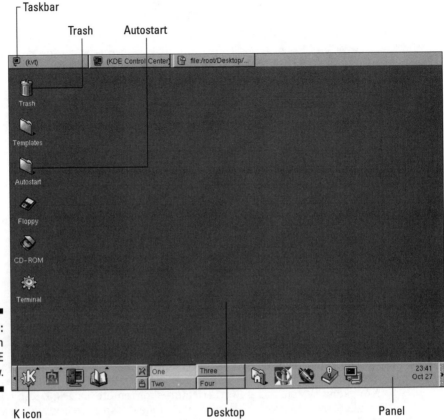

Figure 11-1:
The main
KDE
window.

If you aren't using the graphical login screen in OpenLinux, you can start KDE with the command kde (clever, isn't it?). Of course, if you don't have the X Window System configured yet, KDE can't operate. KDE works on top of the functionality provided by X. (See Chapter 6 for X configuration and Chapter 7 for more on how to log in.)

KDE provides a complete graphical environment for OpenLinux. By using KDE, you can do any of the following things:

- ✔ Explore your desktop with a comfortable interface
- ✔ Start multiple graphical applications
- ✔ Use keyboard and mouse tricks to control getting around in your KDE environment
- ✔ Configure the entire system in the graphical Control Center window

✔ Use a command-line window to execute commands

✔ Smoothly exit the desktop, saving your settings

✔ Create links to launch any application from your desktop

Exploring Your Desktop

The desktop space that you work with in KDE includes several features to help you with different types of programs and to configure your environment. Refer to Figure 11-1 to find each of the items listed here:

✔ **The Taskbar:** This bar appears at the top of your KDE Desktop. The Taskbar contains a button for each open window in KDE. You can make any window active by clicking its button on the Taskbar.

✔ **The Panel:** This bar of icons appears at the bottom of your KDE Desktop. The icons on the Panel represent applications that Caldera assumes you'll want to start up regularly, such as a file browser for your home directory, a Netscape Communicator Web browser, and a command-line window (called a Terminal Emulator). Click an icon on the Panel to start the corresponding application.

✔ **The K icon:** This icon is actually one of the Panel icons (on the far left end), but the K icon deserves special mention. Clicking the K icon opens the KDE main menu, as shown in Figure 11-2. The easiest way to start most programs in KDE (those that don't have an icon on the Panel, as Netscape Communicator does) is to select the program from the KDE main menu. We explore the menu options in the next section.

✔ **The Desktop:** That's the big empty space in the middle. The desktop is where application windows appear as you work. You also can place icons on the desktop for easy access to your favorite programs or most-used data files.

✔ **The Trash:** This icon works just like the Recycle bin in Microsoft Windows or the Trash can on a Macintosh desktop. You can drag and drop file icons onto the Trash icon to discard them. If you're *sure* you want to discard the files, right-click the Trash icon and choose Empty trash.

In most operating systems, you can undelete (or recover) a file that you've erased from the system, even after you empty the Recycle bin or Trash can. Don't plan on undeleting in OpenLinux — call it a security feature. As soon as you delete a file (or empty the Trash), the file is *gone*.

✔ **The Autostart folder:** This icon opens the directory containing programs that you want to start up automatically after you're using KDE. Before you can add an application to the Autostart folder, you must create a KDE Link file for that application. We show you how to do that later in this chapter in "Linking Everything to KDE."

igure 11-2:
The KDE
main menu
contains
submenus
and applica-
tion names.

You also may have a few other icons on your KDE Desktop, especially if you used the KDE Configuration Wizard to set up your desktop after you first logged in to your new OpenLinux system. (See Chapter 7.)

Many features of KDE are accessed by clicking your right mouse button (we call that *right-clicking*). If you're ever wondering how to do something, try right-clicking to see if a handy menu pops up with just the command you need. You can start by trying a right-click on the KDE Desktop or one of the desktop icons.

Getting an Application Started

After you discover how to find your way around the KDE Desktop, you'll probably wonder what to do next. How about starting up an application? Follow these steps to do just that:

1. **Click the K icon to open the main menu.**

   Note: You can also press the Alt+F1 key combination to open the main menu.

2. **Use the arrow keys to navigate the main menu options and then press Enter after the item you want is highlighted.**

For example, click the word Graphics to open the Graphics submenu (you can tell Graphics is a submenu by the little arrow to the right of the word). Then click Fractals Generator. The Fractals Generator starts, showing you the nice mathematically generated graphic, as shown in Figure 11-3.

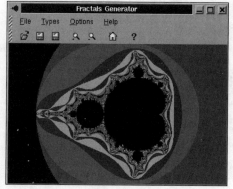

Figure 11-3:
KDE
includes a
fractal
program
on the
Graphics
submenu.

Locate the icon on the KDE Panel that looks like a file folder with a small house on it. That's your home directory. You can click that icon to open a file manager window that displays all the files in your home directory. The file manager window is shown in Figure 11-4.

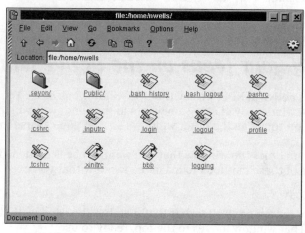

Figure 11-4:
You can
open a File
Manager
window
that shows
your home
directory by
clicking a
KDE Panel
icon.

If you need assistance, open the main menu again and click the KDE Help menu item. The KDE Help menu item isn't a submenu; this menu item immediately opens a KDE help window in which you can search for answers to your most pressing questions about KDE (or read on to get them right here). The help window is shown in Figure 11-5.

Figure 11-5:
The KDE
main menu
includes a
Help item
that opens
this online
help
window.

Window Tricks

The KDE Desktop that you're working on lets you have many application windows open at the same time. But as you may imagine, you quickly can clutter up the KDE Desktop. Fortunately, KDE offers several useful tricks to manipulate windows on the desktop.

Keeping your focus on the active window

If a window is active in KDE, we say that the window has *focus.* You can move the focus to a window by clicking anywhere in the window. A window with focus moves on top of all the other windows so that you can use that window.

Of course, sometimes the window that you want to use is hidden. If that happens, try one of these methods to make the window that you need active in KDE:

- ✔ Click the button on the Taskbar that matches the window that you want to use. That window moves to the top, ready to use.

- ✔ Hold down the Alt key and press the Tab key repeatedly. The first time you press this key combination a small box appears on your screen. As you repeatedly press Tab, the name of each window appears in the box. After the window you want to use is displayed, release the Alt+Tab keys. That window jumps to the top of the heap.

✔ Press the Ctrl+Esc key combination. A window opens that lists all the open windows. Click the name of a window to switch to that window.

Moving day

After you start a new application, KDE guesses where you want the newly opened window. More often than not, you want the window someplace else.

To move a window in KDE, click the title bar (the blue bar across the top of the window), then drag the window to the desired new location and release the mouse button.

Resizing a window

Most KDE windows can be resized to fit better with other windows on your desktop, or to make seeing the window's contents easier. To resize a window, follow these steps:

1. **Move your mouse pointer to any corner of the window.**

   As you position the mouse in just the right spot on the corner of the window, the mouse pointer changes from an arrow to a small angle bracket that matches the corner you're pointing to.

2. **After you see the new mouse pointer, click and drag the mouse to resize the window.**

   If you can't seem to get the mouse pointer to change, you're probably dealing with a window that can't be resized. Most application windows, however, can be resized using the steps in this section.

Making a window a big deal or getting the window out of sight

If you want a really big window, you can maximize the window instead of trying to stretch it by dragging your mouse cursor to the outer limits of your screen.

Each window includes three small boxes or icons on the right side of the title bar. One icon has a line at the bottom; one icon has a box, and one icon has an X. These icons are described in the following list:

🔲 ✔ **The line icon:** This icon *iconifies* the window, meaning that the window still is available but is no longer shown on the desktop. The window remains as an icon on the Taskbar. Click the corresponding Taskbar button or one of the other methods described in "Keep your focus on the active window" to recall a window that's been iconified.

🔲 ✔ **The box icon:** This icon maximizes the window, meaning that the size of the window is changed to the maximum possible size on your desktop. After you've maximized a window by clicking this icon, the icon changes to a set of two overlapping boxes. You can click a second time on this icon to restore the window to its previous size (that is, the size before you maximized it).

🔲 ✔ **The X icon:** This icon closes the window. If you're working with the main window for an application, clicking this icon closes the application; if you're working with a dialog box in an application, clicking the X for that dialog box closes only that dialog box.

Mastering other window tricks

KDE windows have additional features:

✔ Try double-clicking anywhere on the title bar of a window, and the window changes to display only the title bar. If only the title bar is displayed, the window is called *shaded*. Figure 11-6 shows a few windows that are shaded. The position of the shaded windows on the desktop doesn't change; but because the windows are shaded, seeing many windows and their position is easier. As soon as you double-click the title bar of a shaded window, the window is restored to its previous size.

✔ Right-click the title bar to any window to bring up a pop-up menu of options. This menu, sometimes called the *options menu* or the *control menu*, is shown in Figure 11-7.

You can open the control menu for the active window at any time by pressing the Alt+F3 key combination, or by clicking the small icon on the far left end of the title bar.

✔ A feature that we haven't described yet is called the *sticky* option. If you're working with multiple desktops, each window is normally displayed only in one desktop. Any window can be made sticky so that the window appears in all desktops. If you change desktops (by pressing Ctrl+F2, for example), the sticky window is still right where you left it.

The To desktop submenu on the control menu for any window lets you move that window to another desktop. The submenu includes the names of all the desktops as you've configured them (one, two, three, four, by default). After you choose an item from the To desktop submenu, the window suddenly disappears. Move to the desktop where you moved the window to see the window again.

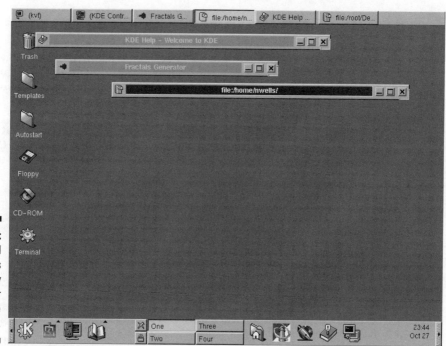

Figure 11-6:
Shaded
windows
include only
the title bar
of the
window.

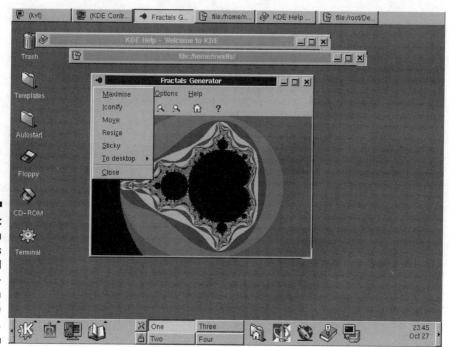

Figure 11-7:
Each
window has
a control
menu avail-
able from an
icon on the
title bar.

Come in, Mission Control

KDE provides a Control Center that lets you configure most features of your environment. You can access the Control Center by clicking the Control Center icon on the Panel (the icon looks like a screen with a computer board on top of it) or just choose Control Center from the main menu.

This section focuses on using the Control Center to set options, but you also can use the Settings submenus of the main menu. The areas of the Control Center that we describe correspond to submenus and menu items under Settings on the main menu.

Figure 11-8 shows the initial Control Center display. To work with options in the Control Center, click the plus sign to the left of a section name. A list of items in that section appears. Click one of the items to begin configuring that item. One or more pages (with a tab at the top for each page) appears in the right side of the Control Center window.

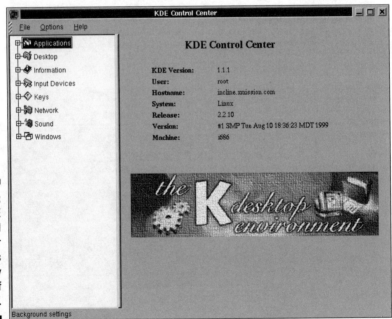

Figure 11-8:
The KDE
Control
Center
configures
many
features of
KDE.

After you've selected an item to configure on the left side of the Control Center, several buttons appear at the bottom of the Control Center window:

- **Help:** Opens an online help screen for the configuration information that you're viewing.

- **Default:** Resets the current configuration screen to its default settings. (*Note:* This may not work for all configuration options.)

- **OK:** Applies the configuration changes that you've made and returns to the original Control Center screen (shown in Figure 11-9).

- **Apply:** Applies (activates) the configuration changes that you've made but leaves the configuration options displayed so that you can make other changes.

- **Cancel:** Ignores the configuration changes that have been made on the current screen and returns to the original Control Center screen (shown in Figure 11-9).

KDE supports hundreds of configuration options, most of which you can access from the Control Center. We describe only the most interesting — those we think you'll want to set up for yourself. You can explore other options by looking at the pages that we don't discuss. Use the Help button or just experiment to see what you can do!

KDE configuration files

The information that you're configuring in the KDE Control Center is stored in plain-text configuration files in the KDE config directory. If you want to explore these files to see how KDE works *behind the scenes*, try looking at files, such as kwmrc and kpanelrc, in the /opt/kde/share/config directory.

Each configuration file applies to a single application. Most of the files end with the letters *rc*, for resource configuration. You can use any text editor to alter these configuration files (after making a backup copy of the file first, of course, just in case a problem occurs). The format of the configuration files is straightforward and should be obvious to you, as you explore each file. Just be certain to try things one step at a time so that you don't make the application unable to operate by choosing strange options.

The files in the /opt/kde/share/config directory apply to all users on the system. The root user can set up these configurations for all users on the OpenLinux system. But each user also can have an individual configuration. These configuration files are stored in the .kde/share/config directory (note that the .kde directory is a hidden directory and starts with a period). If KDE finds a configuration file in a user's home directory, those settings override any settings in the main KDE configuration files. For example, each user probably will set up a preferred color scheme and wallpaper. Because these features are stored in the .kde/share/config directory (in the file desktop0rc and others with similar names), the files in /opt/kde/share/config are not consulted at all. If no configuration file is included for an application in the user's home directory, then the system-wide configurations are used.

Where do you want it?

The basic parts of your KDE Desktop can be positioned in several locations to fit your preferences. To set the location of the Panel and the Taskbar, open the Applications section of the Control Center and choose Panel. Four tabs appear on the right side of the Control Center. The Panel tab (shown in Figure 11-9) lets you select a location for the Panel and the Taskbar.

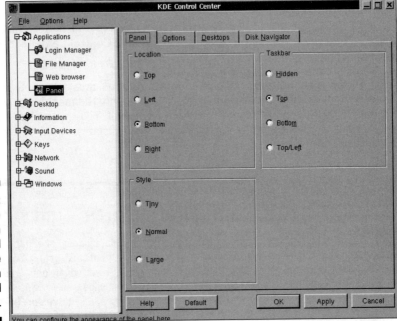

Figure 11-9:
Configure the location of the Panel and the Taskbar in the Panel tab.

The Panel can be on the top, bottom, left, or right side of the screen. Also, the Panel style can be Tiny (using smaller, half-height icons), Normal (as it appears by default), or Large. The Large option uses the same icons as the Normal option but places the icon in a larger box (which is useful if you have a 1600 x 1200 resolution screen). Select a size option in the Style section of the Panel tab. You can see what your selection looks like by choosing Apply.

The Taskbar can be on the Top or Bottom of the screen or in the top-left corner of the screen, in which case the buttons are stacked, as shown in Figure 11-10.

You also can hide the Taskbar, which gives you more room for windows on the desktop. Like the Taskbar, the Panel can be hidden — sort of. Click the arrow that appears at either end of the Panel to slide the Panel off that side of the screen. Click the arrow a second time to make the Panel reappear.

Figure 11-10:
Buttons on
the Taskbar
can be
stacked in
the upper-
left corner
of your
screen.

The Options tab has a setting to hide the Panel or Taskbar automatically after a time, then redisplays the hidden feature whenever the mouse is moved to that edge of the screen.

When one application window is never enough

Imagine that you have four sets of windows all layered on top of the KDE background (the desktop itself, also called the *root window*). You don't want to switch between individual program windows; you want to switch between sets of program windows. What do you do?

Here's where the KDE virtual desktops come in. KDE virtual desktops let you choose which of these sets of windows to view and then allows you to rapidly switch between them. For example, on the first virtual desktop you may have open a full-screen Web browser; on the second, an e-mail reader; on the third, a word processor; and on the fourth, a command-line window for trying new Linux commands that you've read about.

Naming your desktops

The Desktops tab (shown in Figure 11-11) lets you set up how many virtual desktops you want to use and to name each desktop. To change the number of desktops, move the Visible slider. The number of desktops changes in increments of two, up or down. By default, these desktops are labeled One, Two, Three, and Four (and so on, if you've configured additional virtual desktops).

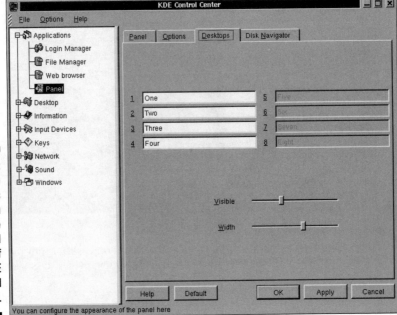

Figure 11-11:
The
Desktops
tab lets you
set the
number and
name of
your KDE
virtual
desktops.

For any of the desktops, click the name field and enter text to set a name. The Width slider below the name fields determines how wide the button is on the Panel for each of the desktop buttons. You can save space on the Panel for program icons by naming your desktops 1, 2, 3, and 4, then making the Width very small. Or, you can use descriptive names, such as "Word processing," to name your desktops and make the Width large.

A short set of names — such as e-mail, browse, xterm, Applix — can be descriptive without taking up a lot of space on your Panel. After you've set up these labels, you quickly get in the habit of pressing Ctrl+F1 through Ctrl+F4 to switch rapidly among the desktops.

Each desktop can have its own name, wallpaper background, and other configuration settings. After you've set up your desktops, you'll want to switch between them so that you can use all the windows that you've opened on each one.

Switching between desktops

You can switch between desktops several ways:

- ✔ Click a desktop button on the Panel.

- ✔ Press Ctrl+F1 for the first desktop, Ctrl+F2 for the second desktop, and so forth.

- ✔ Hold down the Ctrl key and press Tab repeatedly. The names of the desktops appear in a small box. As soon as the desktop that you want to switch to shows up, release the Ctrl and Tab keys.

- ✔ Press Ctrl+Esc. The desktop names are shown in bold, with the window names for each desktop shown below the desktop name. Double-click a desktop name to switch to that desktop.

Colors and all

If you don't care for the default colors used in KDE, then change the colors to something that you like. Just be forewarned: KDE uses both the American "color" and European "colour" spellings in this process. Fortunately, changing the colors (or colours) actually is simple. To change colors, do this:

1. **Open the Desktop section of the KDE Control Center.**

2. **Click Colors to see the Colours tab, as shown in Figure 11-12.**

   The default color scheme used by KDE is a high-contrast set of colors that are easy to read for most users. The Colour Scheme list box contains a list of 13 color schemes to choose from. You can choose something that matches a system that you're accustomed to working with, such as Digital CDE, or something with colors that you'd enjoy looking at all day (maybe a pale gray or a desert red).

3. **Select a color scheme to suit your taste from the list shown.**

   If none of the color schemes suits your taste, choose the Add button, name your own color scheme, and then select items from the Widget list to set the color for each item in your new color scheme. After selecting an item, click the colored bar below the Widget name (such as Inactive title bar). The standard KDE Select Color dialog box appears, as shown in Figure 11-13.

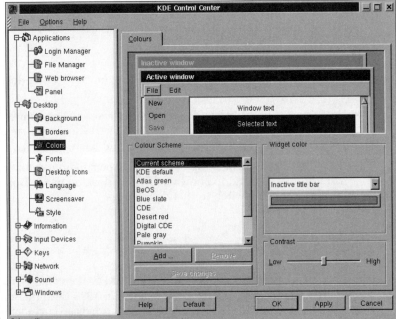

Figure 11-12:
Color
schemes
can be con-
figured in
the KDE
Control
Center
under the
desktop
section
using the
Colors item.

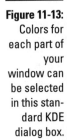
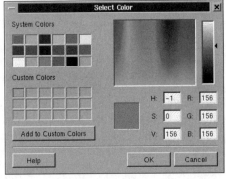

Figure 11-13:
Colors for
each part of
your
window can
be selected
in this stan-
dard KDE
dialog box.

The fonts that are used for your desktop and windows also can be selected by using the Fonts item under the Desktop section of the Control Center. Choose which font you want to alter (most items use the General font). Then select a typeface from the drop-down list of available fonts on your system. Set up bold or italic and the size that you prefer, then press Apply to see what the text looks like. Remember that you can use the Default button to reverse any bad decisions that you make in this box. The Fonts dialog box is shown in Figure 11-14.

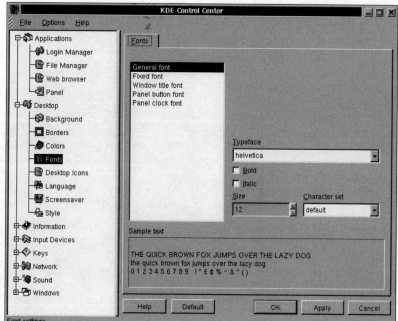

Figure 11-14:
All the fonts used by KDE dialog boxes can be set by using this section of the KDE Control Center.

Paper your walls

Choose the Background item in the Desktop section to bring up the Background tab, as shown in Figure 11-15. Use this tab to set up how your window background appears behind your application windows. On this tab you can set up the color scheme used for the background, or, if you prefer, you can choose a graphic to use as a wallpaper.

Begin by selecting the desktop that you want to configure in the Desktop list. Each desktop can have a separate color and wallpaper configuration (unless, of course, you select the Common Background checkbox, in which case only the currently selected desktop can be configured and all others will match that configuration).

After you've selected the Desktop that you want, keep these things in mind:

✔ Backgrounds can be one color (the default) or two colors (if you choose the Two Colour option). If you choose the Two Colour option, then you can select a second color by clicking the colored box below the Two Colour option button. With Two Colour selected, you also can choose Setup to configure how the two colors are blended together on your background (shown in Figure 11-16). Simple gradients or complex patterns can be selected for the two colors.

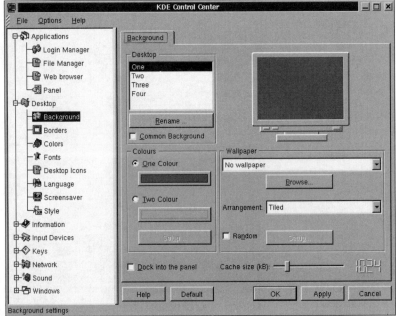

Figure 11-15:
Background
colors and
wallpaper
graphics
can be set
up on this
tab in the
Control
Center.

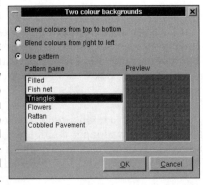

Figure 11-16:
The Two
Colour setup
dialog box
lets you
select how
the two
colors you
chose are
combined
as a back-
ground
image.

✔ If you want to use a wallpaper graphic on your desktop background,
don't bother worrying about the color options — the wallpaper covers
up the background in most cases. The wallpaper can be tiled (repeated
to cover the entire background) or centered (one image in the middle of
the screen). Other options in the Arrangement drop-down list are basically variations on these two ideas.

✔ KDE comes with about a hundred wallpaper graphics. All these wallpaper graphics are small graphics that are intended for use as tiled images. You also may have a large image that you want to use as a single, centered image on your desktop. Any image in a standard graphics format, such as jpg or gif, can be used as a wallpaper graphic. Just choose the Browse button to select the graphic file that you want, and then choose the appropriate arrangement of that graphic from the Arrangement drop-down list.

If you have trouble selecting a wallpaper from among the hundred or so provided with KDE, choose the Random checkbox and then choose the Setup button next to it. Add to the list all the wallpapers you want and then set a delay time for how often the wallpaper images randomly are to be selected from the list you've created in the Setup dialog box.

Choose a screen saver

Choosing a screen saver is not the most important task that you do with your OpenLinux system. Most monitors automatically shut down to an energy-saving mode, so you may not even see the screen saver that you select. But, nevertheless, KDE provides so many fun screen savers that they're worth exploring.

The Screensaver item in the Desktop section of the Control Center is shown in Figure 11-17. In this tab you can choose a screen saver from the list of about twenty screen savers that come with KDE. As you choose an option, a miniature version of the screen saver appears in the window above the list.

In the Settings section to the right of the list, enter the number of minutes of idle time that KDE should wait before launching the screen saver. Also, if you want the screen locked, put a check in the Require password checkbox.

The password option provides good security if you work in a place where strangers may wander by while you're away from your desk. But entering your password twenty times may become annoying if you don't work regularly on your OpenLinux system.

The *funnest* part of screen savers is setting up the screen savers and then testing them. Click the Setup button below the list of screen savers. A different dialog box appears, based on the screen saver that you select. For example, Figure 11-18 shows the setup dialog box for the Science screen saver. In this dialog box you choose the shape, speed, intensity, and size of the distortion used for the screen saver. Not all setup options are this complex, of course.

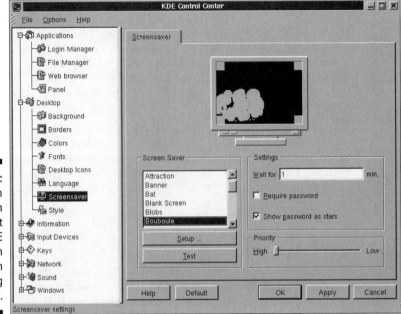

Figure 11-17:
You can choose from about twenty KDE screen savers in this dialog box.

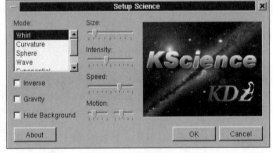

Figure 11-18:
Each screen saver has setup options like the ones in this Science screen saver.

After you've set up the screen-saver options, choose the Test button to see what the screen saver looks like in full-screen mode when activated. Move your mouse to end the test.

The Priority slider in the lower-right corner of the Screensaver dialog box determines how much CPU time is dedicated to running the screen saver. If you choose a screen saver, such as the science example (refer to Figure 11-18), a lot of processor time can be spent calculating the graphical images for the screen saver. Any program that you have running in the background will be slowed down considerably so that the computer can draw fancy pictures for the screen saver. By setting the Priority slider to low, very little CPU time is assigned to the screen saver, thus freeing up your computer for more critical tasks (even when the screen saver is active).

Other Control Center options

Try doing the following for a few other interesting configuration options:

- ✔ Set the language used for all dialog boxes, menus, and so on, in the Language item under Desktop.

- ✔ Change how the buttons on your window title bars are set up in the Titlebar item under Windows.

- ✔ Use Macintosh style menus in KDE (see the Style item under the Desktop section).

- ✔ Set up the positioning of icons on your desktop by using the Desktop Icons item on the Desktop section.

- ✔ Configure how your mouse and keyboard respond by using items under the Input Devices section.

Descending to Text Mode

Maybe you're interested in all this graphical configuration, but maybe you really crave the power of the command line. Memorization, complex commands, and an old-fashioned machine interface are really what you want. Have no fear, for KDE provides this as well.

To work in the text mode (called command-line mode) within KDE, you must open a terminal-emulator window. A terminal is a keyboard interface to OpenLinux that's provided by a shell. (A shell is simply a command interpreter, as you can read about in Chapter 10.)

You can open a window for command-line work at any time in KDE by choosing Terminal from the Utilities submenu or by choosing the Terminal Emulator icon on the Panel (this icon looks like two computer screens overlapping).

Figure 11-19 shows a terminal-emulator window in which you can enter those text commands that are missing when you work in a graphical environment. You can right-click in the terminal-emulator window to set up the font, color, and so on, for the command-line interface window.

To close a terminal-emulator window, use the close button in the upper-right corner of the terminal-emulator window. You also can enter the exit command.

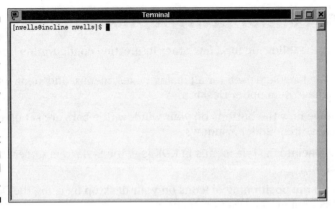

Figure 11-19:
A terminal-
emulator
window lets
you directly
enter com-
mands for
OpenLinux
processing
via the shell
interface.

If you simply need to enter a single command to start a program or check
something on the system, press Alt+F2 to open a pop-up command window.
In this window you can enter a single command and then press Enter to execute the command.

Bye, Bye KDE

When you're ready to exit KDE entirely and return to the graphical login
screen (or the character-mode screen, if that's where you started), gracefully
exit KDE by choosing Logout from the main menu. You also can right-click
anywhere on the KDE Desktop and choose Logout from the menu that
appears.

After you choose Logout, you see a dialog box asking you to confirm that you
want to log out. Any windows that you still have open are listed in the confir-
mation window. You can choose Cancel to close those windows (which you
should do if the windows contain unsaved data).

After you exit, KDE remembers the position of all open windows so that the
next time you start KDE, the same programs are opened again (right where
you left them). Impressive, isn't it? Of course, if you have many non-KDE programs open, then sometimes for your next KDE session, KDE can't reopen the
programs the same way you had them when you ended your last KDE session.

Linking Everything to KDE

You quickly become a fan of the graphical way of life that's provided by KDE.
You'll love choosing color schemes, you'll experiment with wallpaper images,

and you'll play with the fractal generator at lunch time. But some of the programs you need to use aren't included on the KDE main menu. How do you proceed?

KDE uses little configuration files called KDE Link files. These files contain all the information that KDE needs to start an application. KDE Link files are used to create KDE menu items, KDE Desktop icons, KDE Panel icons, KDE Autostart icons . . . you get the idea.

Let's assume you want to access your favorite graphical program, the Gimp, from an icon on your KDE Desktop. Just follow these steps:

1. **Right-click your desktop, then choose New⤳Application from the popup menu that appears.**

   A small window containing a filename pops open.

2. **Change the name from the Program.kdelnk default to something that matches the name of the application you want to add to your desktop.**

   For example, if you were adding the Gimp application, you may use Gimp.kdelnk (just be sure to leave the .kdelnk part intact). Notice that the file extension is *not* kdelink, it's kdelnk.

3. **Choose OK.**

   A properties dialog box appears.

4. **Select the Execute tab of the dialog box (shown in Figure 11-20).**

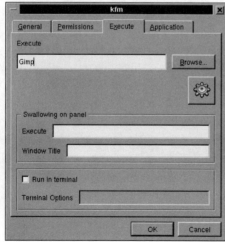

Figure 11-20: The Execute tab of a KDE Link properties dialog box contains the name of the program to execute by using this KDE Link file.

5. **In the Execute field enter the command to start the program as you would from a command line.**

In this example, we enter the command gimp.

6. **Click the picture of a gear to select a new icon for the application that you're configuring access to.**

KDE includes several hundred icons that you can choose from. Explore the other tabs if you want to see what options KDE provides for KDE Link files.

7. **Click OK to close the dialog box and activate the new KDE Link file.**

The icon appears on your desktop. You can click (once) this icon to launch the program that you entered in the Execute tab.

You can use standard drag-and-drop techniques to copy or move this icon and the configuration file it represents to your Panel, to your Autostart folder, or to the menu configuration dialog box. (Choose Panel⇨Edit Menus to alter the KDE menus.)

The KDE Link file is only a configuration file that tells KDE how to use the application. As soon as you delete a KDE Link file, this action has no effect on the application that the KDE Link file was used to access.

Chapter 12

Do Something Useful

● ●

In This Chapter

▶ Using the OpenLinux day planner (KOrganizer)

▶ Counting with the kCalc calculator

▶ Playing tunes from your CD-ROM drive

▶ Enjoying a game or two

▶ Viewing and creating graphics

▶ Running DOS programs in OpenLinux

● ●

*O*penLinux includes quite a few useful graphical programs. Space prohibits us from showing you all the programs that run under KDE, or even all the programs that Caldera includes in a standard installation. But the programs we show you in this chapter are representative of OpenLinux and give you a good idea about how the other programs work.

We have space to show you only the basic features of these programs. You can learn about the more advanced features by exploring the Help menu in each program and other options on the KDE main menu. And if you'd like additional applications, check out the KDE Web site at
`www.kde.org/applications.html`.

Organize Yourself

Most of us need a little help to keep track of a busy life. For many people that means carrying around a day planner of some sort or — for you people who regularly use a computer — keeping track of appointments and people in a program, such as Microsoft Outlook.

KDE provides a similar program that lets you do the same thing in OpenLinux: KOrganizer. And you don't have to pay extra for KOrganizer. To get started, choose Organizer from the Office submenu of KDE. The KOrganizer program window appears, as shown in Figure 12-1.

Reference calendar

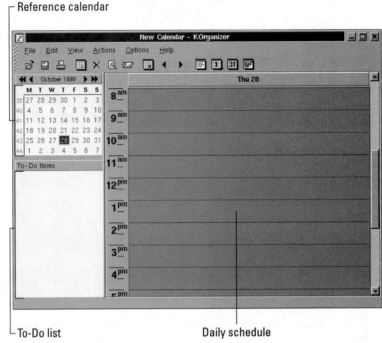

Figure 12-1:
The
KOrganizer
program lets
you set up
calendar
appoint-
ments and
to-do lists.

To-Do list

Daily schedule

When you start the program, the KOrganizer window is divided into three sections:

- ✔ The reference calendar
- ✔ The To-Do list
- ✔ The daily schedule

Setting up simple appointments

You can set up an appointment in the daily-schedule calendar by following these steps:

1. **Right-click the hour of the day when you want the appointment sched-uled, and then choose New Appointment from the pop-up menu that appears.**

   A New Appointment dialog box appears, as shown in Figure 12-2.

2. **Type a name for the appointment in the Summary field.**

3. **Set the Start Time and the End Time in the Appointment Time section.**

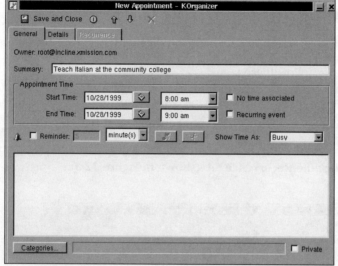

Figure 12-2:
New
appoint-
ments are
set up in
KOrganizer
by using this
dialog box.

After you click the calendar icons next to the Start Time and End Time boxes, calendars appear; just click the appropriate date. Then click the drop-down arrows next to the time boxes and select the appropriate time from the list that pops up.

4. **If you need a little help remembering the appointment, click the Reminder checkbox and set the number of minutes before the appointment for your reminder.**

   At the designated time (just before your appointment), a little pop-up window alerts you to the imminent appointment. This reminder appears even if KOrganizer is closed.

5. **Add any additional details that you want recorded in the large text box in the bottom half of the New Appointment dialog box.**

6. **After you're done, click the Save and Close button at the top of the dialog box.**

   The appointment appears on your daily calendar to remind you about the appointment. You can double-click the appointment to open the dialog box again to review any details. Now you have no excuse for not visiting the dentist.

   If you need to edit an appointment after setting up one, you can right-click that appointment in your calendar view and select Edit Appointment from the pop-up menu to open an Edit Appointment dialog box (which looks exactly like the New Appointment dialog box). From the pop-up menu you also can select Delete to remove the appointment, or check Toggle Alarm (which turns on the reminder alarm if you're worried that you'll miss the appointment).

Scheduling recurring visits

Some of your appointments happen repeatedly (we hope the dentist isn't one of those). KOrganizer automatically can fill in your calendar with a recurring event. Just follow these steps:

1. **Follow Steps 1 through 5, as appropriate, in the preceding section.**

2. **Check the Recurring event checkbox on the General tab.**

   This activates the Recurrence tab.

3. **Click the Recurrence tab (shown in Figure 12-3).**

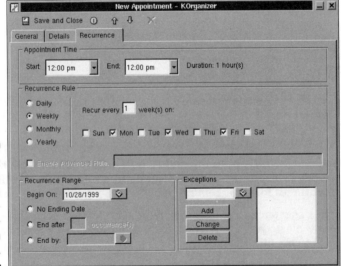

Figure 12-3: Recurring events can be scheduled automatically in KOrganizer.

4. **Check the accuracy of the start and end time for the appointment and make any necessary changes.**

5. **Choose a Recurrence Rule — Daily, Weekly, Monthly, or Yearly — and enter the appropriate information in the right side of the Recurrence Rule box.**

   The information to the right of the Recurrence Rule that you select changes, based on your selection. For example, if you use a Weekly Recurrence Rule (refer to Figure 12-3), then KOrganizer asks you to

   • Choose the number of weeks between recurrences (the default is 1 for something that occurs every week).

   • Choose the days of the week that the event recurs (check as many day-of-the-week boxes as necessary).

6. **Verify the Begin On date in the Recurrence Range area of the dialog box.**

   If the date isn't correct, click the calendar button to the right of the date and select a date from the calendar tool.

7. **Enter the date that the recurring event should end.**

   This date may be never (select No Ending Date), a fixed number of occurrences, or a fixed date (enter in the End by field).

   The End after *xx* occurrence(s) refers to the number of weeks, months, or years that the appointment recurs. For example, if the event you schedule occurs three times per week and you want to schedule the event for 10 weeks, enter 10 as the End after *xx* occurrence(s) number, not 30.

8. **Enter any exceptions to the recurring schedule (a canceled class, a vacation, or whatever else comes up) in the Exceptions area of the dialog box.**

   Click the calendar icon next to the text entry field to select a date, and then choose Add to add the date to the list of exceptions.

9. **Click the Save and Close button at the top of the New Appointment or Edit Appointment dialog box.**

After setting up an appointment you may want to make changes in how the appointment is set up. You can always change an appointment from the calendar view. As soon as you right-click an appointment, a pop-up menu appears in which you can choose Edit to open the Edit Appointment dialog box.

Making a To-Do list entry

The To-Do list in KOrganizer isn't associated with the appointments on your calendar. The To-Do list is a basic list of tasks that you want to record as a reminder about what you need to accomplish.

To add a new To-do item, follow these steps:

1. **Click the To-Do list area of the KOrganizer window.**

   A pop-up menu appears.

2. **Choose New To-Do from the pop-up menu.**

   The cursor appears in a blank line where you can enter a new To-Do list item.

3. **Enter the task and press Enter.**

To edit a To-Do list item, right-click the item in the list and choose Edit To-Do. A dialog box (similar to the one in Figure 12-4) appears. You can't do as much in this dialog box as you can in the Edit Appointment dialog box. Even though the % Completed and Priority fields are active in the dialog box, choosing an item in either field has no effect in this release of the KOrganizer software. You can, however, enter text in the large window to provide more details about the task that you see in the Summary field.

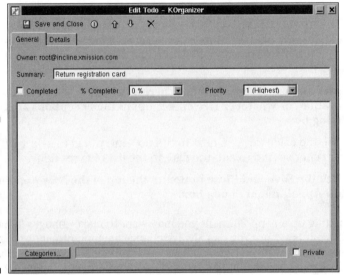

Figure 12-4: Each To-do item can be edited to add more explanation or details to a task description.

Don't forget to click the Save and Close button after entering additional text in the Edit To-do dialog box.

If you have multiple items in the To-Do list, you can click the empty box to the left of each item to mark that item as completed. The item stays in the list, but the checkmark shows you that the item's been completed. After you've completed a few items, you can delete them from the list by right-clicking the list and choosing Purge Completed.

Changing your view

The standard view of your daily calendar that KOrganizer shows isn't the only way to view the world. KOrganizer has several other views. You can select a view either by choosing the View menu of KOrganizer or by clicking a toolbar icon (the icons on the far right end of the toolbar control the view). The Day, Work Week, and Week views are all selected by one icon. You toggle between these three options by clicking repeatedly the third icon from the right on the toolbar.

To see a drop-down list from which you can select the Day, Work Week, or Week view, click and hold down the mouse button on the third icon from the right on the toolbar.

The different views that are available follow:

- **List:** Shows a list of appointments for the current day, as shown in Figure 12-5.

- **Day:** Shows a single day, broken down by hours, with appointments listed for each hour.

- **Work Week:** Shows five days across the calendar area, as shown in Figure 12-6.

- **Week:** Shows seven days across the calendar area (as shown in Figure 12-6, but with Saturday and Sunday added).

- **Month:** Shows a full month without showing the reference calendar or the To-do list, as shown in Figure 12-7.

- **To-Do list:** Shows the To-Do list without showing the reference calendar or any scheduled appointments.

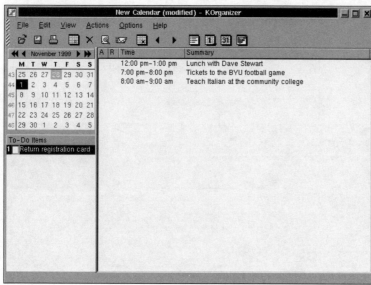

Figure 12-5: The List view shows your appointments without organizing them into an hourly calendar.

An arrow in KOrganizer usually means that you can switch to the next day, week, or month by clicking the arrow.

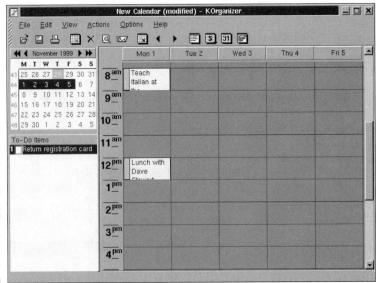

Figure 12-6:
The Work Week view summarizes a week's worth of appointments on one screen.

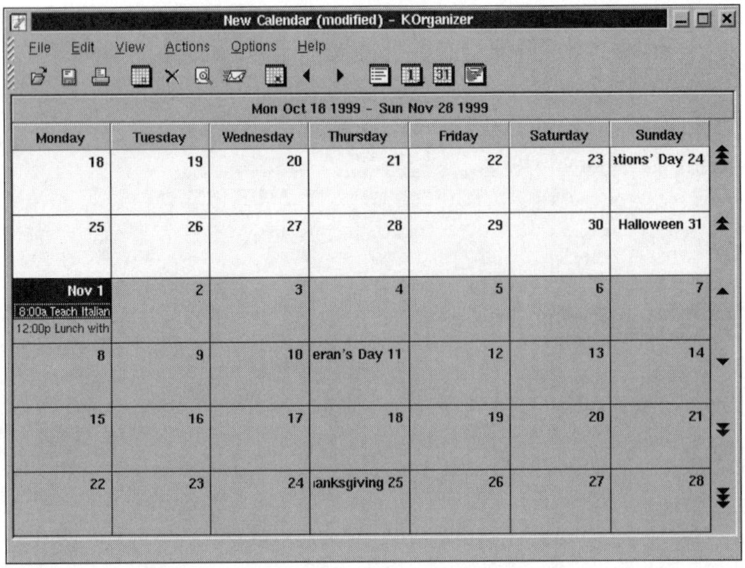

Figure 12-7:
The Month view shows a full month with abbreviated appointments in each day.

KOrganizer has numerous other features and configuration options. You can set up your preferences by choosing Options⊅Edit Options from the menu bar. The Configuration dialog box appears, as shown in Figure 12-8. Choose an item from the list on the left side of the window, then set up those features on the right side.

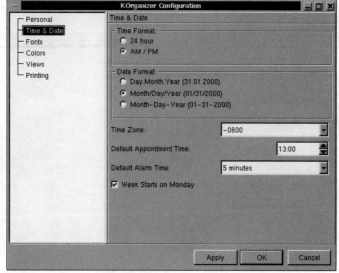

Figure 12-8:
You can set up configuration options for KOrganizer in this dialog box.

As soon as you exit KOrganizer, all your appointments and To-Do list items are saved. You're prompted for a filename to use the first time that you exit KOrganizer. Use a simple filename, such as your first name or the name of a project that the calendar relates to. The next time that you start the program the information loads automatically and is visible immediately.

Track Your Money

Okay, we admit it. This section really isn't about money; this section's about using the calculator. But the numbers that most of us use are for money, so we got your attention, didn't we?

To start the calculator program, choose Calculator from the Utilities sub-menu of your desktop main menu. The calculator, shown in Figure 12-9, is called kCalc.

Playing the market? OpenLinux can play along

OpenLinux supports real money applications for tracking stocks and balancing your checkbook. You can learn about these applications from download sites on the Web, such as www.linuxberg.com or www.kde.org. Try playing with KStocks (good for beginners) or tsinvest (good for professional investors).

Figure 12-9:
KDE
includes a
full-featured
calculator
that you can
start from
the Utilities
submenu.

Using a calculator probably is familiar to you, but we just want to mention a few pointers about kCalc:

- ✔ You can enter numbers by using the mouse, the regular keyboard, or the 10-key keypad on your keyboard.

- ✔ You can copy a number from the calculator's window to the KDE clipboard for use in other applications by clicking in the window containing the number.

- ✔ The letters on the keypad are for working with hexadecimal numbers (base 16 numbers used for computer stuff). You can switch to these numbers by using the Base buttons below the kCalc button.

- ✔ kCalc has separate function keys for trigonometry and statistics functions. To switch between these functions, press F3.

- ✔ You can configure kCalc by clicking the kCalc button. A Help button appears in the configuration dialog box (because no menu bar is included in the kCalc window).

Using the Help button in the kCalc configuration dialog box opens a document with some really handy information, such as how to get pi. Simply press the buttons INV and then EE. But then you probably guessed that.

Figure 12-10 shows the configuration dialog for kCalc, in which you can select colors, default modes, and (by choosing the Display Font tab) the font used to display numbers.

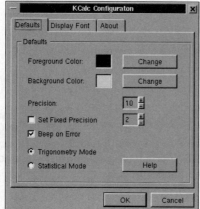

Figure 12-10: To configure kCalc features and display options, click the kCalc button to open this dialog box.

Mr. Music in OpenLinux

People want a little music in their lives, right? That's why you bought a $2,000 computer rather than a $300 stereo system. So you need to set up OpenLinux to play music CDs.

First, you need to make certain that OpenLinux recognizes your CD-ROM drive and sound card. Fortunately, the OpenLinux installation takes care of that for most users. If you have problems playing your CDs and have checked that the speakers are plugged in and turned on (we've missed that part on occasion), check your OpenLinux documentation or contact technical support for assistance with getting the sound system functioning.

With your hardware set up correctly, insert a music CD into your CD-ROM drive. Now choose CD Player from the Multimedia submenu. A nice-looking CD player interface appears, as shown in Figure 12-11. You probably can guess how to use most of the buttons on the player, but a few guidelines may help you get started:

Figure 12-11:
The CD
Player is
included
with
OpenLinux
on the
Multimedia
submenu of
KDE.

- ✔ If you've set up an Internet connection, you can click the i button to select links to Web sites for music concerts, purchase CDs online, and so on.

- ✔ The icon with a little filing cabinet on it opens the CD Database Editor (shown in Figure 12-12). You can enter information about the CD that you're listening to and share that information across the Internet with others who own the same CD. If you have a live Internet connection, then the CD Player tries to update your CD database automatically from data that others have entered.

- ✔ The icon with a question mark starts a random play, selecting tracks at random from the CD.

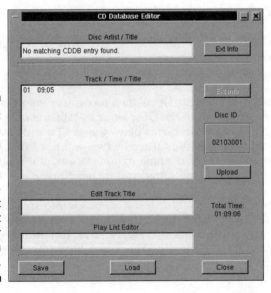

Figure 12-12:
Information
about each
CD is main-
tained in a
CD data-
base that
you can edit
yourself or
update from
the Internet.

✔ The icon with a 1 and a 0 is the *on/off* switch. Click this icon to exit the CD player.

✔ The icon with a hammer and a screwdriver opens a configuration dialog box, in which you can set up many things about how the CD Player operates. The Kscd Options tab, shown in Figure 12-13, has the setting that's most useful to check out.

✔ You also can configure how the CD database is accessed across the Internet by checking out the CDDB tab, shown in Figure 12-14, in the configuration dialog box.

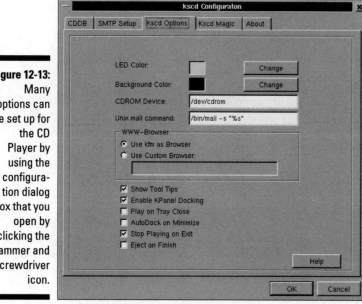

Figure 12-13:
Many options can be set up for the CD Player by using the configuration dialog box that you open by clicking the hammer and screwdriver icon.

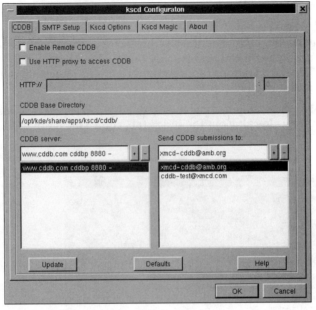

Figure 12-14:
Web access
to the CD
database
can be set
up in the
CDDB tab of
the configu-
ration
dialog box.

How About a Nice Game of Cards?

Most people enjoy playing a computer game at least once in a while. If you don't enjoy computer games, maybe you haven't found the right game yet. OpenLinux includes about 15 games on the Games submenu of your desktop. Each game is worth a few hours of experimentation to help you understand how OpenLinux functions. Tell your boss we said it's okay.

Some games are arcade style, like Asteroids (shown in Figure 12-15). Use the following keys to control your spaceship:

- ✔ Left arrow: Rotate counter-clockwise

- ✔ Right arrow: Rotate clockwise

- ✔ Up arrow: Thrusters (move forward)

- ✔ Spacebar: Shoot a torpedo

You also have favorites, such as Minesweeper or Solitaire, as shown in Figure 12-16. To start a game of Solitaire, choose Patience from the Games submenu. Why they named the game Patience we can't say, unless they're not very good players.

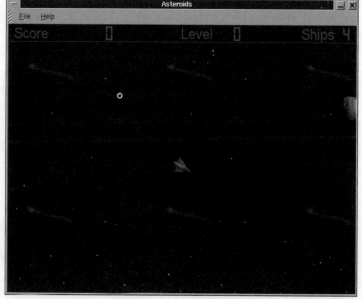

Figure 12-15:
Asteroids
and many
other
arcade-style
games are
included
with
OpenLinux
on the
Games
submenu.

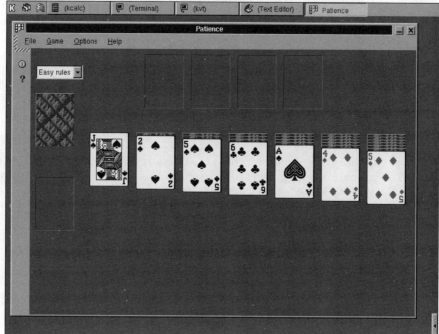

Figure 12-16:
The card
game
Solitaire is
included
with
OpenLinux
(choose
Patience on
the Games
submenu).

If the 15 games on the Games submenu aren't enough to keep you entertained, then check out `www.kde.org/applications.html` where you can download additional games. You can find more card games, more strategy games (including NetHack if you're a fan), arcade games (Pacman, anyone?), and standbys (like chess).

In fact, if you like to play chess, OpenLinux includes everything you need right on your OpenLinux CD. Chess isn't normally installed by default, but you can install Chess and start a game by following these steps:

1. **Make sure you're logged in as root to install the new software.**

2. **Insert your OpenLinux CD into your CD-ROM (use CD 1 if you have the commercial box of OpenLinux).**

3. **Mount the CD with this command:**

   ```
   mount /mnt/cdrom
   ```

4. **Change to the directory containing the software packages with this command:**

   ```
   cd /mnt/cdrom/col/install/RPMS
   ```

5. **Install the chess engine by using the following command:**

   ```
   rpm -Uvh gnuchess-4.0.p180-1.i386.rpm
   ```

6. **Install the chess interface by using this command:**

   ```
   rpm -Uvh xboard-4.0.2-2.i386.rpm
   ```

7. **Start a game of chess by typing the following command:**

   ```
   xboard
   ```

Figure 12-17 shows the chess board ready for your opening move. To move a piece, click, drag, and drop the piece. You can move only your own pieces — you use white pieces by default, so you make the first move. The computer moves as soon as you release your mouse button to drop your piece on a new square.

Figure 12-17:
OpenLinux includes a great chess game based on the powerful gnu chess engine.

Draw Me a Picture

Computers are more visual than ever. With Web pages and all those space shuttle images that you've downloaded (see www.nasa.gov/gallery/index.html) you probably need a good image viewer. OpenLinux has just the thing for you. Choose Image Viewer from the Graphics submenu. The Image Viewer (called kview if you need to start from a command line) isn't much to look at when it opens — just a gray box with a menu bar.

You can load an image by choosing File⇨Open and then selecting a graphics file in your file system. Most common image formats can be viewed, including the following:

- ✔ gif
- ✔ jpeg
- ✔ bmp
- ✔ pcx
- ✔ xbm
- ✔ xpm
- ✔ xwd

If you have a file manager window open to view your home directory or another location in the file system, you can drag the icon for a graphics file from the file manager window and drop the icon on the Image Viewer window, shown in Figure 12-18, to load that image automatically.

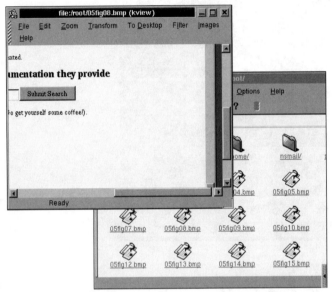

Figure 12-18:
You can drop icons on the Image Viewer window to open a graphics file.

The Image Viewer includes many useful features to adjust your images. This program isn't intended to edit photos or other images (see the next section for that), but you can do the following:

- ✔ Crop a part of the image by clicking and dragging the image, and then choose Edit⇨Crop.
- ✔ Choose an item from the Zoom menu to adjust the size of the image.
- ✔ Rotate or flip the image by using items on the Transform menu.
- ✔ Make the image your desktop wallpaper (temporarily) by choosing an item on the To Desktop menu.
- ✔ Change the image to grayscale on the Filter menu.
- ✔ Print the image by using the File⇨Print option.
- ✔ Adjust the brightness or Gamma of the image by using the Filter⇨Intensity submenu.

The Image Viewer doesn't have a lot of fancy filters as do some graphics programs. However, if you click an icon for a graphics file that Image Viewer can display, then Image Viewer starts up automatically to show the image.

If you want to do more than just view images, then choose Paint from the Graphics submenu. The Paint program is launched, as shown in Figure 12-19.

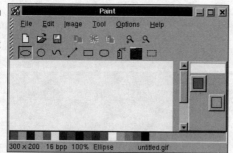

Figure 12-19: The Paint program lets you create your own basic images in OpenLinux.

The Paint program has a set of basic drawing tools plus a color palette to select from. You also can use the menus to zoom in on the image that you're drawing, view information about the image, or select a drawing tool.

The Paint program is very basic. If you need to draw icons for your desktop, try the Icon Editor program on the Graphics submenu.

Two other powerful applications that are installed by default are gimp and XV. You can start either of these programs from the Graphics submenu on your desktop. Gimp is a tool similar to Adobe Photoshop. Gimp includes numerous filters, special effects, and other advanced tools. XV is an older program that is used to view images, not create them. But XV does have a color editor and can view and save files in many graphics formats.

The Old Fashioned Way: DOS

OpenLinux includes a copy of DR-DOS, a better DOS than the one included with Microsoft Windows 98. If you have any old DOS programs that you want to run as you work in Linux, use these steps to start them:

1. **Open a command line window by choosing Terminal from the Utilities menu.**

2. **Type the command** dos.

   After a moment, DOS starts and the C:> prompt appears (shown in Figure 12-20).

   If your screen looks funny when you run a DOS program, try using the command xdos rather than dos. This opens a separate window for DOS that works better when running some DOS programs.

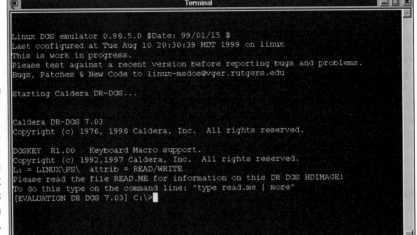

```
                                            Terminal                              _ □ ×
Linux DOS emulator 0.98.5.0 $Date: 99/01/15 $
Last configured at Tue Aug 10 20:30:39 MDT 1999 on linux
This is work in progress.
Please test against a recent version before reporting bugs and problems.
Bugs, Patches & New Code to linux-msdos@vger.rutgers.edu

Starting Caldera DR-DOS...

Caldera DR-DOS 7.03
Copyright (c) 1976, 1998 Caldera, Inc.  All rights reserved.

DOSKEY  R1.00   Keyboard Macro support.
Copyright (c) 1992,1997 Caldera, Inc.  All rights reserved.
L: = LINUX\FS\  attrib = READ/WRITE
Please read the file READ.ME for information on this DR DOS HDIMAGE!
To do this type on the command line: "type read.me | more"
[EVALUATION DR DOS 7.03] C:\>
```

Figure 12-20:
DOS programs can be run in OpenLinux within this emulation mode.

3. **To copy files from drive A: (the floppy disk drive) to your hard disk, use the standard DOS commands that you know.**

   The main OpenLinux filesystem is drive L: in DOS. You can find out how to set up more detailed configurations by reviewing the file `/etc/dosemu. conf`.

4. **Start the DOS programs by using a standard command line entry, such as** `wp51` **to start WordPerfect 5.1 for DOS.**

5. **When you want to exit DOS and return to the Linux command prompt, use the command** `exitemu`.

Part IV
Maintaining Your System

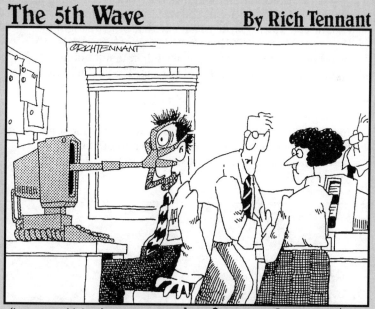

The 5th Wave — By Rich Tennant

"Okay- this is an example of some of the bootup problems you'll incur with Caldera OpenLinux unless you maintain your system properly."

In this part . . .

*E*very outdoorsperson knows the value of maintaining his or her equipment. You wouldn't want to get caught in a downpour with a leaky tent or get caught in the ocean with a leaky kayak. Well, OpenLinux needs to be maintained, too. And the primary job in maintaining OpenLinux is managing its file system. That's the topic of Chapter 13.

But enough talk about maintenance — it's time for some fun stuff. Chapter 14 shows you how to get the most performance out of your system. So, you find out about memory, get to check your disks, and — gasp — rebuild your kernel.

Chapter 13

File System Management

• •

In This Chapter

▶ Making your files available to OpenLinux by mounting a file system

▶ Dismounting a file system

▶ Playing inspector to search for other users

▶ Experiencing the joys of configuration files

▶ Rehabilitating corrupted files

▶ Increasing disk space with a new drive

▶ Using more floppies

▶ Adding a CD-ROM drive

• •

*M*anaging the OpenLinux file system is one of the more important jobs in maintaining and updating your OpenLinux system. You have the responsibility of watching over the OpenLinux file system and seeing to it that users (even if you're the only one) have access to secure, uncorrupted data.

The tasks associated with file-system management include the following:

✔ Mounting and dismounting file systems

✔ Diagnosing hardware failures

✔ Preventing file corruption

✔ Blocking user errors

✔ Connecting and configuring new hardware

✔ Managing disk resources

Some of these tasks are performed automatically, thank goodness. Other tasks you must do manually, as needed. In this chapter, you discover the ins and outs of managing your OpenLinux file system — the easy way.

Mounting and Dismounting

Files are important to OpenLinux and other UNIX-like operating systems in ways that differ from their importance to DOS, Windows, and Macintosh operating systems. In OpenLinux, everything is stored as a file in a predictable location in the directory structure — OpenLinux even stores commands as files. Like other modern operating systems, Linux has a tree-structured, hierarchical, directory organization called a *file system*.

All user-available disk space is combined in a single-directory tree. The base of the system is the *root directory,* which is designated with a slash (/). The contents of a file system are made available to OpenLinux by merging the file system into the system directory through a process called *mounting.*

File systems can be mounted or dismounted, which means file systems can be connected or disconnected to the directory tree. The exception is the *root file system,* which is always mounted on the root directory when the system is running and cannot be dismounted. Other file systems may be mounted as needed, such as ones contained on another hard drive, a floppy disk, or a CD-ROM.

The command syntax

Here's the command syntax for manually mounting a file system:

```
mount block-special-file mount-point
```

where *block-special-file* is the *device driver* file for the partition of the disk drive (such as a hard drive or a CD-ROM) where you've created a file system, and *mount-point* is the directory where the file system is mounted. The term *block-special-file* is often referred to as the device name, because the device is accessed by referring to the block-special-file in the directory structure.

Want to see the `mount` command assign the first floppy drive, which Linux refers to as `/dev/fd0`, (see Chapter 4) to the `/mnt` directory? Hey, did we promise you a good time or what?

```
mount /dev/fd0 /mnt
```

A file system can be mounted in only one place at any given time. The directory where the file system will be mounted *(mount-point)* must exist before you issue the `mount` command. Otherwise, the command won't work. If you need to create the directory, then use a combination of the `mkdir` command (see Chapter 8) and the `mount` command. For example, to create a new directory called `/canadianpolice` and then mount the file system on the disk in the floppy drive (`/dev/fd0`) — onto that directory, you use the following:

```
mkdir /canadianpolice
mount /dev/fd0 /canadianpolice
```

After you're finished or fed up with the file system that you mounted on /canadianpolice, you must dismount the file system by using the umount command. The syntax for the umount command is

```
umount name
```

where *name* is either the name of the *block-special-file* (the device, /dev/fd0) or the name of the directory (that's the *mount-point,* /canadianpolice).

Sleuthing for other file users

Because OpenLinux is a multi-user operating system, sometimes more than one user is logged in to the system at the same time. This feature may mean that multiple file systems are mounted and in use. The umount command works only on inactive file systems. If one of the files in the file system is open or the file system is the current directory, then an error message tells you that the device is busy.

How do you find out which files are being used and by whom? You use the fuser command. (Get it? Find user — fuser.) The command returns a lot of information, identifying which processes are using a particular file or file system and which user is using them. If you use fuser with a filename, then it returns information on only that file. If you invoke fuser with the block-special filename, then fuser reports on all the files in that file system.

The fuser command has two options that you may find useful:

- ✔ -u displays user names along with process IDs
- ✔ -m enables you to specify the file system by name

fuser is a character-cell program. By running fuser with the -u option, you can get the process number of the programs using the file system along with the user name of the person using those programs. For example:

```
/usr/sbin/fuser -u /home
/:        492r(nwells)   503r(nwells)
 504r(nwells)   508r(nwells)   580r(nwells)
 581r(nwells)   585r(nwells)   586r(nwells)
 598r(nwells)   599r(nwells)   601r(nwells)
 879r(nwells)  1287r(nwells)
```

Here you can see that nwells has a series of programs using the home file system. If you want to see what those programs are, then you can use the `ps` command, which shows the process numbers and names of the processes running in the system:

```
ps ax |grep 601
601 p0 S  0:00 /opt/applix/applix
```

We ran `ps ax` to see all the processes in the system in extended mode so that you can see additional information about them instead of just their names. Then, by using the `grep` command with the process number 601 as an argument, we isolated one line from the output of the `ps` command. You can see that the program running is the `/opt/applix/applix` program. This program is just one of the programs that you have to shut down to unmount the root file system.

By repeating the `ps` and `grep` commands, but substituting other process numbers for 601, you can see all the processes and know which programs to shut down. You then can ask the people running those processes to quit their programs, or you can use the `kill` function of `fuser` on the file system.

To use the `kill` function of `fuser`, you simply use the `-k` flag on `fuser` when you list the file systems you're trying to unmount. For example,

```
fuser -ku /home
```

kills all the processes that are using the home file system for any reason.

After all the programs are shut down and no one else is using the file system, you can unmount the file system.

Configuring file systems

Mounting all file systems manually every time you boot the system can quickly become annoying. To avoid manually mounting file systems, you can have the system execute the required mount commands when you boot up. The information needed to execute the required mount commands is in the standard OpenLinux file system configuration file located at `/etc/fstab`. The entries in the file usually follow this format:

```
block-special-file mount-loc type opts dump-freq passnumber
```

in which

✔ *block-special-file* is the name of the special file where the file system resides. This must be the device name for a block device, such as `/dev/hda1` for the first partition on an IDE drive.

✔ *mount-loc* is the directory where the file system will be mounted. If the directory is on a partition used for swapping, then use swap for *mount-loc*.

✔ *type* is the kind of partition. For a native OpenLinux file system, *type* is ext2.

✔ *opts* is the field for listing options, separated by commas. The options may include any of the following:

rw	Allows the file to be read and written to (read-write mode).
ro	Allows the file to be read only (read-only mode).
dev	Treats special files in this file system as special files.
nodev	Treats special files in this file system as filenamess.
exec	Permits execution of binary files from this file systems.
noexec	Prevents the execution of binary files from this file system. This is useful for file systems that contain only data. This option prevents programs from being intro duced by system crackers or to prevent people from trying to execute programs that are meant to run on a dif ferent system, such as MS-DOS.
auto	Allows the file system to be mounted with the a option to the mount command.
nouser	Forbids a nonsuperuser from mounting a file system.
asyne	Writes data to the file system asynchronously. The system is faster, but you can lose data if a system failure occurs.
sync	Writes data to the file system synchronously.
suid	Permits the suid (set user id) access mode (the default).
	The suid access mode enables an executable program with the suid (or setguid) permission bit set to take on the personality and permissions of the owner (or the group) of the executable program. This option can be a security hole; specifying the nosuid option prevents files in this file system from having the set user id (or setguid) access take effect.
nosuid	Does not permit the suid access mode.
noauto	Does not automatically mount this file system when the -a option is used with the mount command.
usrquota	User quotas may be put in effect.
grpquota	Group quotas may be put in effect.
defaults	A combination of rw, suid, dev, exec, auto, nouser, and async.

✔ *dump-freq* is the frequency with which the file system may be backed up by the dump utility (not all systems use this).

✔ *pass-number* is a decimal number specifying the order in which `fsck`, the file system check utility, checks the file systems. A *pass-number* of 1 (one) indicates that this file system should be checked first. This pass-number is assigned to `root`. All other file systems should have a higher number. Two file systems on different drives can be checked in parallel to speed things up, but file systems on the same drive should have different *pass-numbers*. For a swap device, the *pass-number* should be 0 (zero), which disables `fsck` checking.

The following are examples of some typical `/etc/fstab` entries:

```
/dev/hdb1    /     ext2  defaults  1  1
/dev/hdb3    none  swap  sw        0  0
/dev/hda1    /mnt/win98 vfat noauto 0  0
```

The first line enables the mounting of the first partition of the second IDE disk as the root file system. This partition is an OpenLinux native file system and uses the `rw`, `suid`, `dev`, `exec`, `auto`, `nouser`, and `async` options. The first entry in the `/etc/fstab` file also indicates that the root file system should be dumped (backed up) once a week (use the `man dump` command for details on dump). Finally, the first entry of the `/etc/fstab` file indicates that `fsck` should be performed on the root file system immediately after booting the system.

The second line shows that the third partition of the second IDE disk is a swap partition and has the format of a swap file. The swap partition should never be backed up, nor should you ever perform the `fsck` command on the swap partition.

The third line of the `/etc/fstab` file points to the first partition of the first disk, which is a file system to be mounted on the `/mnt/win98` directory. This file system probably holds Microsoft Windows 98 files, and you can read and write to this file system. The file system won't be mounted automatically with the `-a` option of `mount`. You should never use `dump` to back up this file system, nor should you perform a file system check on it.

After you set up the `/etc/fstab` configuration file, file systems can be mounted automatically at boot time. In addition, after you set up the `/etc/fstab` file, the `mount` and `umount` commands require only *mount-point* or *block-special-file* as their argument.

Normally, most of the `/etc/fstab` file is set up during installation, so you only have to update the file over time as you add new disks or disk partitions.

Caldera OpenLinux includes a graphical interface for updating the /etc/fstab file, so that you don't have to edit the file with a text editor (although you still have this option). On the accompanying CD-ROM, you can update the file with a program called fstab, as follows:

1. **Make certain that the KDE desktop is running.**

2. **Open a terminal-emulator (command line) window.**

3. **Change to the root user by entering this command:**

```
su
```

4. **Enter the root password when prompted.**

5. **Type kfstab to start the tool to edit the /etc/fstab file.**

   A dialog box appears, as shown in Figure 13-1.

kfstab						
File Edit Tools Help						
Device	Mount point	Filesystem	Options	Dump	Fsck	C
Device	Preferences...	/dev/hdb2				
Mount Point	Preferences...	/				
Filesystem		ext2				
Options	Preferences...	defaults				
Dump		1				
Fsck		1				
Comment		9999				
Disable Entry ☐		for future use, please wait				
Reload Save Print		Add Delete			Help Exit	

Figure 13-1:
The kfstab utility.

6. **Enter a device name in the Device field.**

7. **Enter a mount point in the Mount Point field.**

8. **Choose the Preferences button next to the Options field, if you want to update the Options from the shown Default.**

9. **Click the Add button to add this device to your file system configuration.**

10. **Click Save to update the /etc/fstab file on disk with the new file system that you have entered.**

Reforming Corrupted File Systems

File systems can become corrupted by anything from a driver error to a hardware crash. The fsck utility can check the file system's consistency, report errors, and make some repairs. Normally, the fsck program is called automatically as the system boots up. Therefore, if your system crashes, fsck runs on all file systems that were mounted when the system crashed.

The repairs that fsck can perform are limited to *structural* repairs of the file system and its data components. The fsck utility can't help if the data in a structurally intact file is corrupt. Also remember that except for the root file system, fsck runs only on unmounted file systems. You must make sure that the system is in single-user mode to use fsck on the root file system.

Here's the syntax for the fsck command:

```
fsck (options) filesystem
```

where *filesystem* names the block-special-file where the file system resides. If *filesystem* is omitted, then the fsck utility checks all the file systems listed in the /etc/fstab file configuration file. If the fsck utility finds any errors, it prompts you for input on what to do about the errors. For the most part, you simply agree with whatever the program suggests.

The fsck command has the following options:

- ✔ -p   Preens the file system. Performs automatic repairs that don't change the contents of files.

- ✔ -n   Answers no to all prompts and only lists problems; doesn't repair the problems.

- ✔ -y   Answers yes to all prompts and repairs damage regardless of how severe.

- ✔ -f   Forces a file system check.

Lots of people run the fsck command with the -y option. If you run fsck with the -p option, some steps are performed automatically for you. Lost files are placed in the lost+found directory, zero-length files are deleted, and missing blocks are placed back on the list of *free blocks,* which are blocks still available for filling with data, among other things.

Suppose your electricity goes out, and your system crashes. As the system reboots, you see messages similar to the following:

```
/dev/hda5 was not cleanly unmounted, check forced
/dev/hda5: Deleted inode 1456 has zero dtime. FIXED
/dev/hda5: Deleted inode 14577 has zero dtime. FIXED
/dev/hda5: Deleted inode 123753 has zero dtime. FIXED
Fix summary information? Yes
/dev/hda5: 46906/308400 files (1.6% non-contiguous),
           767485/1228801 blocks
```

And a little later, you see something like this for each one of your file systems:

```
fsck.ext2 -a /dev/hda7
/dev/hda7 was not cleanly unmounted, check forced
/dev/hda7: Deleted inode 1324 has zero dtime. FIXED
/dev/hda7: Deleted inode 15987 has zero dtime. FIXED
Fix summary information? Yes
/dev/hda7: 47266/356000 files (1.6% non-contiguous),
           765217/1283507 blocks
```

This message is `fsck` running with the `-a` option, which answers all the questions with yes. For the most part, this option corrects any errors that occur when the power fails or when something breaks inside your computer, causing your computer to crash. After `fsck` runs, it reports whether any file systems were modified.

Adding Elbow Room to Your System

Sooner or later, you're likely to want to add more hard-disk storage to your OpenLinux system to hold more programs, to hold more data, or to enable more users to log on. You usually increase storage by adding one or more hard disks to your system; each hard disk can have one or more disk partitions.

A hard-disk partition is the basic file storage unit for OpenLinux. First you create the file systems on the disk partitions, and then you combine the file systems to form a single directory-tree structure. The directory-tree structure can be on one disk or spread across many.

You can define hard-disk partitions when adding a new hard disk or at a later time. In most cases, disk partitions are defined for you during your original OpenLinux installation. You may divide a disk into one, two, four, or more partitions, each of which may contain a file system or be used as a swap partition. Swap partitions allow very large programs or many small programs to run even if they take up more memory than you have as RAM in your computer. The total of all your swap partitions and RAM is called *virtual memory*.

After you create a hard-disk partition, you must create a file system. The file system occupies a single space on the disk that has a unique block-special-file (device) name. This unique name accesses the file system, regardless of whether the data is stored on all or only part of a physical disk or is an aggregation of multiple physical disks.

OpenLinux regularly adds support for new file systems. The following are the major file system types:

- **Local:** ext, ext2, hpfs
- **NFS:** nfs
- **Samba:** SMB
- **CD-ROM:** iso9660
- **DOS and Windows:** msdos, umsdos, vfat
- **Other:** sysv and minix

If you want to add one of these types of file systems, you have to make a new partition, which may mean adding a new disk drive, which just happens to be the subject of the next section.

Setting Up That New Hard Disk

The first step to increasing your disk space is to add a new hard-disk drive. The following tasks are required to add a disk to your system (regardless of whether the disk is SCSI or IDE) and to make the disk accessible to users:

- Attach the hard-disk drive to your computer system.
- Provide a suitable device driver for the disk's controller in OpenLinux. This may mean rebuilding the kernel of the OpenLinux operating system (see Chapter 14 for details).
- Define at least one partition.
- Create a file system(s) on any partition(s) to be used for user files.
- Enter the new file systems into /etc/fstab, the configuration file.
- Mount the file systems (you may have to make a directory for a mount point).

The following sections take you through the process of configuring a hard disk, a floppy drive, and a CD-ROM drive after they are physically installed.

Configuring a drive

The business of adding a hard disk to your microcomputer is broken down into two steps:

- Physically adding the hard drive
- Logically making OpenLinux aware of the hard drive

The first step is beyond the scope of this book because your drive may be either IDE or SCSI, and the setup of the physical disk is dependent on the rest of the hardware in the system. We suggest you consult the hardware manual that came with your system or have a reseller install your new disk. The OpenLinux system is complicated by the fact that several operating systems — such as DOS, OpenLinux, and SCO UNIX — may share the same disk.

To complete all the steps necessary to install and configure your new disk, you must know the total formatted drive capacity and the number of heads and cylinders, among other details. You can usually find this information in the documentation or from the manufacturer.

You may want to keep a record of the data from the partition table (as displayed by fdisk), such as:

- ✔ Partition numbers
- ✔ Type
- ✔ Size
- ✔ Starting and ending blocks

Installing a drive

After the drive is attached to the system, OpenLinux should recognize it when you boot up. To review the booting messages in a slower fashion than they're displayed, use the dmesg command. If you added a new IDE drive, then look for the mention of a new hdx drive, where the *x* is replaced with the letter *b, c, d,* or *e*. This information tells you that your kernel saw the new disk as it booted, so rebuilding the kernel is not necessary in order to add this drive. Likewise, if you're adding a new SCSI disk drive, then you see a boot message indicating a new disk drive bearing the designation sdx, where *x* is a letter. In either the IDE or SCSI case, you may see other messages with additional information.

The messages for an IDE drive may look like this:

```
hdb: HITACHI_DK227A-50, 4789MB w/512KB Cache,CHS=610/255/63
```

Sometime later, a message appears that looks like the following, which describes the existing partitions on the new disk (if any):

```
hdb: hdb1 hdb2 < hdb5 hdb6 hdb7 hdb8 >
```

A SCSI disk drive has messages that look like this:

```
SCSI device sdb: hdwr device= .......
sdb: sdb1
```

If you see these messages, the kernel has seen your new disk, and you don't have to rebuild the kernel to use the new disk.

The OpenLinux product on the CD-ROM included with this book features block-special-files for each of eight IDE disks (hda–hdh) with nine partitions each (1–9). OpenLinux also has block-special-files for seven SCSI hard-disk drives (sda–sdg), which can have eight partitions each (1–8). In addition, OpenLinux has a block-special-file for a SCSI CD-ROM (scd) with eight partitions (0–7). If you've got more disks than this (we're jealous), then you may have to create one or more additional block-special-files for the device, like this:

```
cd /dev; makedev sdg
```

This command creates the block-special-files for SCSI disk 7. Note that in both IDE and SCSI disks, the letters and disk numbers correspond: *a* is for the first disk, *b* is for the second disk, and so on.

If you add a SCSI disk drive with a lower ID number than one you have already, then the new disk drive takes on that number. Suppose you have SCSI disk drives with hardware ID numbers of 0, 2, and 3. OpenLinux gives these disks the names sda, sdb, and sdc, respectively. You make your partitions and your file systems and create your entries in /etc/fstab to show where you want the file systems mounted. Now you get a new disk drive and set the hardware ID number to 1. When you reboot, the new disk drive gets the sdb designation, and the disk drives with ID numbers of 2 and 3 are renamed to sdc and sdd, respectively. You must now, at the very least, change your /etc/fstab table. For this reason, we recommend adding SCSI disk drives to your system starting with ID 0 and working up the number chain, with no gaps in the numbering.

Partitioning a drive

Now that you've created block-special-files, you can use fdisk to partition the drive. The command to call this utility is /usr/bin/fdisk.

For example, if you want to invoke fdisk for partitioning the first SCSI disk on your system, you type the following:

```
/sbin/fdisk /dev/sda
```

To find out how to use fdisk, refer to Chapter 5. Using fdisk is not too difficult; you can partition the drive fairly easily.

Making the file system

Every disk partition is simply an empty space with a beginning and an ending. Unless the partition is being used for swap space, you have to put some type of file system on the partition before the partition can become useful. The mkfs (for make file system) command is used to create the file system on the partition. Normally, the file system is a native OpenLinux file system, which at this time is called ext2. The OpenLinux version of mkfs has been nicely streamlined and requires hardly any input. To create a file system on the disk-drive partition sda1, for example, you enter the following command:

```
mkfs -t ext2 /dev/sda1
```

If you want to create an MS-DOS file system on the disk partition, you use this command:

```
mkfs -t msdos /dev/sda2
```

You can continue to execute mkfs commands to create file systems for every partition on your new disk. Or you can leave some partitions without file systems (for future use), as long as you remember to perform the mkfs command on the partitions before trying to attach them to your file system by using either the mount command or the /etc/fstab table.

Congratulations! Your disk has been physically added to your system and partitioned, and you've added file systems to the hard disk. Now the hard disk is ready to join the rest of the file system — simply use either the mount command or the /etc/fstab file, which we describe earlier in this chapter.

Living with Floppy Disks

Floppy disks are treated a little differently than hard disks, mostly due to their size and fragility. Floppy disks normally are not mounted and used for hours and days on end to hold gigabytes of data. More often, floppy disks are used to transfer data to other computers or to back up a few files.

Although you can create OpenLinux file systems on floppy disks, using floppy disks in other ways is more advantageous. For example:

- Floppy disks can be mounted as DOS file systems, which can then be accessed with the standard OpenLinux utilities, such as cp and ls.
- Floppy disks can be used as raw devices with commands, such as tar and cpio.
- Floppy disks can permit the use of special utilities that read and write to DOS disks.

On OpenLinux systems, the block-special-file for the first floppy drive is /dev/fd0. The default density is 1,440 kilobytes. We assume you're using standard, 3 ½-inch, preformatted floppy disks.

The following commands mount a floppy disk and write a DOS file to the floppy, (replace *any-dosfile.txt* with a real filename):

```
mount /dev/fd0 /mnt/floppy
cp any-dosfile.txt /mnt/floppy
umount /mnt/floppy
```

These commands are ways to move files back and forth to an MS-DOS (Windows 3.1, 95, 98) or Windows NT machine. You can add the file to a floppy disk, insert the floppy in the MS-DOS machine, and the MS-DOS machine can read the file from the disk. Likewise, by mounting a floppy disk created on an MS-DOS machine, you can read and manipulate the files by using OpenLinux.

The mtools package installed on your system enables you to access DOS disks and files without first mounting the floppy disk and adding it to your file system. Table 13-1 presents some mtools commands, which are probably familiar to DOS users.

Table 13-1	The mtools Utilities
Command	**What It Does**
Mformat	Formats a floppy disk in DOS format
mlabel	Labels a DOS floppy disk
mcd	Changes the current directory location on a DOS floppy disk
mdir	Lists the directory contents on a DOS floppy disk
mtype	Displays a DOS file's contents
mcopy	Copies files between a DOS floppy disk and OpenLinux
mdel	Deletes files on a DOS floppy disk
mren	Renames files on a DOS floppy disk
mmd	Creates a subdirectory on a DOS floppy disk
mrd	Removes a directory from a DOS floppy disk
mattrib	Changes DOS file attributes

Configuring a CD-ROM Drive

You treat CD-ROM drives similar to — but not exactly like — hard-disk drives. The block-special-file for CD-ROMs in OpenLinux is usually /dev/cdrom, /dev/hdc, /dev/hdd, or /dev/sr0, depending on factors such as the CD-ROM's type, how the CD-ROM is connected to the controller, and the CD-ROM's drive number.

The most common type of CD-ROM is ATAPI, and OpenLinux recognizes ATAPI CD-ROM drives at boot. SCSI CD-ROMs are also normally recognized as the kernel boots. If you installed OpenLinux from the accompanying CD-ROM, then OpenLinux will have recognized the CD-ROM, which is probably called /dev/cdrom.

We mention that CD-ROMs aren't exactly like other disk drives because CD-ROMs are read-only (which means that you can't change their contents) and typically have only one file system to a disk. Therefore, you don't partition a CD-ROM drive, nor do you make a file system before mounting it. The manufacturer already did these things. You simply have to determine where you want to mount the CD-ROM and which drive you want it attached to. We assume your CD-ROM drive is /dev/cdrom, which is really just a pointer to another special-device file. This extra pointer (called a *link*) enables you to call the CD-ROM by the name /dev/cdrom, rather than having to call it /dev/scda on some systems (because it happens to be a SCSI device) and /dev/hdc on other systems (because it happens to be an IDE-based device).

Here is the command for mounting a CD-ROM on your OpenLinux system:

```
mount /mnt/cdrom
```

If you're having trouble getting this command to work, it's probably because the OpenLinux installation didn't correctly identify your CD-ROM drive and place information about it in the /etc/fstab file. In that case, you can try the following more cryptic command that provides OpenLinux with all the relevant details to access the CD-ROM drive.

```
mount -r -t iso9660 /dev/cdrom /mnt/cdrom
```

The OpenLinux system dismounts file systems automatically when you shut down the machine and — if you've put all the necessary information into the /etc/fstab file — automatically mounts them when you start up the system.

Chapter 14

Customizing OpenLinux

· ·

In This Chapter

▶ Finding out about different types of memory

▶ Unearthing how much RAM your system has

▶ Checking out the performance of your disks

▶ Rebuilding your kernel

· ·

*Y*our OpenLinux system is a mélange of hardware and software, and you have choices to make about both. So how do you tune your system for good performance? Follow this chapter, that's how.

 Tuning operating systems can become a life-consuming task. If you're obsessed about squeezing the most from your hardware and software, you won't have time for anything else. Take advantage of the tips in this chapter, take a deep breath, and get on with the rest of your life.

Tuning Your OpenLinux System

Most UNIX-like systems don't have many knobs and buttons you can change to make the systems work faster, or better. OpenLinux, however, has a few special features that you can tweak for better performance. More important, if you follow a few guidelines, you can help your OpenLinux system perform at its best.

You can never have enough memory

Although having too much memory theoretically is possible, most people have too little — in their systems, that is. Today, memory is so inexpensive that few excuses for not having enough hold up.

Not having enough RAM is a holdover from memory prices, such as $23,000 per megabyte. I paid $400 for 4 kilobits (.004MB) of main memory about the same time that I purchased a new pickup truck for $2,000.

Real versus virtual memory

When we talk about *real memory,* we're referring to the semiconductor RAM (random-access memory) in your machine. You may have as little as 4MB or as much as 128MB of RAM in your machine. Some power users (or their servers) have 1GB (1 billion bytes) of RAM in their PCs.

If semiconductor RAM is the only type of memory you have, OpenLinux and all programs running under OpenLinux have to fit into that RAM. You can run OpenLinux in 32MB of memory, but more is better. 128MB, a standard on many newer systems, sounds like a lot of memory, but even that amount of memory fills up pretty quickly.

Virtual memory is hard-disk-drive space that OpenLinux uses as if it were real memory. Only the programs don't know the difference. Apart from the fact that hard-disk-drive space is much cheaper than RAM, virtual memory offers two big benefits:

- More programs and files can run at the same time.

- Programs and files can exceed the size of actual RAM.

The drive space that simulates real memory is called *swap space.* (When you installed OpenLinux, you may have been asked to select a swap space. If not, rest assured it was done automatically for you.) Here's how the swap space is used:

- When OpenLinux needs more RAM to start a new application or allow an open application to expand, some disk space may be substituted for the necessary RAM. An existing section of RAM is copied onto the swap space. Moving part of an inactive application to the swap space frees RAM for the new data.

- When OpenLinux needs the information from the swap space, OpenLinux must make room in RAM. Therefore, OpenLinux may write some other program's data to the swap space before recalling data. This process is called *demand-paging,* because the data is in RAM only when a *demand* exists for it to be there. Otherwise, data tends to stay on the swap area of the disk.

- When the computer doesn't have enough RAM to do its normal tasks efficiently, the computer is memory bound; the CPU must wait while portions of virtual memory are brought back into RAM. If this happens a lot, the computer is *thrashing* and becomes very slow.

Do I have enough RAM?

The `procinfo` and `vmstat` commands can help determine whether you have enough RAM. Using these commands by themselves or with each other can tell you whether you're over-utilizing your RAM memory. If so, your CPU is waiting for RAM to be available.

Measuring performance with vmstat

The `vmstat` command displays information about memory utilization, the status of a process, the status of the I/O system, and CPU utilization. The `vmstat` command also tells you whether the swap partition is being used, and if so, how much is being used.

The following is a sample output of the `vmstat` command:

```
vmstat
procs       memory swap      io system      cpu
r b w swpd free buff cache si so bi bo in cs us sy id
1 0 0    0 2100 2372 13248 0 0 4 1 123 52 3 2 95
```

The details are:

- The r (run) number indicates the number of processes that are capable of being run but are waiting for the CPU to pay attention to them. The more processes you have in this segment, the slower the system.

- The b (blocked) number indicates processes waiting for something to happen (usually some type of I/O). The processes can't be run, even if you have some free CPU.

  Too many processes in the block number may mean that you have an I/O bottleneck. We discuss how to alleviate I/O bottlenecks later in the chapter.

- The w number is the number of processes that are *swapped* out. Processes are swapped out if there's not enough memory to run them efficiently, or if they've been idle for more than 20 seconds.

  A large w value may indicate a lack of memory. Processes that are inactive for a long time (waiting for I/O, for example) may be swapped automatically by OpenLinux to conserve real memory space and other system resources.

- swpd is the amount of virtual memory used, in kilobytes.

- free is the amount of idle memory, in kilobytes.

- buff is the amount of memory in I/O buffers, in kilobytes.

- cache is the I/O cache, in kilobytes.

- ✔ si (swapped in) and so (swapped out) monitor the program pages swapped in and out. In a heavily loaded, memory-bound system, you see high numbers here.

- ✔ bi (blocks in) and bo (blocks out) indicate I/O activity on disks.

- ✔ The in value reports interrupts per second (including the clock).

  Normally, the number of interrupts ranges from the low hundreds on a single-user system (most of these are due to the system clock) to the low thousands on a busy server system.

  The number of interrupts per second is useful if you have a device that has gone crazy. An improperly wired serial line, for example, can eat CPU time with thousands of interrupts per second. Although hundreds of interrupts per second are not uncommon on most systems today, sudden unexplained jumps in the number of interrupts (for example, thousands of interrupts per second on an otherwise unused machine) may be worth investigating.

- ✔ cs reports the number of context switches per second.

- ✔ us, sy, and id (user, system, and idle) CPU numbers are the percentages of time the CPU is running your program, doing some type of system service (perhaps requested by your program), or standing idle, respectively. Note that a system with lots of idle time is not necessarily the best tuned; the CPU may be idle because programs are waiting on I/O.

vmstat can output a one-line summary automatically while OpenLinux runs. Enter a command in the following form (just substitute the time interval, in seconds, for *x*):

```
vmstat x
```

The programs that you see are the programs inside the system, minus the activity of vmstat (although running vmstat does have some slight effect).

Measuring performance with the Task Manager

The Task Manager is another program used to measure system performance. In many ways, the Task Manager is nicer to use than vmstat because the Task Manager lists more information in one place and is better formatted (for human eyes). vmstat still has its uses, though, because vmstat's lack of formatting makes it easier to use inside shell scripts.

You can start the Task Manager from the main menu of KDE by choosing System⇨Task Manager. The Task Manager has two tabs:

- ✔ The Processes List tab (shown in Figure 14-1)

- ✔ The Performance Meter tab

The Processes List tab includes all the processes (programs) running on your OpenLinux system. You can select whether to show only the programs you started or everyone's programs. The screen is refreshed every few seconds as the status of processes changes.

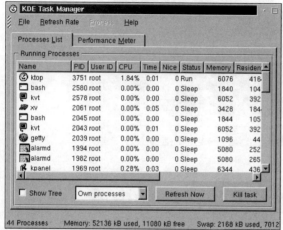

Figure 14-1:
The Task
Manager
Processes
List tab.

To change the priority of any process, select the process from the list, then choose an item from the Processes menu. You can also use the Kill button to end any process that's causing you trouble.

Running a command (especially in the background) at a lower priority is a *nice* thing to do and makes the system more reactive to interactive jobs.

The Performance Meter tab (shown in Figure 14-2) shows the system performance over time. You can see that this system hasn't been running very long, but the colored graphs (really, they are) show the load on the CPU (how busy it's been handling program requests) and the use of system resources, particularly memory and swap space (virtual memory).

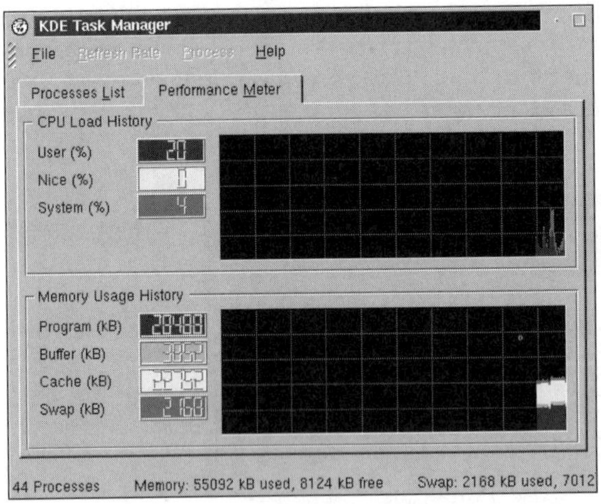

Figure 14-2:
The Task
Manager
Performance
Meter tab.

Enhancing Disk Performance

After your system has enough main memory, you may want to look at how well your disks are performing. OpenLinux (like a lot of UNIX operating systems) is very disk-oriented. Many programs that OpenLinux users execute come from disk, execute for a short time (creating swap space on the disk and then releasing it), and then terminate. In particular, when you create a long pipeline in shell programming, the last few programs on the command line may never do any work because the programs depend on data flowing through to them before the programs do anything. If no data reaches the last programs in the pipeline, the programs can't do anything and will terminate.

Suppose that the last program is the sort program. The sort program's job is to sort the output into a particular order and then allow the display of the output on the screen. If no data to sort comes through the pipeline, the sort program's job is very short (kind of nonexistent), and all the work that the sort program did preparing to do the sort is useless.

OpenLinux also does a lot of work with temporary files. The C compiler generates many temporary files while it's compiling a program, and the sort routine does the same thing while sorting (darn that sort routine). All these temporary files may flush data out to the disk or bring data in from the disk, creating a bottleneck through the disk subsystem.

OpenLinux sets aside a certain amount of main memory in its dynamic buffer cache to hold data moving from the disk to the CPU and vice versa. When data is read from the disk, the data first goes into the dynamic buffer cache. Usually, more data than was originally requested goes into the cache (in a process known as *read-ahead*). When more information is needed, the CPU often can just go to the buffer cache and quickly get the data, without having to wait for the disk. When data is written to the disk, the data often goes only as far as the buffer cache. Data sits in the buffer cache until it's needed again or until the buffer cache is told to write out its data to disk.

Multiple swap partitions

If your system is paging and swapping heavily and you can't afford more memory, try creating multiple swap partitions (rather than having only one) and then distributing the swap partitions across your disk drives. Doing so helps to alleviate disk contention because then your programs are swapped and paged across multiple disks.

Older versions of OpenLinux were limited to 128MB per swap partition. The latest versions don't have this limitation. But performance improvements still come from creating multiple swap partitions instead of a single large swap partition to reduce head contention, as information is moved to and from the swap space. An OpenLinux system can support up to 16 swap partitions.

Create Your Very Own Kernel

One of the items that may be slowing down your system can be a kernel that isn't tailored to your hardware or your needs. A kernel that's not set up for your system has two major disadvantages:

✔ You may have your kernel compiled for a processor that you don't have.
✔ You have more instructions and data than you need in your kernel.

This section describes both situations and what you can do to change them.

Tailoring a kernel for your processor

The kernel of OpenLinux is prepared to install and function well on the largest reasonable range of systems. Therefore, the kernel is compiled to run on the slowest processor: An Intel 386. That's what you have, right? Oh, well, let's fix that.

To take advantage of the power waiting inside the Pentium-class system that you have sitting next to you, you need at least to rebuild the kernel portion of OpenLinux, specifying the processor that you have. To do this:

1. **Log in as root.**

2. **Insert the *Caldera OpenLinux For Dummies* CD-ROM in your CD-ROM drive.**

3. **Mount the CD-ROM drive with this command:**

```
mount /mnt/cdrom
```

4. **Change to the packages directory on the CD-ROM:**

```
cd /mnt/cdrom/col/install/RPMS
```

5. **Install the kernel source code with these two commands. (Press <TAB> after typing the information shown before pressing Enter. Doing so fills in the rest of the package name):**

```
rpm -Uvh linux-source-common<TAB>
rpm -Uvh linux-source-i386<TAB>
```

If you see an error message from either of these commands stating that the packages are already installed, you can ignore the message (knowing that you're a step ahead of the game) and continue with the next step.

6. **Type** cd /usr/src/linux **at the system prompt.**

7. **Type** make menuconfig.

The screen appears, as shown in Figure 14-3.

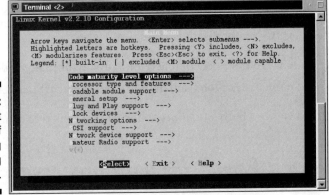

Figure 14-3:
The first menu of menuconfig for tailoring the kernel.

8. **Use the arrow keys to go to General setup and press Enter.**

The General setup menu appears, as shown in Figure 14-4.

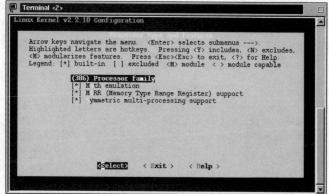

Figure 14-4:
The General
setup menu.

9. **Use the arrow keys to move down to Processor family (the screen scrolls), and press Enter.**

   A menu of all supported processors appears, as shown in Figure 14-5.

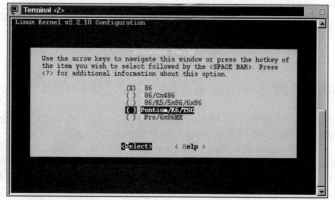

Figure 14-5:
The list for
choosing
your
processor.

10. **Use the arrow keys to move your cursor to the processor that you have in your system, and then press the spacebar to select it.**

    You're automatically moved back to the preceding menu, and the processor you selected shows under Processor.

11. **Press the Tab key once to move the cursor to Exit, and then press Enter.**

    The first menu appears.

12. **Press the Tab key once to move the cursor to Exit, and then press Enter to close the menu.**

13. **If you don't want to save your changes, press the Tab key once to select No, and then press Enter to exit the menu.**

14. **To save your new kernel configuration file, do the following:**

    a. **Press the Enter key.**

    The following message appears:

    ```
    The Linux kernel is now hopefully configured for your
         setup. Check the
    top level Makefile for additional configuration, and do a
         "make dep ;
    make clean" if you want to be sure all the files are
         correctly remade.
    ```

    b. **Type** make dep; make clean **as the message directs.**

    c. **Finally, type** make zlilo **to make the new kernel.**

We've taken you through a very simple reconfiguration of your kernel, changing only one small item. You've invoked the program that configures the kernel, allowed OpenLinux to recognize and make all the dependencies for creating a new kernel, cleaned up old files lying in your kernel directory structure, and then made the kernel. But you're probably not finished at this point, so in the next section you take another, larger step by redefining what you need in the kernel.

Instructions and data not needed

Although remaking the kernel and changing only the processor type typically makes your system go faster by utilizing new instructions in the CPU architecture, just changing the processor type doesn't do anything for the size of the kernel (which may be very large if you've requested support for features you don't use). Simply changing the CPU architecture also won't support functionality or devices not listed in the installation kernel.

For example, perhaps OpenLinux is not tuned to support your sound card. (Sound boards are tricky because so many of them look *almost* like the software.) So, you may want to make a new kernel that works efficiently with your sound card. Fortunately, a lot of support for different kernel functionality and device drivers is in modular form and is available through both loadable kernel modules and loadable device drivers. Because of these two features, a standard kernel in OpenLinux handles a great many devices and features without having to be rebuilt. If a specific feature doesn't seem to be working, however, a look at the kernel configuration is probably in order.

1. **Log in as root.**

2. **Change to the** /usr/src/linux **directory.**

3. **Type** make menuconfig.

   The screen appears (refer to Figure 14-3).

4. **Use the arrow keys to go to General setup, and press Enter.**

5. **Move the cursor to an option of interest and type ? (question mark).**

   The configuration program attempts to tell you what the option means, why the option is important, and the option's possible pitfalls and advantages. The configuration program also makes suggestions regarding whether to include each option as a module (or whether to include the option at all).

6. **Move down the menu items by using the arrow keys and select what you want to include.**

   Referring to the elements in Figure 14-3, you can see that the entries with square brackets ([and]) in front of them have two possible values. By moving the cursor to these entries, you can choose blank (which means unselected) or * (which means selected). If the selection has < and > brackets, you have three possible values: Unselected, selected, or module.

7. **Press the Tab key to move to the Exit option, then press Enter.**

8. **Tell the system to save your new kernel configuration file.**

9. **Type** make dep; make clean **as the message directs.**

10. **Finally, type** make zlilo **to make the new kernel.**

As in the preceding section, you invoked the program that configures the kernel, allowed OpenLinux to recognize and make all the dependencies for creating a new kernel, cleaned up old files lying in your kernel directory structure, and then made the kernel. But this time, the kernel probably has all the features you want it to have, so you can continue putting the new kernel in place by following the procedures in the next section.

Finishing the kernel rebuild

After the kernel is rebuilt the way you want it, you probably have to remake any modules that you want to use. These modules are the ones that you specified in the kernel as *loadable*. The easiest way to remake the modules is to type **make modules** and **make modules install** after the basic kernel is built.

In addition to making the kernel the way you want it, you have to tell the system where you want to put the new version of the kernel. One way to do this is by using /etc/lilo.conf, which is the configuration file for the LILO boot loader. If you edit /etc/lilo.conf, you see a file that looks similar to this:

```
boot=/dev/hda
map=/boot/map
install=/boot/boot.b
prompt
timeout=50
other=/dev/hda1
    label=dos
    table=/dev/hda
image=/boot/vmlinuz
    label=linux
    root=/dev/hda2
    read-only
```

The first line, boot=/dev/hda, means the master boot block is on device /dev/hda. If you want to create a LILO boot file on a floppy disk, you make this line boot=/dev/fd0. The second line names a file that shows how Linux looks inside the kernel. The third line shows where to get a boot block. For now, let's leave these three lines alone.

The prompt line means you want to be prompted for multibooting operations (using LILO to boot more than one operating system), and you want the LILO program to wait at the prompt at least 50 seconds before booting the default operating system, which in this case is dos. When this system was installed, dos was loaded on the first partition of /dev/hda1, and when you press the Tab key after the first boot prompt appears, you see dos as one of the labels for which operating system to choose and linux as the other label. The next section of the /etc/lilo.conf file, which starts with image=/boot/vmlinuz, describes the Linux part of the boot process. Note here that the image is located in /boot/vmlinuz. You may want to change this to place the image in /vmlinuz, which is more standard in OpenLinux systems, and which is where the make zlilo command ends up putting the new kernel.

The final two entries tell LILO that your root file system is /dev/hda2 and that it should be mounted read-only until it has a chance to be checked by fsck.

Please remember that all disk names, such as /dev/hda2, as well as the layout are only examples; your system may have a different layout and no DOS to act as a second operating system to boot. In this case, your lilo.conf file will be a lot smaller and simpler, but just as effective.

After you've updated the /etc/lilo.conf file to reflect the configuration of your system and a new copy of the kernel is at /vmlinux (you may want to check the date and time stamp on the file to make sure it's the latest one), you can type the lilo command and update the master boot record. The next time you boot, you'll be running your rebuilt kernel.

Part V
Going Online

The 5th Wave   By Rich Tennant

"It's called 'Caldera OpenLinux Poker.' Everyone gets to see everyone else's cards, everything's wild, you can play off your opponents' hands, and no one loses except Bill Gates, whose face appears on the Jokers."

In this part . . .

It's time to hit the great outdoors, starting in your back-yard and moving out from there. Chapter 15 shows you how to find an Internet service provider (ISP) and then make the necessary connection between your ISP and your system.

You're also ready to venture into uncharted territory, oth-erwise known as the Web. Chapter 16 shows you how to browse the Web with a program called, naturally, a Web browser. The *Caldera OpenLinux For Dummies* CD-ROM already contains one of the best Web browsers available, Netscape Communicator.

Okay, now that you're out in the wilds of computerdom, how will you communicate? Smoke signals? Yodeling? E-mail? That's the ticket, and in Chapter 16 you also find out how to send and receive e-mail.

Chapter 15

Setting Up Your Internet Connection

· ·

In This Chapter

▶ Finding an Internet service provider

▶ Connecting with your modem

▶ Making the connection between your modem and your Internet service provider

▶ Starting and stopping the Internet service software

· ·

*O*ne of *the* things to do these days is to surf the Net. You connect to the Internet and tie up your phone line for hours, looking for obscure information and sending e-mail to people you barely know and never speak to on the phone.

Now, you too can go to a party and drop the casual phrase "I found this while surfing the Net this afternoon . . . [which will draw bored looks] . . . on my OpenLinux system." The mention of OpenLinux immediately shows that you're truly a person of class and standing in the Internet community.

First, though, you have to find a *good* Internet service provider, hook up your phone to the computer (using a device called a modem), and set up a few simple items on your OpenLinux system (to satisfy the networking gods) to make the connection.

The Search for an ISP

We categorize Internet service providers (ISPs) into those that specialize only in Windows and Windows NT products and those that are good. By *good,* we mean ISPs that also can handle UNIX and Linux accounts.

To find a good ISP, first look in the local Yellow Pages under Internet or Internet Service Providers. List the names and telephone numbers of any ISPs that you find. These companies probably are local companies, which is fine if you want to communicate only from your home. If you do a lot of traveling, you may want to call the following national providers:

AT&T WorldNet: 800-967-5363

IBM Global Network: 800-888-4103

CompuServe: 800-336-6823

Next, talk to some friends who live close to you and ask them which ISP they use and what they think of the service. If a service has overused local access numbers, you often get busy signals. Also ask about the technical help, which in some services is poor or nonexistent.

Finally, call the ISPs and tell them you have a Linux system and are interested in PPP services, with e-mail and newsgroups. Find out whether the ISPs have access numbers in your local calling area. Otherwise, you end up making a long-distance call each time you connect. Check their prices and whether they have unlimited service (a flat rate no matter how many hours you're logged in). A typical price for unlimited service is $20 to $30 per month. ISPs that host Web pages are a plus, as are ISPs that can filter junk e-mail, or *spam*.

Now is a good time to verify that your own telephone service is billed at a flat rate and not metered.

Tell the ISP the highest speed of your modem. You'll probably also need to supply a login name and a password for the ISP's server, so you may want to write these down ahead of time.

A young friend of mine from Poland came to visit me. He had obtained a nationwide ISP service to keep in touch through the Internet with family and friends back home. Unfortunately, the closest number to his ISP connection site was a long-distance call from my house. I cautioned him to watch his connection time, so that I wouldn't have a lot of long-distance charges. He assured me that he would. The month after he went back to Poland, I received my phone bill — with $70 in long-distance telephone charges to his Internet provider. Hi Antoni!

After you choose your Internet service provider and arrange payment, the ISP provides you with certain pieces of information, including the following:

✔ Telephone access numbers

✔ A username (usually the one you want)

✔ A password (usually the one you supply)

✔ An e-mail address, which is typically your username added to its domain name

✔ A primary Domain Name Server (DNS) number, which is a large number separated by periods into four groups of digits

✔ A secondary Domain Name Server (DNS) number, which is another large number separated by periods into four groups of digits

✔ An SMTP (mail) server name

✔ An NNTP (news) server name

✔ A POP3 server name, which is used to download e-mail from the ISP's server to your machine

The ISP may also give you software on a CD-ROM or a floppy to help you get your account working, but this software probably works only with Microsoft operating systems. That's okay because OpenLinux has more than enough software to use with the Internet and to help you get your account working.

Connecting Your Modem

To use OpenLinux with the Internet, you must have at least one of these devices:

✔ A serial modem

✔ An ISDN line

✔ A digital subscriber line (DSL)

✔ A broadband connector of some type (such as Ethernet, FDDI, a cable modem, or ATM)

For the second and third items, you or someone you know (your boss, your systems administrator, or your 10-year old) probably arranged for you to get the connection and even set up your computer for it. The serial modem is a device that you may have chosen yourself, or it may have come with your computer, in which case you may have little knowledge of how to use it with OpenLinux. For the rest of this chapter, we assume that you're connecting your system to the Internet by using a serial modem and a telephone line.

Modems, quite simply, do three main functions:

✔ Convert digital information into tones that go across telephone lines (and vice versa)

✔ Dial the telephone number you want to reach and make the connection with a modem at the other end

✔ Negotiate with the modem at the other end for the speed to use when sending bits of information

Types of modems

Modems can be either internal or external. An *external modem* stays in its own little box and usually plugs into a wall outlet for power, into the telephone line for the connection, and into a serial connector on the back of your computer. An *internal modem* usually is plugged into a slot on the motherboard inside the computer case. (Some internal modems are built directly onto the motherboard.) To the computer and operating system, an internal modem appears as if it were two or more serial ports. Internal modems draw their power from the computer system, and they plug into the phone jack.

Usually internal modems are less expensive than their external counterparts, but some people like external modems because they can hook them up to different computer systems simply by unplugging the serial line from one system box and plugging it into another.

A third type of serial-line modem is a PCMCIA card (sometimes called a PC card). These cards are used most often with laptop computers.

Finding the serial line

After you connect your modem, you have to tell OpenLinux which serial line (or simulated serial line) the modem is connected to. If your modem was already installed on your system when you installed OpenLinux, a /dev/modem link was already created for you by the installation program as it scanned your system and located the modem.

The /dev/modem device is a standard location for the modem. OpenLinux creates a symbolic link (a pointer, really) from the actual modem device to /dev/modem. The modem itself may be located on /dev/ttyS0, /dev/ttyS1, or another serial-port device.

If you need to locate a modem that you've installed after installing OpenLinux, try using each serial port in turn (ttyS0 to ttyS3) to see which one works for you. You can make a link from one of the serial devices to the /dev/modem device name by using the ln command with the -s option, like this:

```
ln -s /dev/ttyS0 /dev/modem
```

After you've set up the /dev/modem link, you can try using the link with the kppp program described in the next section. If the modem doesn't respond (you normally hear it dialing when it works), try creating a link to a different device by using the above command.

Some newer computers already have a modem installed, but the modem is a WinModem, which isn't a true modem — it requires software control to function. Because specifications haven't been released for this type of device, WinModems can't be accessed from OpenLinux (or any version of Linux).

Rather than try each serial-port address in turn, if you have Windows 98 on your system, you can see which port or COM line the modem connects to by reviewing the information in the Windows configuration. Reboot your computer into Windows and follow these steps:

1. **Choose Start⇨Settings⇨Control Panel.**

   The Control Panel window appears.

2. **Click the Modem icon.**

   The Modems Properties dialog box appears.

3. **Click the Diagnostics tab.**

   You see your modem listed, with a COM-line number beside it. This number is the Windows designation for your modem's serial communications line.

Setting Up kppp

You have a modem connected and have established an account with an ISP, but that's not all you have to do. You need to set up a program that uses the PPP communications protocol to connect to your ISP using the modem device that you just set up. KDE includes the perfect utility to do this: kppp.

To start kppp, choose it from the Internet menu in KDE. The main connection window appears, as shown in Figure 15-1. This window includes fields where you can select which account to connect to and then enter your username and password for that account before clicking the Connect button. But, before you can use kppp, you need to set up your account and tell kppp how to use your modem.

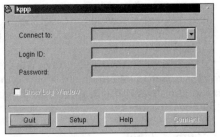

Figure 15-1:
The kppp
main
window
includes
places to
enter your
username
and
password.

Setting up an ISP account

To begin setting up kppp, follow these steps:

1. **Choose the Setup button on the main kppp window.**

   The kppp Configuration dialog box appears, as shown in Figure 15-2. The dialog box contains several tabs. You can set up information about your ISP in the Accounts tab. This tab shows all the accounts that you have configured (and maybe some you haven't — delete those).

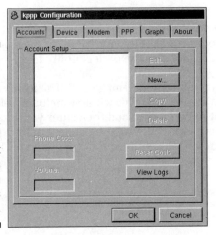

Figure 15-2:
The kppp
Configur-
ation
dialog box
includes
tabs to set
up accounts
and modem
access
information.

2. To set up your ISP account, choose New on the Accounts tab of the kppp Configuration dialog box.

A New Account dialog box appears. This dialog box includes six tabs in which you can set up the properties of your ISP account. Happily, you normally don't have much to do in most of the six tabs, so setting up the account is fairly easy. The most important tab is the Dial tab, shown in Figure 15-3.

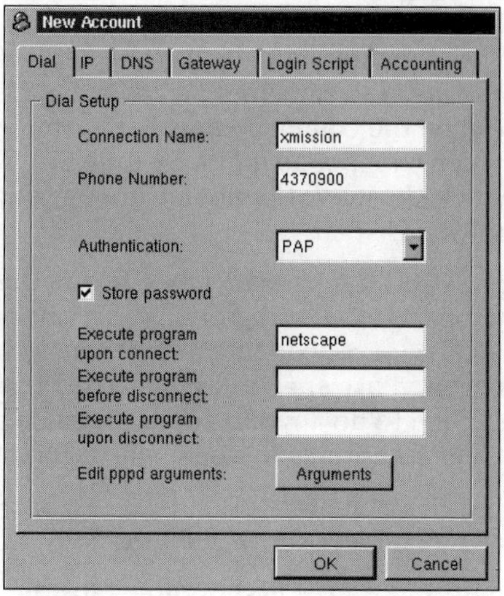

Figure 15-3: In the Dial tab of the New Account dialog box, you set up how to reach your ISP.

3. In the Dial tab, do the following:

a. **Enter a name for the account in the Connection Name field.** This name can be anything you choose but try to use something you can associate with your ISP name, in case you later have multiple accounts to keep track of.

b. **Enter the number to call to reach your ISP server (not the tech support number, please) in the Phone Number field.** kppp doesn't have fancy dialing options, so if you need to dial 9 first or dial special codes when you're away from home and calling long distance, you need manually to enter those features as part of the Phone Number field.

c. **Indicate how you want kppp to identify you to the ISP server in the Authentication field.** The four options are Script-based, Terminal-based, PAP, and CHAP. Almost all ISPs use PAP or CHAP because PAP and CHAP are easier and more secure than the other two methods. We explain later how to set up Script-based authentication by using the Login Script tab. Ask your ISP which method to use for a connection to its server.

d. **Check the Store password checkbox if you want kppp to remember the password you enter for this account when you connect.** This feature is handy for quick connections, but it has two disadvantages. First, others may try snooping around your system and locating your password (though it doesn't appear on screen in plain text). Second, you're likely to forget the password if you don't type it regularly (which makes using your ISP account from another system difficult).

e. **Enter the name of a program to start automatically after the connection is established.** Three fields let you execute a program at different points: When you first connect, before disconnecting, or right after disconnecting. You can enter any command in these fields just as you can on the command line. For example, you could enter the program name `netscape` in the Execute program upon connect field to launch Netscape Communicator as soon as the ISP connection is established.

f. **Edit the pppd arguments (if necessary) by clicking the Arguments button.** pppd is the background program that manages the PPP protocol and connects you to your ISP. Unless your ISP indicates that you need to use special arguments to connect successfully, you don't need to do anything here. If you do, choose the Arguments button and enter the additional information to use when running pppd.

4. **Click the IP tab and make any necessary selections.**

The IP tab (shown in Figure 15-4) is the first of three tabs that you can use to determine how your system configures networking after attaching to the ISP server. The IP tab lets you choose to use a dynamic IP address (one automatically assigned by your ISP) or a static IP address. A few people have arranged with their ISP to have a static IP address to make configuration of some OpenLinux services easier. In general, though, this is more work than you want to worry about. Choose Dynamic IP Address and forget about it.

5. **Click the DNS tab (shown in Figure 15-5) and configure how your computer resolves names to IP addresses.**

You must indicate a DNS server that will convert `www.yahoo.com` and all your other URLs (*Uniform Resource Locators,* the technical term for Web addresses) into an IP address that the Internet can understand — like 207.29.12.1. Do the following:

a. **In the Domain Name field, enter the domain name that you're using.** This name may be the domain of your organization, or the domain of your ISP. In most cases the domain name isn't highly relevant. The only potential problem you have is being connected to both an internal network (via your Ethernet card, for example) and an ISP (via your modem). If so, use your internal domain name.

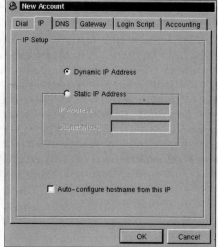

Figure 15-4:
You select a
dynamic or
static IP
address in
the IP tab of
the New
Account
dialog box.

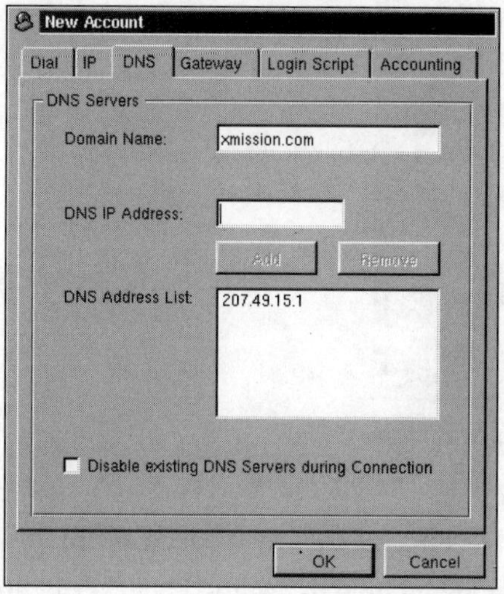

Figure 15-5:
Configure
how to
access a
DNS server
at your ISP
by using the
DNS tab.

   **b. Enter the IP address that your ISP provided for accessing a DNS
   server in the DNS IP Address field, then click Add.** This part of
   this tab is key. The address is a cryptic-looking set of numbers
   (again, like 201.207.68.30). After you click Add, the IP address is
   added to the DNS Address List field. If your ISP gives you two DNS
   server addresses, so much the better. Enter both the server
   addresses. If one DNS server is down, then you still can reach
   the Web.

6. **Click the Gateway tab (shown in Figure 15-6) and click the Default Gateway button, unless you have a good reason not to.**

The Gateway tab tells your system how to route information (network data packets, to be precise). Your ISP normally acts as a gateway to the rest of the world — to the Internet. By choosing Default Gateway, your ISP's gateway is used for your connection. If you need to use a different gateway, choose Static Gateway and enter the ISP address of the gateway computer. A static gateway would be needed only if you have an internal network connection where most of your traffic can be sent. However, using a static gateway address in this tab may make it hard to browse the net by using your ISP connection. You can enter a static gateway address and then deselect the checkbox to Assign the Default Route to this Gateway.

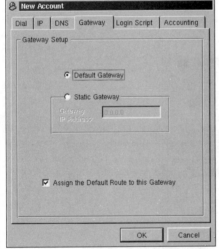

Figure 15-6: The Default Gateway is configured in the Gateway tab.

7. **Click the Login Script tab and create any desired scripts.**

We promised that we'd explain how to use the Login script authentication method. Welcome to the Login Script tab. This method of authentication uses a script of exchanges between your computer and the ISP computer to log you in and start the pppd daemon. The purpose of the script is to define what lines of text to expect from the ISP server and what commands to send in return. In general, these lines involve sending back your username and password.

To create a login script, you choose a type of message from the drop-down list, such as Expect or Send (most lines will be one of these two — you may not have any others). Then enter the text in the blank field next to the drop-down list and choose Add or Insert. The lines of your login script appear one by one in the bottom section of the Login Scrip tab.

Your ISP provides you with sample lines to show what the login script looks like to connect to its server. Figure 15-7 shows a simple version of a login script in the Login Script tab.

Figure 15-7:
A simple login script can be used for some ISPs in place of PAP or CHAP authentication.

If your ISP specifies PAP or CHAP authentication, you don't need to enter anything in the Login Script tab.

8. **Click the Accounting tab and make any necessary selections.**

   This tab provides the ability to track how much data you exchange with your ISP and how long you're connected, computing charges based on the telecom provider that you're using. This information only applies outside the United States, where telecom providers normally charge per time unit or number of bytes for an Internet connection.

   If you're outside the United States, you can select the Enable accounting checkbox and then choose a telecom provider in your country. Then choose the method of accounting from the Volume accounting drop-down list. You see in the Accounts tab of the kppp Configuration dialog box a summary of the costs associated with the account that you've configured, based on how much you've used the account. This summary lets you track expenses between billings. Figure 15-8 shows how the Accounting tab appears with a telecom provider selected.

9. **After you've entered all the account information in these six tabs (well, hopefully not all six are needed), click OK to close the New Account dialog box and finish configuring kppp.**

   From the kppp Configuration dialog box you can choose New multiple times to set up numerous ISP accounts. You also can select an account from the list and choose Edit to change the properties of that account.

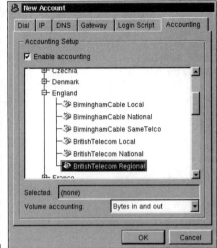

Figure 15-8:
The
Accounting
tab for
tracking
telecom
expenses
based
on units
of time
or bytes
transferred,
for users
outside
the U.S.

After you've set up a new account, the features on the Accounts tab of the kppp Configuration dialog box become a little more meaningful. Below the list of accounts and the buttons that are used to set up accounts (you can delete them if you want), you see fields labeled Phone Costs, Volume, Reset Costs, and View Logs. These fields refer to the information determined by the Accounting tab in the Accounting Setup information.

But before you can use that new account, you have to finish setting up kppp and then get connected.

Finishing kppp configuration

To put the finishing touches on your new ISP account, follow these steps:

1. **Click the Device tab of the kppp Configuration dialog box (shown in Figure 15-9) and define how to access your modem device.**

   This tab contains several key areas:

   - In the Modem Device drop-down list, choose the device name for your modem. This is normally /dev/modem if OpenLinux was able to locate the modem during installation or you created a link afterward. You also can select various specific serial ports (such as /dev/ttyS0) from the drop-down list.

   - The Flow Control and Line Termination settings can be left alone unless you have trouble connecting when everything else seems to be correct.

Figure 15-9:
Configure
how your
modem is
accessed
using the
Device tab
of the kppp
Configur-
ation
dialog box.

- The Connection Speed field determines how fast kppp tries to send information to the modem. Choosing a number that's too high is better than choosing one that's too low in this field. If you choose a high number, kppp tries to push out data and ends up waiting for the modem to catch up. If you choose a low number, the modem waits for more data to send, which takes your transmission speed lower than it can be. If you have a 28.8 modem, you can choose 57600 as the speed; if you have a 56K modem (that really works at 56K in your area), choose 115200.

- The Use Lock File checkbox indicates that kppp should lock the modem so that other programs can't use it while kppp uses it. This is a good thing.

- The Modem Timeout field sets how long kppp tries to look for the modem and waits for the modem to respond before giving up (timing out, as we say). The 60-second value is a little long but gives time for slower modems. You can reduce this lag time if your modem appears to respond quickly when you start a connection.

2. **Click the Modem tab (shown in Figure 15-10) to define modem-specific options.**

   The Busy Wait field defines how long kppp waits when a busy signal is detected before retrying the connection. The Modem volume slider determines how loud the dialing sound is (though this may not effec- tively silence some modems).

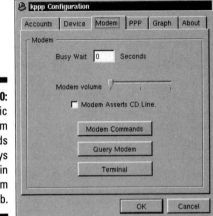

Figure 15-10:
Specific
modem
commands
and delays
are set in
the Modem
tab.

The Modem Commands, Query Modem, and Terminal buttons let you
manually interact with the modem for testing purposes. The Modem
Commands button includes all the commands that kppp uses to communicate with your modem. If you're using nonstandard commands, then
you can edit the list shown in Figure 15-11 by choosing Modem
Commands and modifying any of the fields shown.

Edit Modem Commands

Pre-Init Delay (sec/100):	50
Initialization String:	ATZ
Post-Init Delay (sec/100):	50
Init Response:	OK
Dial String:	ATDT
Connect Response:	CONNECT
Busy Response:	BUSY
No Carrier Response:	NO CARRIER
No Dialtone Response:	NO DIALTONE
Hangup String:	+++ATH
Hangup Response:	OK
Answer String:	ATA
Ring Response:	RING
Answer Response:	CONNECT
Escape String:	+++
Escape Response:	OK
Guard Time (sec/50):	50
Volume off/low/high	M0L0 M1L1 M1L4

OK   Cancel

Figure 15-11:
The com-
mands used
to communi-
cate with
your modem
can be
altered in
the Modem
Commands
list.

3. **Click the PPP tab (displayed in Figure 15-12) and specify how you want the pppd program to act as it tries to connect to your ISP (under the control of kppp).**

   The pppd Timeout field indicates how long to wait for a connection. This number is not related to the Modem Timeout value in the Device tab. The Modem Timeout value in the Device tab determines how long kppp waits for the modem to respond to a command; the pppd Timeout determines how long pppd waits for the ISP server to respond with connection information.

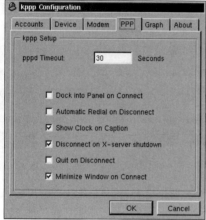

Figure 15-12: Options for how the pppd program responds to connection attempts are set in the PPP tab.

The PPP tab also includes several checkboxes. The following list describes what these options do:

- **Dock into Panel on Connect:** Tells the program to display a small icon on the KDE panel to show the connection (but don't display the main kppp window after connecting).

- **Automatic Redial on Disconnect:** Automatically attempts to redial and reestablish the connection with the ISP if the connection is lost for some reason.

- **Show Clock on Caption:** Shows a clock with the length of the ISP connection.

- **Disconnect on X-server shutdown:** After KDE is shut down and the kppp program closes, exits the background pppd program to exit the connection. (If this option isn't selected, you may think you've disconnected because kppp is no longer visible, when in fact the background connection — and associated charges — are still active.)

- **Quit on Disconnect:** Exits kppp when the connection is ended.

- **Minimize Window on Connect:** Minimizes the kppp window after a connection is established. This gets the kppp window out of the way so that you can use Netscape Communicator. The kppp window still can be accessed from the Taskbar, of course.

4. **Click the Graph tab (shown in Figure 15-13) and choose the colors used for the throughput graph that is displayed as long as you're connected (if the Throughput graph checkbox is selected).**

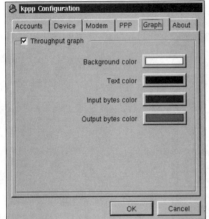

Figure 15-13:
Colors for the through-put graph can be selected on the Graph tab of the kppp Configur-ation dialog box.

By clicking any of the color boxes, you can select a new color from the standard KDE color selection dialog box.

Fire it up!

After you've set up your account and device information, you can connect to your ISP with just a few mouse clicks. Follow these steps:

1. **Select an account in the main kppp window (refer to Figure 15-1) from the Connect to drop-down list.**

2. **Type your Login ID for that ISP account in the Login ID field and press Enter.**

3. **Type your password for that ISP account in the Password field and press Enter.**

4. **Click Connect and wait a few moments for the connection to be established.**

To actually surf the Net, read e-mail, and otherwise interact with others on the Net, check out Chapter 16, where you find out how to configure and use a major tool of the Internet, the Netscape Communicator program.

Chapter 16

Surfing the Web

• •

• •

*O*nce upon a time a company called Netscape created a browser called Mozilla. Despite the fact that the company spelled the name *Netscape,* you were supposed to pronounce it *Mozilla.* Crazy, isn't it? (We're just going to use the names interchangeably in this chapter.) In any case, the browser was one of the best in the world (if not *the* best), and the folks at Netscape made the browser even better by turning it over to the Open Source community.

Over time, Mozilla not only could surf the Web but also could read e-mail, gather files using the File Transfer Protocol (FTP), run simple programs using Java, and even read Netnews (a discussion group made up of thousands of categories on the Net), all through a single graphical interface.

In this chapter, you set up Netscape Communicator for your system. Then, with the information from your ISP, you finally surf the Web and send and receive e-mail.

Customizing Netscape Communicator

Your *Caldera OpenLinux For Dummies* CD-ROM has a copy of Mozilla, which you can activate by typing the following from a Terminal Emulator window while KDE is running:

```
netscape&
```

Or, if you prefer to take it easy today, click the Netscape Communicator icon on the KDE Panel, or choose Communicator from the Internet submenu. A screen like the one in Figure 16-1 appears, and Mozilla is set free!

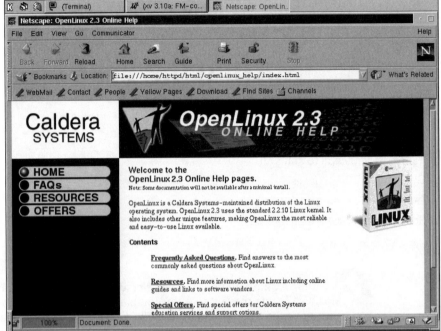

Figure 16-1:
Netscape
(Mozilla) in
its initial
invocation.

The initial screen (the default Netscape Home Page) shows you the online help for OpenLinux, which you can refer to for links to the Caldera Systems Web site or other information. Netscape has three main screens:

- Navigator screen, (refer to Figure 16-1)
- Mail and Discussions screen
- News screen

The first thing that you want to do is to tailor Netscape to your preferences. You can do this *offline,* which is certainly preferable if you have only one phone line. Follow these steps:

1. Choose Edit⊏>Preferences.

The Preferences window appears, as shown in Figure 16-2.

Note that on the left side of the Preferences window is the Category item, which is a map of where you are in the Preferences window. You skipped over the Appearance window (it's self-explanatory) and are concentrating now on the Navigator window. The Navigator window is where you determine what initial window appears when you start Netscape; most people select either a home page or the last page they viewed.

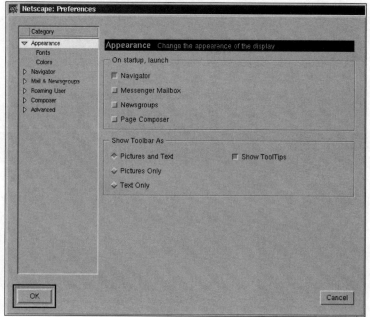

Netscape: Preferences

Category
- ▽ Appearance
  - Fonts
  - Colors
- ▷ Navigator
- ▷ Mail & Newsgroups
- ▷ Roaming User
- ▷ Composer
- ▷ Advanced

Appearance Change the appearance of the display

┌─ On startup, launch ──────────────
☐ Navigator
☐ Messenger Mailbox
☐ Newsgroups
☐ Page Composer

┌─ Show Toolbar As ─────────────────
◆ Pictures and Text   ☐ Show ToolTips
◇ Pictures Only
◇ Text Only

OK   Cancel

Figure 16-2:
The first major Preferences window for Netscape.

2. **In the Home Page area of the Navigator window, fill in the Location field.**

   Make sure that you fill in the home page location so that you can access it easily by clicking the Home Page icon at the top of the Navigator screen. If you change the home page, then you may want to note somewhere the default location in case you need to find the OpenLinux online help page.

3. **If you want, select a History number.**

   Netscape remembers where you've been and lets you select (and go to) a previous location. How long Netscape remembers (and how big the list becomes) depends on how many days of history you choose.

4. **In the Category window, click Mail & Newsgroups, and then click Identity. Fill in any necessary information.**

   The Identity window, shown in Figure 16-3, is where you add your e-mail address, return address, and organization name, and specify your signature file (the file that holds additional information included as a signature at the end of each e-mail message).

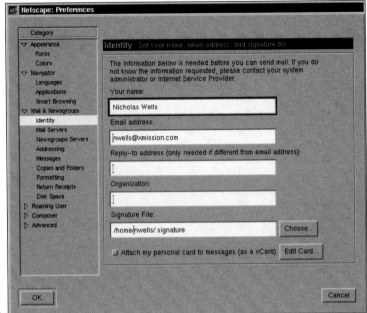

Figure 16-3:
The Identity
window in
all its glory.

5. In the Category window, click Mail & Newsgroups, and then click Messages. Fill in any necessary information.

You may want to deselect the option that automatically quotes and includes the original message in a reply. (Some folks think that this habit is a bit obnoxious.) To deselect an option, just click to remove the check mark.

The screen shown in Figure 16-4 appears. You use this screen to set defaults for outgoing messages, such as whether messages are wrapped and include original messages in replies.

This window is where you can select the option of automatically quoting e-mail you reply to, which means the original message gets included (quoted) in your reply. This feature often is useful when you want to comment on what someone has written.

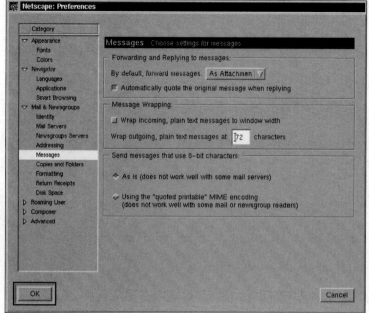

Figure 16-4:
The
Messages
window
offers
options for
sending
e-mail.

6. **In the Category window, click Mail & Newsgroups, then click Formatting, and fill in any necessary information.**

   Watch the sections on how to respond to HTML messages. Using HTML is fine if you know that the recipient reads e-mail by using a browser rather than an ASCII e-mail reader.

7. **In the Category window, click Mail & Newsgroups, then click Mail Servers, and fill in any necessary information.**

   The window in Figure 16-5 appears. Because you'll probably be attached to the Internet for relatively short periods of time, your Internet Service Provider supplies you with machines called *servers,* which send and deliver your e-mail even when you're not connected to the Internet. Then when you do connect to the Internet, your computer tells the server to deliver the e-mail or send your messages.

   Your ISP gives you a login name for the mail server (usually the same as your other login name), and you're told what the name is for both your incoming and outgoing mail server. These two names are usually the same, but if you're using a special mail service called POP (Post Office Protocol), which allows you to download e-mail to your system from the server, then your ISP gives you a name for the POP server. IMAP4 is an even newer protocol for doing similar procedures as POP, and if your ISP has an IMAP4 server, it should tell you that also.

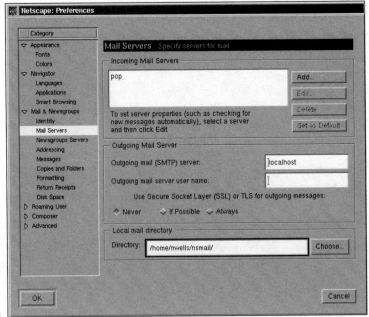

8. **In the Category window, click Mail & Newsgroups, and then click Newsgroups Servers; if you want to participate in a news server, fill in the fields.**

   Netscape enables you to read Netnews, which is a series of discussion groups that have been active for many years. Discussion groups were one of the first uses of the Internet, and they've been disseminating information (and misinformation) for many years. To participate in a discussion group, fill in the name of your news server (provided by your ISP), as well as the working area where your messages can be downloaded for you to read. Message groups can be quite active, so you should fill in the last option in the window, which specifies how many messages you want to receive before being asked. These fields are shown in Figure 16-6.

9. **At this point, you're set to run Netscape and see the world, so click OK and go, go, go!**

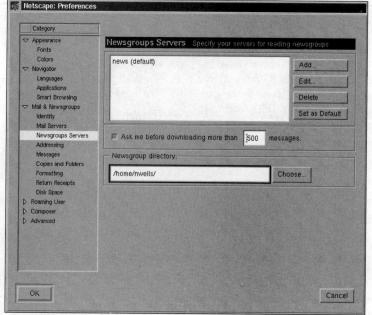

Figure 16-6:
Setting up
Netnews
server
information
to partici-
pate in
newsgroup
discussions.

Ready, Set, Go!

Now that you've configured your browser properly, you can connect to the Internet by typing the following in a Terminal Emulator window (or by using the kppp utility described in Chapter 15):

```
/sbin/ifup ppp0
```

You have to wait a few seconds (or even a minute) to connect with your ISP (hearing your modem dial is reassuring). Try using the ping command to see whether the www.calderasystems.com server is *visible* over the network, indicating that you have a working connection:

```
ping www.calderasystems.com
```

Now type the following:

```
netscape http://www.linuxjournal.org&
```

Netscape starts and displays the URL you just supplied (http://www. linuxjournal.org). The screen appears similar to Figure 16-7.

Surfing with the proper footing

Before you start to surf the Web, you need the proper footing. To navigate to a Web site, you type or click a URL (Uniform Resource Locator). After you know at least one URL, moving to other places on the Web is usually easy. URLs look like this:

```
http://www.openlinux.org/
```

or this:

```
www.openlinux.org/
```

Some browsers let you omit the `http://`. Some browsers also allow you to omit the trailing slash, unless the final segment is a filename.

In the old days spotting a link on a Web page was easy because the link was underlined and usually in blue text. Now it's not that simple. The best way to locate a link is to move your mouse pointer to a part of the Web page and see if the pointer changes from an arrow to a hand with a pointing index finger. If so, the hand indicates a link that you click to jump to a different Web page. If your browser doesn't take you to another Web page location when you click, the culprit is usually one of the following:

- The page that you're viewing hasn't been updated recently, and the page to which it's pointing no longer exists.

- The server system that the page is on is inoperative. You may see the message `the server is down`.

- The server system is running, but it's under too much of a load because too many users are trying to get to that page. For example, this problem happens when the eBay auction server gets a new load of Beanie Babies to sell.

- Your network connection is down, either from you to your ISP or from your ISP to the requested Web site.

When surfing the Net, be patient. Even on the best days downloading certain pages can take several minutes.

On the left side of the page are numerous links to the sections of the Linux Journal Web site. Click a link, such as "What is Linux?" You're taken to a page that looks similar to the one in Figure 16-8.

Note that near the top of the Netscape window is a box that contains the URL for the page you're viewing.

Use your cursor or keyboard to delete the URL in the Location field and replace the URL with another one. Then press the Return key, and you send the browser off to another Web page. Here are some interesting URLs to try:

Figure 16-7:
Netscape
Navigator
viewing the
home page
of the Linux
Journal.

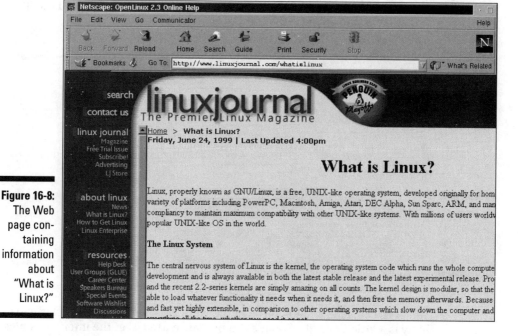

Figure 16-8:
The Web
page con-
taining
information
about
"What is
Linux?"

```
http://www.slashdot.org
http://www.linuxworld.com
http://www.linuxberg.com
```

Another way of opening a new Web page is to choose File⇨Open Page. The browser displays the Open Page dialog box, shown in Figure 16-9, where you can type the new URL and then choose whether you want to use that URL for the Navigator (most of the time) or the Composer (perhaps to use the Web page that the URL points to as part of a new Web page). You can also use this dialog box to open a file of HTML code (the language that Web pages are written in) local to your system, either to read that file as documentation or to treat it as a new Web page.

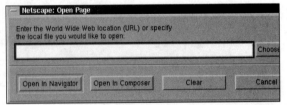

Figure 16-9:
The dialog box for opening a new page.

If you choose to load a local file and click the Choose File button, another dialog box springs up so that you can search the file system to find the file you want, as shown in Figure 16-10.

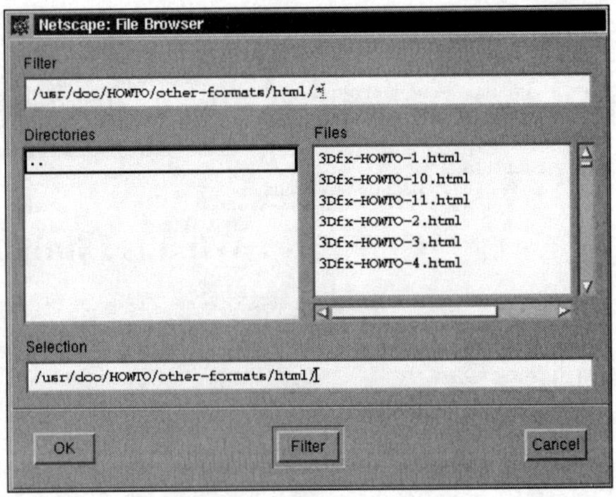

Figure 16-10:
Navigating through local files.

You even can send sounds through the Web (although illustrating this capability is a little difficult). Sounds can be transmitted over the Internet as files and then played after they reach your browser, computer, and sound card.

Getting E-Mail

Now that you can surf the Net, you probably want to tell people about your adventures. Well, Netscape can send and receive e-mail, too.

Go to the main window of Netscape, and you see a menu item labeled Communicator. On the Communicator menu choose the Messenger option. The browser takes you to the Mail side of Netscape Communicator, as shown in Figure 16-11.

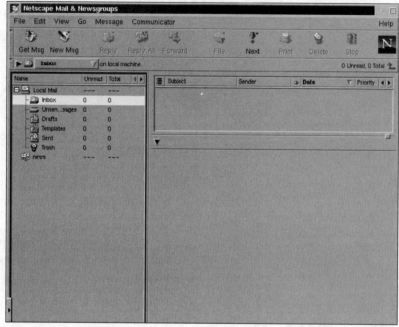

Figure 16-11:
The
Netscape
Mail &
Newsgroups
window.

To get your mail, simply click the Get Msg icon. This icon tells Netscape to make contact with your mail server and see whether any e-mail messages are waiting for you. If you have no new e-mail, a message at the bottom of the screen tells you so. If you do have e-mail, then the subject and sender appear in the center of the screen, and the e-mail message appears in the bottom of the screen, as shown in Figure 16-12.

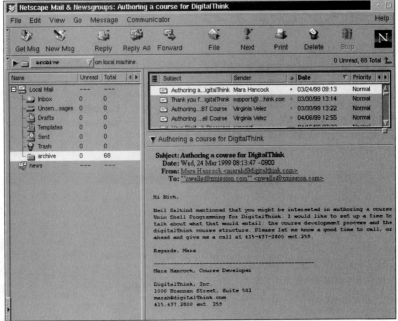

Figure 16-12:
Receiving
an e-mail
message.

If you have multiple e-mail messages, you can see each message by clicking the Subject line in the middle window. You may reply to, forward, or delete a particular message by highlighting its Subject line and clicking the appropriate icon (Reply, Forward, or Delete). When you click the Reply icon, the address of the person you're replying to appears automatically in the To field of the reply. When you forward a message, a copy of the message is sent as an attachment to the address you specify.

Sending E-Mail

To send an e-mail message, you have to know the recipient's e-mail address. Just as a URL consists of certain components, an e-mail address is made up of the person's e-mail name (often the same as his or her login name) and domain name. For example, to send an e-mail to the President of the United States, you address your message to president@whitehouse.gov. (Give him our regards.)

Your ISP should have given you an e-mail address, and you can ask your friends for their e-mail addresses. The irony is that to get your friends' e-mail addresses initially, you invariably spend a lot of time calling them on the telephone.

With the Mail & Newsgroups window on the screen, click the New Msg icon. A window similar to the one in Figure 16-13 appears.

To field   Subject field   Message body

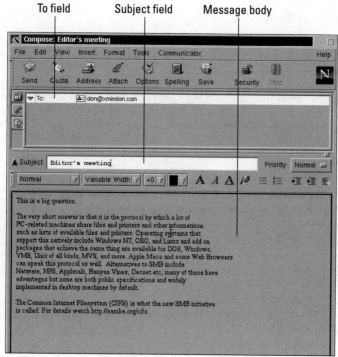

Figure 16-13:
The
Compose
window
for new
messages.

Below the row of icons near the top of the window is the word *To*. To the right is a white space where — after you click in it — you can type the e-mail address of the person you're trying to reach. Just for fun, try sending a letter to your own e-mail address. Then if you receive it, you'll know you did everything correctly. Just follow these steps:

It slices, it dices, it even . . .

Netscape can do much more than what we describe in this chapter, such as get (download) files from the Internet and keep an address book. These topics are beyond the scope of this book.

For more information, we recommend *The Internet For Dummies*, 6th Edition, by Levine, Young, and Baroudi (published by IDG Books Worldwide, Inc.).

1. **Click in the To field and type your own e-mail address.**

2. **Click in the Subject field and type a suitable subject.**

3. **Click in the body of the message and type your message.**

4. **Click the Send icon.**

   If you're sending a message to yourself, the message won't appear instantaneously. It still has to go down the telephone line, be analyzed by the server, and then sent back to you, so be patient.

You also can attach a file, an image, or even a sound to your message and send it to friends who also use Netscape (or another MIME-compliant mail reader). To attach a file to your letter, simply click the Attach icon at the top of the Compose window. A dialog box similar to the one in Figure 16-14 appears, allowing you to search the file structure of OpenLinux looking for the file you want to send.

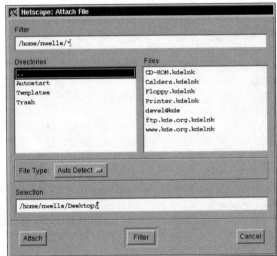

Figure 16-14:
The Attach file dialog window for selecting a file to attach to an e-mail.

At this point, you can do basic functions with the Internet, but so much more is available. For starters, use the Help facility in Netscape to read about the different options. Out across the Net is a wealth of data to which you now have access. Remember, however, that data can be good data or bad data, and you have to use your common sense to figure out whether your data source is knowledgeable or unreliable. Happy surfing!

Part VI
The Part of Tens

The 5th Wave   By Rich Tennant

"I don't think it's so much the Caldera OpenLinux OS
she's fascinated with, as much as the association it
has with a small flightless bird."

In this part . . .

Ah, the part you find in every *For Dummies* book: The Part of Tens. Here's where we get to rummage around and come up with ten of this and ten of that.

In Chapter 17, we list ten important places to find help. Also, you can use some of these sources to enhance and widen your knowledge of Linux in general and OpenLinux in particular. The things you can find out about these great technologies is endless.

In Chapter 18, we put together ten of the most frequently encountered problems people have after installing OpenLinux. If you're having trouble, turn here first.

Chapter 17

Ten Sources of Help

. . . .

. . . .

*B*y now, you're probably wondering whether any end exists to the amount of information and knowledge needed to run an OpenLinux (or any Linux or UNIX) system. The answer is yes, an end does exist to the knowledge you *need* to run a system well, but not to the knowledge you can accumulate if you want to understand how things work and interact. In this chapter, we suggest several ways to get additional training and support.

Books and More Books

When we started working with computers 20+ years ago, the number of books about computers filled only one bookshelf and were mostly about hardware electronics. One rarely saw books on computers in the popular-press bookstores. Today, thousands of books on computers are available; most computer books describe the software and its interactions, with the hardware now taking a back seat.

Perhaps you looked at other books before you bought this one but were intimidated by their use of technical terms. Or you thought the other books too general for what you wanted to do, because you wanted something more task-oriented. You may want to look over those books again after reading this one, because your knowledge level will have soared. TCP/IP networking, Web server administration, graphical interfaces, system administration, and regular old computer programming are all topics you can study in greater depth with a background in OpenLinux.

Lots of books specific to the UNIX operating system are either partially or completely applicable to OpenLinux, such as books on Perl, which is a comprehensive programming language. By getting one (or more) books on Perl and sitting down with your OpenLinux system, you can have both a new tool for doing your work and a new appreciation for a complete programming language. If you want to find out how to write Perl, then simply check out the source code.

MADDOG SAYS

Becoming a geek

As long as you're coming up to speed on all this technical knowledge, you should know that true UNIX (and Linux) geeks have their own way of saying things. The jargon used by Linux geeks mostly makes life easier for them, rather than more cryptic for the rest of the world, but some of their sayings, well . . . here are some examples:

✔ "Eff Ess Check" the file system rather than "run EF ES C K on the file system"

✔ "VEYE" (rhymes with "eye") rather than "vee eye," when talking about the editor "vi"

Linux geeks know that a word like fsck (the disk checking utility) can be used as a noun, a verb, and an adjective, so they say:

✔ I ran fsck.

✔ I fscked the file system.

✔ I moved the files into the fscked file system.

Your English teacher (and our editor) shudder at this concept.

Linux geeks talk about *disks,* when they mean *disk drives,* and they interchangeably use the words *X, X11,* and *X Window System* (and sometimes *KDE*), assuming that everyone who hears these terms knows their precise meanings.

I also want to point out that geeks are not nerds. Geeks are people who love technical topics, but they typically also have a wide range of other interests. Geeks are often outgoing, and many (but not all) enjoy being with people. One of my favorite T-shirts (I have more than 3,000 XL T-shirts) reads: "It is hard being a Geek, but it is getting easier."

Linux HOWTOs

Don't forget about the Linux HOWTOs, which are included on this book's CD-ROM. These excellent guides to Linux are applicable to your OpenLinux system. The HOWTOs are covered under the Linux Documentation Project copyleft, which means that you can print them. You also can read the HOWTOs by using a more(1) or less(1) command.

School Days

Another way to find out more information about OpenLinux is to take a course, perhaps at a local community college or a vendor near you. Lots of colleges offer courses on UNIX, and some use Linux to teach their UNIX courses.

Many Linux and OpenLinux courses are popping up all over the world. You can take computer-based training courses, video training, or old-fashioned instructor-led training courses where you sit at a computer and an instructor guides you through the material. Some places where you can look for these resources are:

✔ Caldera Systems' Web site at www.calderasystems.com. Look under the Education headings to find lists and links to Caldera Systems training centers all over the world.

✔ Traditional training companies, such as Learning Tree (www.learningtree.com) and ExecuTrain (www.execvtrain.com), and technology companies, such as Hewlett-Packard (www.hp.com), offer Linux training courses. Most of what you're taught in these courses is generic to Linux but also applies to OpenLinux.

✔ LinuxCare University is a part of the LinuxCare commercial support program. Visit www.linuxcare.com for details.

✔ Regional offerings from companies, such as ALC Press (www.alcpress.com), provide various specialty or introductory courses that last from two to five days.

✔ Video training is available from Keystone Learning Systems (www.klscorp.com).

Many of these training programs (and many of the myriad books about Linux that appear monthly) are aimed at Linux certification. Several programs currently are vying for the lead in a career and business-oriented Linux certification program, similar to the MCSE from Microsoft and the CNE from Novell. For details, visit the SAIR Linux Certification site (www.linuxcertification.com) or the Linux Professional Institute (www.lpi.org).

In the News

You can obtain additional information on Linux and OpenLinux from the Internet. A facility called *netnews* has tens of thousands of newsgroups, and each newsgroup is about a special topic. More than 30 newsgroups are devoted to Linux topics.

An ISP (Internet service provider) usually provides access to netnews. You can use a newsreader (such as krn, trn, tin, or pine) or one of several Web browsers on your KDE Desktop (such as Netscape) to read netnews. Both Netscape and the tin text-based newsreader are installed by default from this book's companion CD-ROM.

User Groups

User groups are springing up all over the country. Some groups are more active than others, but most hold meetings at least once a month. Some groups are Linux only, whereas other groups are connected to a larger computer group — either UNIX or a more general computer-user association. User groups provide great opportunities to ask questions, and they stimulate news ideas and ways to do things.

You can find out if a Linux user group is in your area by checking with GLUE (Groups of Linux Users Everywhere), which is a service run by SSC (publishers of the *Linux Journal*). GLUE is an automated map of user groups and you can find it at the following address:

```
www.linuxjournal.com
```

After you open the site, check out the Resources section to find out where the user group closest to you meets.

No user group in your area? Just post a note in a Linux-oriented newsgroup (see the previous section about netnews) saying that you want to start a user group; then, perhaps, other people in your area will join you. A good newsgroup to post this sort of message in is `comp.os.linux.advocacy`. Terrified at the thought of trying to start a user group? User-group leaders often are not the most technically knowledgeable people in the group but are simply good planners. They organize the meeting space, find (hound) speakers, send out meeting notices, locate sponsors, arrange refreshments, and perform other organizational tasks. Sometimes being a leader is a thankless job, but when the meeting goes well, then all the hard work seems worthwhile. So, as a newbie to Linux, you may not know a grep(1) from an awk(1), but you still may make a good chairperson.

Bring in the Cavalry

Some people want to be able to hire people to manage or fix their systems, which is what the commercial computer world calls *support*. Often the place where you bought your computer — whether it's a store, a value-added reseller (VAR), or the manufacturer — provides that support.

Linux has been criticized in the past for not having a high level of support, but nowadays that's a tough argument to swallow. The first group that offers support are the vendors of Linux products. Caldera Systems has complete support packages for OpenLinux, as do other Linux vendors. These support packages range from e-mail to telephone and on-site consulting. If you purchase your OpenLinux system as a complete hardware bundle from a Linux specialist, such as VA Research (www.varesearch.com), then be sure to ask your hardware vendor what support your system includes.

Another group that offers support are people who resell OpenLinux systems. These people typically install OpenLinux on hardware that you purchase from them. They will repair your system if it breaks and help you with knotty problems (usually for a fee).

The final group of people who offer support are independent consultants who have learned about OpenLinux and are now in the business of offering support for the system. You can find a list of consultants in a document called the Consultants HOWTO, which is available at the following address:

```
www.linuxhq.com/HOWTO/Consultants-HOWTO.html
```

You can also visit the Question Exchange to submit a technical question to a qualified online expert. You can indicate whether you're willing to pay a fee to get your question answered (which can speed up the response). Visit www.questionexchange.com.

You can find a not-as-current copy of the consultants' list on the accompanying CD-ROM, which includes a copy of the Consultants HOWTO in the directory /usr/doc/HOWTO/other-formats/html.

Commercial Applications

Because we're talking about commercial support, we need to mention something about *commercial applications*. Many OpenLinux users are frugal (we prefer that term over *cheap*) and often want or need to use only freely distributable software. Often, the freely distributable software is very good and does exactly what you want it to do. Other times, however, the application that you want is available only as a commercial application.

Some OpenLinux users buy the latest and greatest hardware and want the same commercial applications on OpenLinux that they have on their other operating systems, no matter what the price.

For commercial application vendors everywhere who may be reading this book, we cannot stress this point enough: You need to look at the market for OpenLinux applications as you do the market for *any other operating system*. You can sell your applications to a market that not only is appreciative but also believes, for various reasons, that its operating system should be developed as an OpenSource product. That doesn't need to affect how they view your application.

If you're wondering why commercial software is still viable with all the free software we've talked about, consider the powerful feature list of programs, such as Applixware by Applix, Inc. (www.applix.com). Applixware has a word processor, a spreadsheet, a presentation package, a mail front end, an HTML-authoring program, a graphical program for drawing pictures (usually to include in your presentation or paper), an application-building program, and a scripting language that allows you to tie these and other programs together.

We wrote this book by using Applixware Words. We chose Applixware Words rather than Microsoft Word, because with Words, we could easily cut examples of code directly from the OpenLinux screen and paste them into the text of the book. After finishing a chapter in Applixware Words, the text is easily exported to Microsoft Word 97 format, and then e-mailed to our editor.

I also use Applixware Presentation Editor to make presentations about Linux on Linux. When I'm talking about Linux at a show or a convention, I can demonstrate what I'm talking about by using the X Window System while showing the presentation slides on the screen. If I used Microsoft PowerPoint, in order to do a demo, I'd have to reboot the system to Linux — an awkward approach at best. Applixware has many of the same features that Microsoft products have. Recent editions of Applixware can read and create PowerPoint output, so now I can run my system truly FAT-free.

Other office suites are also available. The StarOffice suite includes a word processor, spreadsheet, presentation and graphics software, simple database, and complete Internet integration. You can read e-mail, browse and edit Web pages, and visit FTP or news sites all within StarOffice. StarOffice was originally developed in Germany by StarDivision, and then acquired in late 1999 by Sun Microsystems, which has released it freely over the Internet. (Visit www.sun.com and search for StarOffice.)

WordPerfect for Linux from Corel also has a strong following and includes server and personal editions, as well as a free downloadable version. Corel has committed many resources to developing additional Linux products. The Web site for Corel Linux products is linux.corel.com.

Visit Web Sites

A variety of Web sites are available for help. Some of these Web sites provide technical information, some provide news about the Linux community, and others furnish a bandstand for the Linux community to voice its opinions. Here are some Web sites that you may want to check out:

- ✔ **Linux International:** www.li.org
- ✔ **LinuxHQ:** www.linuxhq.com
- ✔ **Linux World:** www.linuxworld.com
- ✔ **Linux Today:** www.linuxtoday.com
- ✔ **Linux Documentation Project:** www.metalab.unc.edu/LDP
- ✔ **Linux Now:** www.linuxnow.com
- ✔ *Linux Journal, Linux Gazette, Linux Resources:* www.linuxjournal.com
- ✔ **Linux Focus:** www.linuxfocus.org
- ✔ *Linux Weekly News:* www.lwn.net
- ✔ **Slashdot:** www.slashdot.org
- ✔ **Freshmeat:** www.freshmeat.net
- ✔ **File Watcher:** www.filewatcher.org

This list is not exhaustive. You can find links to many more sites in some of the Web sites mentioned here.

Some of the lists offer opinions that are for mature audiences only. Most of the lists are moderated and most of the opinions are mature, but people sometimes get carried away. Don't judge technology by the radical opinions you may hear expressed about it. Be aware and form your own opinions.

Attend Conferences

You can attend a number of conferences and trade shows for more information on Linux. New shows appear regularly, so keep an eye on the Linux-related Web sites listed above to see what events are coming up in the near future. Where possible, we list the more general Web addresses for these events. You may have to do a little Web surfing to find the next event of the year. If you get stuck, try the Linux International Web site, which has an Events page that lists new events.

Linux World Conference and Expo

Linux World Conference and Expo is the first and largest of the Linux shows sponsored by a major trade show producer, IDC, who has been doing computer industry trade shows for years. The Linux World conference is intended for both technical audiences (with a conference track) and business audiences (with keynote speakers and trade show booths). Visit www.linuxworldexpo.com for details about upcoming dates and locations.

Linux Business Expo

Linux Business Expo is part of the Comdex show put on by ZD Net events twice a year in the spring and fall. Though perhaps diluted by the Comdex crowd, Linux nevertheless continues to make a strong showing at this event. The Linux Business Expo is a new part of the event; Linux International and numerous Linux vendors have created a Linux Pavilion at the show for many years. Check out its Web site at www.comdex.com.

Linux Kongress

Linux Kongress is the oldest Linux event. Held in Germany every year, Linux Kongress is a technical conference for Linux developers with a small collection of trade show booths. The Web site is www.linux-kongress.de.

Linux Expo

Linux Expo is held in the Raleigh/Durham, North Carolina, area every spring. Linux Expo is a technical conference, trade show, and all-in-all good time. In 1998, more than 2,000 attendees and numerous vendors participated. The Web site is www.linuxexpo.org.

USENIX/FREENIX

USENIX, a technical organization that has long supported UNIX users, has several technical conferences and small trade shows every year on various topics. A few years ago, a separate set of presentations called FREENIX was created for freely distributed operating systems, such as Linux. If you're interested in a good technical conference that attracts UNIX giants (such as Dennis Ritchie, one of the two principal creators of UNIX long years ago) or if you're a Linux developer, you may want to take a look at www.usenix.org.

CeBIT

CeBIT, the largest computer trade show in the world, is held yearly in Hannover, Germany. It often draws more than 600,000 people. In recent years, Linux International (www.li.org) has had a booth along with several other Linux vendors. The Linux area at CeBIT drew thousands of visitors. CeBIT is mostly a trade show, with very little (if any) conference sessions on Linux. To find out more about CeBIT, check out www.messe.de.

Try to Help Others

After you've exhausted all avenues of help (or maybe even before), you should just try to do whatever you can. Often, you find that the pieces fit together or that the software is not as difficult as you thought it would be. Here are some tips:

✔ **If you're investigating a large software package, scan the documentation one time and then concentrate on the necessary topics.**

I still remember the first time I tried to learn groff(1), a powerful text-processing system. The documentation was daunting, and I thought I'd never learn the package. I was right; I never learned it. But I did learn enough to do a few simple things, which was all I needed. With those "few simple things" (less than 2 percent of the power of the package), I can write letters, create overhead slides, and process necessary text. If I need another command, I look it up in a reference book.

✔ **Create a small sample of what you want to do.**

If you're working with a new command or part of OpenLinux, create a small example of the one part of the command or software that you don't know and see how that works.

✔ **Keep it small.**

A friend of Maddog's named Mike Gancarz (Hi Mike!) wrote a book called *The Philosophy of UNIX*. In this book, Mike talks about how UNIX systems were created and programmed in the early days, utilizing lots of the small, cryptic (we prefer the word *terse*) commands that lurk below the glossy interface of the graphical interfaces we now use. With these commands, you can create powerful programs called shell scripts, or you can just use the commands one at a time to transform your data. The main tenet of Mike's book is to keep things small and simple.

✔ **Remember that OpenLinux is only a piece of code, and your computer is only a machine.**

So what if you make a mistake? You're probably running OpenLinux on a machine that has only one user, you. That's the great thing about OpenLinux. It runs on such inexpensive machinery that for under $50 you can buy an old 486 computer with enough disk and memory in it to run OpenLinux as a practice system. (We've run Linux on just such machines. They work nicely, thank you very much.) So even if you have to reinstall your system because of some mistake that you made, no one else on your practice machine will be disturbed. You now know how to install OpenLinux, so that no one but you ever has to know when something goes wrong.

We also want to suggest that you help someone else. "What?" say you. "How can I help anybody else? I'm just a beginner!"

We all started that way. No one is born with a knowledge of computer science. We all pick it up over time. The way to cement a thought or an idea, however, is to explain it clearly to someone else. Helping others install OpenLinux on their PCs will help cement some of the concepts that you've discovered. Another thing you can do is to attend a Linux Install Fest at a local user group meeting or trade show conference. At these events lots of people go (with their machines) to install Linux. That way you not only get to help someone else, but you'll probably pick up a few pointers from some of the other attendees.

A main tenet of OpenLinux is the word *open*. *Open*Linux is open and is best when shared. You can start helping people (and asking questions) immediately by joining the Caldera Systems mailing list. On this mailing list hundreds of OpenLinux users exchange information and help each other with problems. The Caldera Systems Web site has instructions for subscribing; check it out at `www.calderasystems.com/support/forums`.

Chapter 18

Ten Problem Areas and Solutions

● ●

In This Chapter

▶ I can't boot OpenLinux anymore

▶ My disk numbers changed after installation

▶ The sound doesn't work

▶ My CD-ROM isn't detected

▶ I don't know how to remove LILO and restore my MBR

▶ I can't use LILO to boot

▶ The ls command doesn't show files in color

▶ OpenLinux can't find a shell script (or a program)

▶ I see a gray screen when I start KDE

▶ I never seem to have the correct time

● ●

*I*n any complex, technical situation, people have problems and issues that they need help with. The problems in this chapter are taken from a database of hundreds of questions and answers. Many of these questions are answered in other parts of this book, but because you may not have run across those sections, we repeat some of the information here.

I Can't Boot OpenLinux Anymore

Problem: You install OpenLinux and everything is fine (naturally). Then one day you make a change to your Windows or Windows NT system, and OpenLinux stops working. You no longer see the lilo boot prompt, so you no longer can specify that you want to boot OpenLinux.

Solution: Various operating systems tend to think that they are the only operating systems on the disk or on the system. Therefore, when these operating systems are installed or updated, they write things to an area of the system called the Master Boot Record (MBR). This process overlays the Linux boot loader (called LILO) and stops you from booting OpenLinux. The best correction requires an ounce of prevention: Make a boot-emergency floppy disk, as you're instructed to do during installation (see Chapter 5). Keep this disk handy when updating your system (or during any other significant system event, such as repartitioning disks or rebuilding your kernel). Then, if you make a mistake, you can boot the floppy, which enables you to reboot your OpenLinux operating system. After you've rebooted your system by using the floppy, just log in as root and type **lilo** on the command line. This process repairs the MBR by reinstalling LILO.

If you're installing multiple operating systems on a new machine, do yourself a favor and install OpenLinux last. Otherwise, you have to keep reinstalling LILO.

My Disk Numbers Changed after Installation

Problem: Each time OpenLinux boots, it numbers disks, calling SCSI disks names like sda, sdb, sdc, and so on. Suppose that sda holds your Microsoft system, sdb holds the bulk of OpenLinux, sdc holds your user files, and sdd holds your swap space. Now you add another disk and your user files are on sdd and your swap space is on sde. The new disk is called sdc, but the disk is empty. What happened?

Solution: SCSI disks are lettered according to the SCSI IDs set on each disk. OpenLinux names the disks using this ordering scheme. If you insert a new disk into the SCSI bus with a SCSI ID that is lower than an existing disk, then you rename all disks with a SCSI ID number above the SCSI ID number that you just installed. Installing your SCSI disks starting with a SCSI ID of 0, 1, 2, and so on, is best; then you install additional SCSI devices at the other end of the SCSI bus (SCSI IDs 6, 5, 4, and so on). Note that most SCSI controllers are set to SCSI ID 7 by default.

IDE disks are numbered according to their IDE controller and whether they're a master or a slave on that controller. Therefore, adding a new disk to a set of IDE controllers doesn't change the existing names, as shown here:

Controller	Disk	Linux Name
ide0	master	hda
ide0	slave	hdb
ide1	master	hdc
ide1	slave	hdd
ide2	master	hde
ide2	slave	hdf

Controller	Disk	Linux Name
ide3	master	hdg
ide3	slave	hdh

ide0 = primary controller

ide1 = secondary controller

ide2 = third controller

ide3 = fourth controller

The Sound Doesn't Work

Problem: You install OpenLinux, but the sound card in your system isn't recognized. You can't use the multimedia features to play audio CDs, .wav files, or video clips with sound.

Solution: The OpenLinux installation program attempts to locate and configure your sound card, but sound hardware is a problematic area of Linux. You can try the following command, which works with most SoundBlaster-compatible sound cards:

```
modprobe sb io=0x220 dma=1 mpu_io=0x330 irq=5
```

If this doesn't do the trick, browse the Sound-HOWTO document, located at /usr/doc/HOWTO/otherformats/html on your OpenLinux system. Or check the Caldera mailing lists and Web site for hints about your particular hardware setup. You also can find help with laptops (which are notoriously difficult to install anyway) on the Linux for Laptops page, at www.cs.utexas.edu/users/kharker/linux-laptop.

My CD-ROM Isn't Detected

Problem: You're installing OpenLinux, but OpenLinux doesn't find your CD-ROM.

Solution: Most of the newer CD-ROMs are either EIDE (ATAPI) or SCSI, and most of the newer computer systems have enough support to see either the ATAPI CD-ROMs or the SCSI CD-ROMs, so CD-ROM support is not the issue it was in earlier days. Many older CD-ROM drives don't use ATAPI or SCSI interfaces; instead they use proprietary interfaces that work only with a specific vendor's CD-ROM drive. Fortunately, most of these special CD-ROM drives are supported in OpenLinux. Many will even be auto-detected by the installation program.

Some early CD-ROMs pretended to be other devices (such as tape drives or floppies) to fool the computer system into using them, but those CD-ROMs were hidden from the detection system. If your system has a hidden CD-ROM, don't despair: You can supply information that helps OpenLinux find your CD-ROM.

Refer to the previous section about disk numbering. Then apply the information in this section to figure out the name that OpenLinux would have given your CD-ROM if OpenLinux had known about it. If you have an EIDE/ATAPI CD-ROM, then type the following line wherever you see the `boot` or `lilo` prompt while booting or installing your system:

```
linux hdX=cdrom
```

where X is the number that your CD-ROM has if the CD-ROM can be detected.

I Don't Know How to Remove LILO and Restore My MBR

Problem: You don't know how to replace the boot record that was on your system before you started installing OpenLinux.

Solution: You can log in to OpenLinux as root, and then type the following command:

```
/sbin/lilo -u
```

Another solution is to boot MS-DOS or Windows 3.1, 95, 98, or NT to an MS-DOS prompt and type the following:

```
fdisk /mbr
```

I Can't Use LILO to Boot

Problem: You need to put OpenLinux on a disk or a partition that is beyond the 1023rd cylinder, the second IDE disk, or the second SCSI ID number; or you need to do something that makes it difficult for OpenLinux to boot by using LILO. Can you boot OpenLinux another way?

Solution: You can use a program called LOADLIN to boot from your MS-DOS or Windows system:

1. **Copy your configured Linux kernel to the C drive of your MS-DOS or Windows system.**

   The easiest way is to install OpenLinux, log in as root, and type

   ```
   grep image /etc/lilo.conf
   ```

   A line similar to the following appears:

   ```
   image=/boot/vmlinuz-2.2.10
   ```

   which points to your compressed kernel (located in this example at `/boot/vmlinuz-2.5.10`).

2. **Copy the compressed kernel to a floppy disk, as follows:**

   ```
   mcopy /boot/vmlinuz-2.2.10 a:\vmlinux.gz
   ```

   The kernel name `vmlinuz-2.2.10` refers to a specific version of the Linux kernel. Except for the `/boot/vmlinuz-` part, which remains constant, the name may be slightly different on your system.

   Next copy LOADLIN from the CD-ROM accompanying this book.

3. **Boot MS-DOS or Windows and put the *Caldera OpenLinux For Dummies* CD-ROM in your CD-ROM drive.**

4. **Go to the DOSUTILS directory and copy LOADLIN.EXE to your C drive.**

   If you're using MS-DOS or Windows 3.1, then copy the LOADLIN16 file, which is the 16-bit version of the program.

5. **Copy the kernel image you just made on the floppy disk to your C drive.**

6. **Exit Windows, go to the MS-DOS prompt, and then type the following (assuming your root partition is on partition `/dev/hda5`) to boot OpenLinux:**

   ```
   C:\> loadlin vmlinux.gz root=/dev/hda5 ro
   ```

The ls Command Doesn't Show Files in Color

Problem: Using OpenLinux from the accompanying CD-ROM, you can't get the ls command to show files in color.

Solution: You have to edit the .bashrc file in your home directory to add the following line to the end of the file:

```
alias ls ='ls - color=auto'
```

Log off and then back on to reexecute your `.bashrc` file (assuming you're using the bash shell), and bingo, `ls` shows different file types in different colors.

OpenLinux Can't Find a Shell Script (Or a Program)

Problem: You type a command name, but OpenLinux can't find the command, even if the file matching the command name is in the current directory.

Solution: When you type a shell or binary command name, OpenLinux looks for the name in specific places and in a specific order. To find out what directories OpenLinux looks in, and in what order, type the following command:

```
echo $PATH
```

You see a stream similar to the following:

```
/bin:/usr/bin:/usr/local/bin
```

OpenLinux looks in these directories to find the command, program, or shell that you want to execute. You may see more directories, depending on your distribution or how your system administrator (if you have one) set up your system.

Now suppose you create a shell or a program called flobnob and want to execute it (assuming you've set the permission bits to make flobnob executable by you). You have two choices (well, you have more than two choices, but we're listing the safest ones). One choice is to type the following on the command line:

```
./flobnob
```

This command tells OpenLinux to look in this directory (`./`) and execute flobnob.

Your second choice is to move flobnob to one of the directories shown in the PATH variable, such as `/usr/local/bin`.

When I Start KDE, I See a Gray Screen

Problem: You configure the X Window System (the graphical foundation of KDE), but when you log in as a general user (that is, not as root) and type **startx**, all you get is a gray screen with a big X in the middle. You wait a long time, but nothing happens.

Solution: First, understand that you may have to wait a long time if you have a slow CPU with a small amount of main memory (about 8MB). Some machines with small amounts of memory take as long as 6 minutes to start the X Window System. But, assuming that you're starting the X Window System on a machine with a faster CPU and more memory, you may have problems with permissions on your home directory. This problem is particularly true if the X Window System works if you're logged on as root (that is, as superuser) but not when you're logged on as a general user.

To correct this problem, log in as root and go to the home directory of the user who's having problems. For example, suppose that lembree is the login name of the user. After you're in the user's home directory, issue the ls -ld command to see who owns that directory and what that directory's permissions are:

```
cd ~lembree
ls -ld .
drwxrwx— root bin 1024 Oct 31 16:00 .
```

Note that in this example, the directory is owned by root and the group ownership is bin, which doesn't allow lembree to have access to the directory structure inside the directory. Because the shells and terminal emulators needed by the X Window System require access to that directory structure, the X Window System (and thus KDE) can't fully work.

To correct this problem, use the chown and chgrp commands to change the ownership of the lembree home directory to lembree and to change the group ownership of the lembree home directory to users:

```
chown lembree ~lembree
chgrp users ~lembree
```

Make sure you replace the lembree login name that we use in this example with the login name you're having difficulty with.

I Never Seem to Have the Correct Time

Problem: After you boot OpenLinux, the time is wrong, so you set it with the `date(1)` command. Then you boot Windows and its time is wrong, so you reset it. When you reboot OpenLinux, its time is wrong again.

Solution: Most UNIX systems keep their time using Universal Time (also known as Greenwich Mean Time, or GMT), but Microsoft systems keep their time as local time. When you set the time in either system, you set the CPU clock to that version of the time. Then when you boot the other system, the other system interprets what is in the CPU clock differently and reports a different time.

OpenLinux enables you to store and think of the clock as either GMT or local time. You make this choice when you install the system. To change your choice, follow these steps:

1. **Log in as root.**

2. **Type** lisa.

3. **Choose System Configuration from the menu.**

4. **Choose System Configuration from the next menu as well.**

5. **Choose Configure Time Zone.**

6. **Choose Local Time from the menu that appears.**

   This setting prevents the conflict between OpenLinux and Windows that causes you to have problems setting the clock correctly.

7. **Select your time zone from the list that appears.**

8. **Repeatedly choose Continue to back out of the lisa menus and exit this utility.**

9. **Reset the time to the proper value using the** date **command if you reboot OpenLinux or through the Windows system if you boot Windows.**

Part VII
Appendixes

The 5th Wave   By Rich Tennant

MODERN MARRIAGE

©RICHTENNANT

WE'RE AGREED ON THE SILVER PATTERN, WALLPAPER AND CARPET SCHEME, BUT WE'RE STILL HASHING OUT THE OPERATING SYSTEM.

In this part . . .

Appendix: That useless vestige of the human anatomy that certainly shouldn't be applied to the important information in this part. Appendix A is a real cliff-hanger — a list of all the hardware we could find that's compatible with the version of OpenLinux on the accompanying CD-ROM (Version 2.3, by the way).

Here and there throughout the text, we mention man pages. In Appendix B, you find out what all those sections in a man page mean and how to find the right man page for you. The final appendix is about installing your *Caldera OpenLinux For Dummies* CD-ROM. For those of you accustomed to short installation instructions — surprise. We use Appendix C to refer you to the real installation instructions (which take up most of Part II).

Appendix A

Hardware Compatibility

• •

*T*he version of OpenLinux on the *Caldera OpenLinux For Dummies* CD-ROM supports a wide range of hardware but, like any other Linux product, it doesn't support *all* types of hardware.

To learn what hardware OpenLinux supports, you can visit the Caldera Systems Web site (www.calderasystems.com) or check out the voluminous documentation on your accompanying CD-ROM. The Caldera Web site includes a comprehensive list that's updated as new hardware support is released for OpenLinux. The information in this appendix provides a list of many hardware options (including a few to avoid), but it doesn't list all the latest hardware devices — many of which you can use with Linux. Still, having everything on a Web site doesn't help you if you're not connected to the Net at the moment. Also, writing down things on paper is nice once in a while, just for reference. For these reasons, we provide this appendix.

We make every attempt to present correct material in this appendix based on what Caldera Systems, Inc., believes to be the hardware currently supported by OpenLinux 2.3. Problems still may occur, however. In addition, new hardware is introduced all the time, and some of the new hardware that may work with OpenLinux may not be listed here.

After you have your system running, review some of the hardware HOWTOs located in the directory /usr/doc/HOWTO to see whether any other hardware is listed that you may want to use in your OpenLinux system.

Hardware Architectures

OpenLinux runs on a variety of hardware architectures. These architectures are usually defined by the model name of the main CPU's manufacturer, such as the Intel architecture, the Alpha (Compaq) architecture, and the SPARC (Sun) architecture. This book and its CD-ROM cover only the Intel architecture, which includes AMD and Cyrix CPUs all the way from the x386 configurations to the class of CPUs for the Pentium IIs.

In addition to the hardware architecture of the CPU, you have to consider the *bus structure*. A bus is made up of electrical paths, wires, and sockets that transmit electrical impulses to and from the CPU.

ISA, EISA, VLB, and PCI buses have been around a long time and are all supported in OpenLinux. Although the Microchannel bus has support in the OpenLinux kernel, OpenLinux does not support Microchannel by default, although if you're brave you can try to add this support by recompiling the kernel. Most new systems today are PCI-based, with one or two ISA slots for backward compatibility.

In addition, the AGP bus is supported as a graphics-card interface. The number of video cards available for AGP and supported under OpenLinux continues to grow. In addition to the information provided in this appendix, you may want to check the Caldera System Web site or the XFree86 Web site (www.xfree86.org) to learn about additional AGP cards that are supported by the standard XFree86 software in OpenLinux.

The combination of the CPU architecture and the bus structure loosely can be termed the motherboard (often pronounced "muthaboard"). If OpenLinux doesn't work on your system and you suspect that the motherboard is the problem,check with the motherboard's manufacturer to see whether it has a newer BIOS (the code that ties the CPU to the bus structure and devices).

Laptops

Laptops and OpenLinux are problematic for a few reasons. Although newer laptops have hard disks and memory large enough to accommodate OpenLinux easily, laptop manufacturers continue to use the newest electronics in an effort to make laptops smaller, faster, and cheaper. That's great, except that the newest hardware may not have support yet from OpenLinux.

The greatest ongoing problem with laptops is that the video chipset used by many laptop manufacturers is not recognized and configured easily by the OpenLinux installation program. Some of these chips — especially in older laptops — simply are not supported. Other peripheral can also cause problems. Strange PCMCIA SCSI cards and CD-ROM interfaces — again more common on older laptops — can make installing OpenLinux a challenge.

Many older laptops had swappable floppy disk drives and CD-ROM drives. You couldn't have both devices in the machine at the same time. The CD-ROM drives also weren't bootable in many cases. The manufacturers obviously weren't thinking of any users who may want to install a new operating system. A system without both a floppy drive and a CD-ROM drive makes it impossible to start the installation program from a boot floppy and then install OpenLinux from the CD-ROM. I've spent countless hours figuring out how to circumvent the limitations of these early systems by using network connections, additional peripherals, or even a different laptop.

SMP Systems

The kernel on the *Caldera OpenLinux For Dummies* CD-ROM supports symmetrical multiprocessors (SMPs), although this support isn't enabled by default (it requires that you recompile the Linux kernel). In OpenLinux 2.3, support is limited to either two or four CPUs.

Memory

All memory typically found in PC computer systems works with OpenLinux. However, when your system has large amounts of main memory, you may have to add the following to the /etc/lilo.conf file, depending on how smart your BIOS is:

```
append="mem=<number of Mb>M"
```

In any case, if OpenLinux is having trouble seeing all the memory that you have, use a line like the one shown here. (For a machine with 256MB of memory, for example, add the following line below the line with the name that's used to start the OpenLinux operating system — this line usually contains the text label=linux):

```
append="mem=256M"
```

Video

In character-cell mode, OpenLinux works with all video cards. Therefore, at a minimum, you're able to get your system up and running. Likewise, most cards work in VGA or SVGA mode, so you're able to have KDE running, although KDE will be a little slow and course-grained with huge icons and little space in which to maneuver.

As a general rule, both the earliest and the latest models of video cards are not supported. Early video cards were obsolete before OpenLinux was introduced, and XFree86 (the people who provide most of the support for the video cards) never had time to retrofit support. The very latest cards often are not supported right away because getting the code ported to the video card takes time and effort. But with help from vendors, lead times are becoming shorter.

Accelerated cards and unaccelerated cards also are available. Accelerated cards typically work faster than unaccelerated cards because the software can take advantage of the capability of the hardware to display the images more quickly.

Some accelerated cards that are known to work are ARK Logic (ARK1000PV/VL, ARK2000PV/MT), ATI Mach8, ATI Mach32, ATI Mach64, Chips & Technologies 64200, 64300, 65520, 65525, 65530, 65535, 65540, 65545, 65546, 65548, 65550, 65554, Cirrus Logic 5420, 542x/5430, 5434, 5436, 544x, 546x, 5480, 62x5, 754x, Diamond Viper 330, Gemini P1 (ET6000 chip), IBM 8514/A, IBM XGA-I, XGA-II, IIT AGX-010/014/015/016 (16 bpp), Matrox MGA2064W (Millennium), Matrox MGA1064SG (Mystique), Number Nine Imagine I128, Oak OTI-087, S3 732 (Trio32), 764 (Trio64), Trio64V+, 801, 805, 864, 866, 868, 86C325 (ViRGE), 86C375 (ViRGE/DX), 86C385 (ViRGE/GX), 86C988 (ViRGE/VX), 911, 924, 928, 964, 968, S3 card families, SiS 86c201, 86c202, 86c205, Trident 9440, 96xx, Cyber938x, Tseng ET4000/W32/ W32i/W32p, ET6000, Weitek P9000 (16/32 bpp), Diamond Viper VLB/PCI, Orchid P9000, and Western Digital WD90C24/24A/24A2/31/33.

A variety of unaccelerated boards are available as well: Alliance AP6422, AT24, ATI VGA Wonder series, Avance Logic AL2101/2228/2301/2302/ 2308/2401, Cirrus Logic 6420/6440, 7555, Compaq AVGA, DEC 21030, Genoa GVGA, MCGA (320x200), MX MX68000/MX68010, NCR 77C22, 77C22E, 77C22E+, NVidia NV1, Oak OTI-037C, OTI-067, OTI-077, RealTek RTG3106, SGS-Thomson STG2000, Trident 8800CS, 8200LX, 8900x, 9000, 9000i, 9100B, 9200CXr, 9320LCD, 9400CXi, 9420, 9420DGi, 9430Dgi, Tseng ET3000, ET4000AX, VGA (standard VGA, 4 bit, slow), Video 7/Headland Technologies HT216-32, Western Digital/Paradise PVGA1, and WD90C00/10/11/30.

Also available are a series of boards supported by companies, including S.u.S.E., Red Hat Software, and Metro Link. These boards include the following: Elsa GLoria X-Server, ELSA GLoria L, GLoria L/MX, Gloria S video cards with the Alliance Semiconductor AT3D (also AT25) chip, Hercules Stingray 128 3D, NVidia X-Server (PCI and AGP support, NV1 chipset and Riva128), ASUS 3Dexplorer, Diamond Viper 330, ELSA VICTORY Erazor, STB Velocity 128, XSuSE Matrox, Mystique, Millennium, Millennium II, Millennium II AGP, Trident, 9685 (including ClearTV) and latest Cyber chipset, XSuSE Tseng, W32, W32i ET6100, and ET6300.

Hard Drive Controllers

OpenLinux works with standard IDE, EIDE, and SCSI disk controllers. In addition, OpenLinux supports many SCSI controllers found on early sound cards (particularly the Sound Blaster and Media Vision cards).We recommend that you stay away from the sound-card-based SCSI and some of the older SCSI cards because they're slow and the booting process has difficulty determining where they are. Try to find a PCI-based SCSI controller instead.

Following are some of the supported SCSI controllers: AMI Fast Disk VLB/EISA (BusLogic compatible), Adaptec AVA-1502E (ISA/VLB) (AIC-6360), Adaptec AVA-1505/1515 (ISA) (Adaptec AHA-152x compatible), Adaptec AHA-1510/152x (ISA/VLB) (AIC-6260/6360), Adaptec AHA-154x (ISA) all models, Adaptec AHA-174x (EISA) in enhanced mode, Adaptec AHA-274x (EISA) (AIC-7771), Adaptec AHA-284x (VLB) (AIC-7770), Adaptec AHA-2920 (PCI), Adaptec AHA-2940AU (PCI) (AIC-7861), Adaptec AHA-294x/U/W/UW/D/WD (AIC-7871, AIC-7844, AIC-7881, AIC-7884), Adaptec AHA-3940/U/W (PCI) (AIC-7872, AIC-7882) (since 1.3.6), Adaptec AHA-398x/U/W (PCI) (AIC-7873, AIC-7883), Adaptec PCI controllers with AIC-7850, AIC-7855, AIC-7860, Adaptec on-board controllers with AIC-777x (EISA), AIC-785x, AIC-787x (PCI), AIC-788x (PCI), Advansys 5140 (ISA), Always IN2000, BusLogic (ISA/EISA/VLB/PCI) all models, DPT PM2001, PM2012A (EATA-PIO), DPT Smartcache/SmartRAID Plus, III, IV families (ISA/EISA/PCI), Future Domain TMC-16x0, TMC-3260 (PCI), Future Domain TMC-8xx, TMC-950, Future Domain chips TMC-1800, TMC-18C50, TMC-18C30, TMC-36C70, ICP-Vortex PCI-SCSI Disk Array Controllers (many RAID levels supported), Media Vision Pro Audio Spectrum 16 SCSI (ISA), NCR 5380 generic cards, NCR 53C400 (Trantor T130B) (use generic NCR 5380 SCSI support), NCR 53C406a (Acculogic ISApport/Media Vision Premium 3D SCSI), NCR chips 53C7x0, NCR chips 53C810, 53C815, 53C820, 53C825, 53C860, 53C875, 53C895, Qlogic/Control Concepts SCSI/IDE (FAS408) (ISA/VLB), Quantum ISA-200S, ISA-250MG, Seagate ST-01/ST-02 (ISA), SoundBlaster 16 SCSI-2 (Adaptec 152x compatible) (ISA), Tekram DC-390, DC-390W/U/F, Trantor T128/T128F/T228 (ISA), UltraStor 14F (ISA), 24F (EISA), 34F (VLB), and Western Digital WD7000 SCSI.

Boards that aren't supported include SCSI adapters that fit into the parallel port and DTC boards, such as the 327x and 328x that aren't Adaptec compatible.

Serial, Parallel, and Joystick Interfaces

Any standard expansion card that provides serial ports, parallel ports, joystick ports, or a combination of these cards can be used to extend the hardware connectivity of OpenLinux. OpenLinux supports cards using the following chipsets (which you can identify from either looking on the card itself or checking with the vendor or documentation): 8250, 16450, 16550, and 16550A UARTs.

Other Controllers (Multiport)

Some cards are used to increase the number of serial lines that a PC-style system can support above the one or two serial/parallel lines that come with most computers by default. Multiport serial cards can be classified as intelligent or nonintelligent. Intelligent cards have storage for information coming to and from the serial ports on the card and can also send control signals to each port on the card. Intelligent cards can cut down on the overhead of having a huge flow of data coming into the system every second from numerous serial ports and, therefore, relieve part of the load on the main CPU. Some nonintelligent cards also use an IRQ for every port, which can use up a lot of the system's resources for little gain. Try to get a card that's intelligent and uses only one IRQ.

Nonintelligent cards

Some of the nonintelligent cards are AST FourPort and clones (4 port), Accent Async-4 (4 port), Arnet Multiport-8 (8 port), Bell Technologies HUB6 (6 port), Boca BB-1004, 1008 (4, 8 port) - no DTR, DSR, and CD, Boca BB-2016 (16 port), Boca IO/AT66 (6 port), Boca IO 2by4 (4 serial/2 parallel, uses 5 IRQs), Computone ValuePort (4, 6, 8 port) (AST FourPort compatible), DigiBoard PC/X, PC/Xem, PCI/Xem, EISA/Xem, PCI/Xr (4, 8, 16 port), Comtrol Hostess 550 (4, 8 port), PC-COMM 4-port (4 port), SIIG I/O Expander 4S (4 port, uses 4 IRQs), STB 4-COM (4 port), Twincom ACI/550, and Usenet Serial Board II (4 port).

Intelligent cards

Some of the supported intelligent cards are Computone IntelliPort II (4/8/16 port), Cyclades Cyclom-8Y/16Y (8, 16 port) (ISA/PCI), DigiBoard PC/Xe (ISA), PC/Xi (EISA) and PC/Xeve, Equinox SST Intelligent serial I/O cards, Hayes ESP 1, 2 and 8 port versions, Stallion EasyIO (ISA), Stallion EasyConnection 8/32 (ISA/MCA), Stallion EasyConnection 8/64 (PCI), Stallion EasyConnection 8/64 (ISA/EISA), Stallion ONboard (ISA/EISA/MCA), and Stallion Brumby (ISA).

Network adapters

If you're going to use Ethernet, make sure you buy a good Ethernet card. Some of the earlier cards were flaky and made the system stop working from time to time. Most of the new cards are 100 Mbit/second as well as the older 10Mbit/second, so they'll work now in your current environment and later in your newer environment.

Supported cards are 3Com 3C503, 3C505, 3C507, 3C509/3C509B (ISA), 3C579 (EISA), 3Com Etherlink III Vortex Ethercards (3C590, 3c592, 3C595, 3c597) (PCI), 3Com Etherlink XL Boomerang Ethercards (3c905) (PCI), 3Com Fast Etherlink Ethercard (3c515) (ISA), AMD LANCE (79C960)/PCnet-ISA/PCI (AT1500, HP J2405A, NE1500/NE2100), AT&T GIS WaveLAN, Allied Telesis AT1700, Allied Telesis LA100PCI-T, Ansel Communications AC3200 EISA,

Apricot Xen-II/82596, Cabletron E21xx, Cogent EM110, Crystal Lan CS8920, Cs8900, Danpex EN-9400, DEC DE425 (EISA), DEC DE434, DEC DE435 (PCI), DECDE450, DECDE500 (DE4x5 driver), DEC DE450/DE500-XA (Tulip driver), DEC DEPCA and EtherWORKS, DEC EtherWORKS 3, DEC QSilver's (Tulip driver), Fujitsu FMV-181, 182, 183, 184, HP PCLAN (27245 and 27xxx series), HP PCLAN PLUS (27247B and 27252A), HP 10/100VG PCLAN (J2577, J2573, 27248B, J2585) (ISA/EISA/PCI), ICL EtherTeam 16i/32 EISA, Intel EtherExpress, Intel EtherExpress Pro, KTI ET16/P-D2, ET16/P-DC ISA (works jumperless and with hardware-configuration options), NE2000/NE1000 (be careful with clones), Netgear FA-310TX (Tulip chip), New Media Ethernet, PureData PDUC8028, PDI8023, SEEQ 8005, SMC Ultra/EtherEZ (ISA), SMC 9000 series, SMC PCI EtherPower 10/100 (Tulip driver), SMC EtherPower II (epic100.c driver), Schneider & Koch G16, Western Digital WD80x3, Zenith Z-Note, IBM's ThinkPad 300 built-in adapter, and 312 Etherarray (Tulip driver).

Sound cards

OpenLinux supports many sound cards, including the following: 6850 UART MIDI, Adlib (OPL2), Audio Excell DSP16, Aztech Sound Galaxy NX Pro, Crystal CS4232/CS4236 (PnP) based cards, ECHO-PSS cards (Orchid SoundWave32, Cardinal DSP16), Ensoniq SoundScape, Gravis Ultrasound, Gravis Ultrasound 16-bit sampling daughterboard, Gravis Ultrasound MAX, Gravis Ultrasound ACE (no MIDI port and audio recording), Gravis Ultrasound PnP (with RAM), Logitech SoundMan Games (SBPro, 44kHz stereo support), Logitech SoundMan Wave (Jazz16/OPL4), Logitech SoundMan 16 (PAS-16 compatible), MediaTriX AudioTriX Pro, Media Vision Premium 3D (Jazz16), Media Vision Pro Sonic 16 (Jazz), Media Vision Pro Audio Spectrum 16, Media Vision Pro Audio Studio 16, Microsoft Sound System (AD1848), OAK OTI-601D (Mozart), OPTi 82C924/82C925. OPTi 82C928/82C929 (MAD16/MAD16 Pro/ISP16/Mozart), OPTi 82C931, Sound Blaster, Sound Blaster Pro, Sound Blaster 16, Sound Blaster 32/64/AWE (configure like Sound Blaster 16), Sound Blaster AWE63/Gold and 16/32/AWE PnP, Turtle Beach Wavefront (Maui, Tropez), Wave Blaster (and other daughterboards), cards based on the ESS Technologies AudioDrive chips (688, 1688), MPU-401 MIDI, and PC speaker/parallel port DAC.

Tape Drives

When backing up your system, you get lots of storage on one device (2 or 4GB or even higher) by using a tape drive. OpenLinux supports most SCSI tape drives. Other drives sometimes use the floppy controller (such as the Colorado FC-10/FC-20, Mountain Mach-2, or the Iomega Tape Controller II) or hook up to the IDE controller (Seagate TapeStor 8000 and Conner CTMA 4000 IDE ATAPI Streaming tape drive).

Note that OpenLinux doesn't support tape drives that plug into the parallel port.

CD-ROM Drives

You may think that any CD-ROM device works under OpenLinux, and most do. Early CD-ROM drives, however, usually were attached to the sound board and used for multimedia instead of high-capacity data drives. Linux supports most SCSI and EIDE (ATAPI) CD-ROM drives, particularly the newer ones that read data at 2x, 4x, 6x, and on up to 40x speeds.

CD-Writers

Frustrated singers, photographers, and choreographers would love being able to make their own CD-ROMs filled with music and pictures. Well, you can with OpenLinux! OpenLinux supports CD-writers, and a variety of software is available to instruct you on writing to write-once (WO) CDs. Programs, such as cdwrite and cdrecord, can be used for writing to a CD-WO; and graphical front-ends, such as X-CD-Roast and KreateCD, make the job even easier. The following CD-writers are supported: Grundig CDR 100 IPW, HP CD-Writer+ 7100, HP SureStore 4020i, HP SureStore 6020es/i, JVC XR-W2010, Mitsubishi CDRW-225, Mitsumi CR-2600TE, Olympus CDS 620E, Philips CDD-522/2000/2600/3610, Pinnacle Micro RCD-5020/5040, Plextor CDR PX-24CS, Ricoh MP 1420C, Ricoh MP 6200S/6201S, Sanyo CRD-R24S, Smart and Friendly Internal 2006 Plus 2.05, Sony CDU 920S/924/926S, Taiyo Yuden EW-50, TEAC CD-R50S, WPI (Wearnes) CDR-632P, WPI (Wearnes) CDRW-622, Yamaha CDR-100, Yamaha CDR-200/200t/200tx, and Yamaha CDR-400t/400tx.

Modems

Modems are simple things on the surface. Modems either are external to your system and plug into an existing serial line, or they're internal to the system and look like another serial line to the system. Alas, some modems are made only for Windows and, therefore, don't work with OpenLinux. These modems are generally known as WinModems — stay clear of them.

Mice

Here's another case where you may say "Surely there aren't any issues with mice working, because they're so simple." Well, when we start thinking of the vagaries of mice and men, we know that nothing is simple. OpenLinux supports the following mice: Microsoft serial mouse, Mouse Systems serial mouse, Logitech Mouseman serial mouse, Logitech serial mouse, ATI XL Inport bus mouse, C&T 82C710 (QuickPort) (Toshiba, TI Travelmate), Microsoft bus mouse, Logitech bus mouse, PS/2 (auxiliary device) mouse, and Alps Glidepoint.

Printers and Plotters

All printers and plotters connected to the parallel or serial port should work — except those printers made to work only with Microsoft products. Do you see a pattern here?

Many OpenLinux programs output PostScript files. Non-PostScript printers can emulate PostScript Level 2 by using Ghostscript, in particular: Apple Imagewriter, Itoh M8510, Canon BubbleJet BJ10e (bj10e), Canon BubbleJet BJ200, BJC-210 (B/W only), BJC-240 (B/W only) (bj200), Canon BubbleJet BJC-600, BJC-610, BJC-4000, BJC-4100, BJC-450, MultiPASS C2500, BJC-240, BJC-70 (bjc600), Canon BubbleJet BJC-800 (bjc800), Canon LBP-8II, LIPS III, DEC LA50/70/75/75plus, DEC LN03, LJ250, Epson 9 pin, 24 pin, LQ series, AP3250, Epson Stylus Color/Color II/500/800 (stcolor), HP 2563B, HP DesignJet 650C, HP DeskJet, Deskjet Plus (deskjet), HP Deskjet 500, Deskjet Portable (djet500), HP DeskJet 400/500C/540C/690C/693C (cdj500), HP DeskJet 550C/560C/600/660C/682C/683C/693C/850/870Cse (cdj550), HP DeskJet 850/870Cse/870Cxi/680 (cdj850), HP DeskJet 500C/510/520/5540C/693C printing black only (cdjmono), HP DeskJet 600 (lj4dith), HP DeskJet 600/870Cse, LaserJet 5/5L (ljet4), HP Deskjet 500/500C/510/520/540/550C/560C/850C/855C, HP Deskjet 720, 820 and 1000 series, HP PaintJet XL300, Deskjet 600/1200C/1600C (pjxl300), HP LaserJet/Plus/II/III/4, HP PaintJet/XL, IBM Jetprinter color, IBM Proprinter, Imagen ImPress, Mitsubishi CP50 color, NEC P6/P6+/P60, Oki OL410ex LED (ljet4), Okidata MicroLine 182, Ricoh 4081/6000 (r4081), SPARCprinter, StarJet 48 inkjet printer, Tektronix 4693d color 2/4/8 bit, Tektronix 4695/4696 inkjet plotter, and Xerox XES printers (2700, 3700, 4045, and so on).

Scanners

OpenLinux has an interface called SANE that enables you to attach and control many types of scanners. The scanners currently supported are A4 Tech AC 4096/AS 8000P, Adara Image Star I, Conrad Personal Scanner 64, P105 handheld scanners, Epson GT6000, Fujitsu SCSI-2 scanners, Genius ColorPage-SP2, Genius GS-B105G handheld scanner, Genius GeniScan GS4500, GS4500A handheld scanners, HighScreen Greyscan 256 handheld scanner, HP ScanJet II series SCSI, HP ScanJet IIc, IIcx, IIp, 3c, 4c, 4p, 5p, 5pse, plus, Logitech Scanman+, Scanman 32, Scanman 256 handheld scanners, Microtek ScanMaker E3, E6, II, IIXE, III and 35t models, Mustek M105 handheld scanner, Mustek HT800 Turbo, Matador 105, Matador 256 handheld scanners, Mustek Paragon 6000CX, Nikon Coolscan SCSI 35mm film scanner, Pearl 256 handheld scanner, and UMAX SCSI scanners.

Touch Screens

As if we don't have enough stuff to spend money on, the Metro Link X-server supports the following touch-screen controllers: Carrol Touch serial touch screen, EloGraphics, Lucas Deeco, and MicroTouch.

Video Capture Boards, Frame Grabbers, and TV Tuners

Video capture boards, frame grabbers, and TV tuner cards enable you to capture images and send them over the wire, only in real time. A few programs are available that support TV tuners: BTTV (`www.thp.Uni-Koeln.DE/~rjkm/linux/bttv.html`), Xawtv and Xtvscreen. The CMOS Video Conferencing Kit comes with a video capture card and a CCD camera. Other boards that are supported are Data Translation DT2803, Data Translation DT2851 Frame Grabber, Data Translation DT3155, Diamond DTV2000 (based on BT848), Dipix XPG1000/FPG/PPMAPA (based on TI C40 DSP), Epix SVM, Epix Silicon Video MUX series of video frame grabbing boards, FAST Screen Machine II, Hauppage Wincast TV PCI (based on BT848), Imaging Technology ITI/IC-PCI, ImageNation Cortex I, ImageNation CX100, Imaging Technology IC-PCI frame grabber board, Matrox Meteor, Matrox PIP-1024, MaxiTV/PCI (based on ZR36120), Miro PCTV (based on BT848), MuTech MV1000 PCI, MuTech MV200, Pro Movie Studio, WinVision B&W video capture card, Quickcam, Sensus 700, Smart Video Recoder III (based on BT848), STB TV PCI Television Tuner (based on BT848), Tekram C210 (based on ZR36120), Video Blaster, Rombo Media Pro+, and VT1500 TV cards.

UPS and Miscellaneous Devices

Many people have a little surge protector on the power to their computer system. Although it's better than nothing, that surge protector offers only so much protection from surges and no protection from brownouts or black-outs. As you'll come to know, OpenLinux systems just hate having their power turned off before a nice, orderly shutdown of services. And when the system does come back up, you have this long wait while the system checks to see whether the file system was corrupted. An uninterruptible power supply (UPS) uses batteries to provide power to the computer system, allowing the computer system to shut down in an orderly way if the power starts to fail. A good UPS also gives you the ability to tie the computer into the UPS and, therefore, have the UPS judge when your OpenLinux system should go to complete shutdown. Some of the UPS units mentioned are APC SmartUPS, APC-BackUPS 400/600, APC-SmartUPS SU700/1400RM, UPS with RS-232 monitoring port (genpower package), and MGE UPS.

Many other hardware devices are supported, and some don't fit into any other category than *strange* . . . er . . . *miscellaneous.* These devices include Mattel Powerglove, AIMS Labs RadioTrack FM radio card, Reveal FM Radio card, and Videotext.

PCMCIA Cards

PCMCIA cards are used to get extra features into very small places. Most PCMCIA cards are supported by OpenLinux.

Here are some Ethernet cards that work under OpenLinux: 3Com 3c589, 3c589B, 3c589C, 3c589D, Farallon EtherWave, EtherMac, CONTEC C-NET(PC)C, Eagle NE200 Ethernet, Labs EPX-10BT, EPX-ET 10BT, Fujitsu FMV-J181, FMV-J182, FMV-J182A, Towa LA501, Hitachi HT-4840-11 EtherCard, NextCom NC5310, RATOC REX-9822, REX-5588A/W, TDK LAC-CD02x, LAK-CD021, LAK-CD022A, LAK-CD021AX Ethernet, New Media EthernetLAN, Accton EN2212, EN2216 EtherCard, Addtron Ethernet, Allied Telesis CentreCOM CE6001, LA-PCM, AmbiCom AMB8002, Apollo RE450CT, Asante FriendlyNet, Billionton LNT-10TB, California Access LAN Adapter, CeLAN EPCMCIA, CNet CN30BC, CN40BC Ethernet, Compex/ReadyLINK Ethernet Combo, Compex LinkPort Ethernet, Connectware LANdingGear Adapter, Danpex EN-6200P2 Ethernet, Datatrek NetCard, Dayna Communications CommuniCard E, Digital DEPCM-AA, PCP78-AC Ethernet, Digital EtherWORKS Turbo Ethernet, D-Link DE-650, DE-660, DynaLink L10C Ethernet, Edimax Technology Ethernet Combo, EFA InfoExpress 205, 207 Combo, Labs EPX-ET10T2 Combo, ELECOM Laneed LD-CDWA, LD-CDX, LD-CDNIA, LD-CDY, EP-210 Ethernet, Epson Ethernet, EtherPRIME Ethernet, Explorer NE-10000 Ethernet, 4109 Ethernet, Fiberline FL-4680, Gateway 2000 Ethernet, Genius

ME3000II Ethernet, Grey Cell Ethernet, GVC NIC-2000P Ethernet Combo, Hypertec HyperEnet, IBM CreditCard Ethernet Adapter, IC-Card Ethernet, Infotel IN650ct Ethernet, I-O Data PCLA/T, Katron PE-520 Ethernet, KingMax Technology EN10-T2 Ethernet, Kingston KNE-PCM/M, KNE-PC2, KTI PE-520 Plus, LANEED Ethernet, LanPro EP4000A, Lantech Ethernet, Linksys EtherCard, Logitec LPM-LN10T, LPM-LN10BA Ethernet, Longshine ShineNet LCS-8534TB Ethernet, Macnica ME-1 Ethernet, Maxtech PCN2000 Ethernet, Melco LPC-TJ, LPC-TS, Micronet EtherFast Adapter, NDC Instant-Link, Network General Sniffer, /National NE4100 InfoMover, OvisLink Ethernet, Panasonic CF-VEL211P-B, Planet SmartCOM 2000, 3500, Pretec Ethernet, PreMax PE-200 Ethernet, Proteon Ethernet, Relia RE2408T Ethernet, Reliasys 2400A Ethernet, RPTI EP400, EP401 Ethernet, SCM Ethernet, Sky Link Express, Socket Communications Socket EA LAN Adapter, SuperSocket RE450T, Surecom Ethernet, SVEC PN605C, -Conrad Ethernet, Trust Ethernet Combo, Volktek NPL-402CT Ethernet, Megahertz XJ10BT, XJ10BC, CC10BT Ethernet, New Media BASICS Ethernet, Ositech Four of Diamonds, Compaq Ethernet Adapter, Xircom CreditCard CE2, D-Link DFE-650, Linksys EtherFast 10/100, NetGear FA410TXC, Compaq Netelligent 10/100, Intel EtherExpress PRO/100, and Xircom CreditCard CE3.

Wireless network adapters are neat. They enable you to roam about but still be connected with your other systems. OpenLinux supports the following wireless network adapters: AT&T GIS/NCR WaveLAN version 2.0, DEC RoamAbout/DS, and Xircom CreditCard Netwave.

Most modem and serial cards should work. Unfortunately, some manufacturers have made cards that work only with Microsoft software. These cards are typically called WinModems (avoid them).

SCSI adapters enable you to attach any number of SCSI devices (disks, tapes, scanners, CD-ROMS, and CD-Writers) to your notebook. Supported controllers are Adaptec APA-1460, APA-1450A, APA-1460A, APA-1460B SlimSCSI, Iomega Zip and Jaz Cards, New Media Bus Toaster SCSI, New Media Toast 'n Jam (SCSI only), Noteworthy Bus Toaster SCSI, Sony CD-ROM Discman PRD-250, Future Domain SCSI2GO, IBM SCSI, Simple Technologies SCSI, Eiger Labs SCSI, MACNICA mPS110, mPS110-LP SCSI, NEC PC-9801N-J03R, Qlogic FastSCSI, Panasonic KXL-D740, KXL-DN740A, KXL-DN740A-NB 4X CD-ROM, Raven CD-Note 4X, RATOC REX-9530 SCSI-2, Toshiba NWB0107ABK, SCSC200B, Digital SCSI II adapter, IO-DATA PCSC-II, PCSC-II-L, IO-DATA CDG-PX44/PCSC CD-ROM, Logitec LPM-SCSI2, Logitec LCD-601 CD-ROM, Melco IFC-SC2, IFC-DC, Pioneer PCP-PR1W CD-ROM, and Taxan ICD-400PN.

Supported ATA/IDE CD-ROM adapters include the following: Argosy EIDE CD-ROM, Caravelle CD-36N, Creative Technology CD-ROM, Digital Mobile Media CD-ROM, EXP Traveler 620 CD-ROM, H45 Technologies Quick 2X CD-ROM, H45 Technologies QuickCD 16X, IO-DATA CDP-TX4/PCIDE, CDP-TX6/PCIDE, CDV-HDN6/PCIDE, IO-DATA CDP-TX10/PCIDE, MOP-230/PCIDE, and TEAC IDE Card/II.

The following multifunction cards are supported: 3Com 3c562, 3c562B/C/D, 3c563B/C/D, 3Com 3CCEM556, 3CXEM556, Motorola Marquis, D-Link DME336T, Grey Cell GCS3400, IBM Home and Away, IBM Home and Away 28.8, Linksys LANmodem 28.8, 33.6, Gateway Telepath Combo, Megahertz/U.S. Robotics EM1144, EM3288, EM3336, Motorola Mariner, Ositech Jack of Diamonds, and Xircom CreditCard CEM28, CEM33, and CEM56.

Appendix B

The OpenLinux man Pages

*A*ll UNIX and Linux systems are largely made up of small, terse commands that are executed on the command line. Typically, each command is associated with at least one man page, which has nothing to do with gender. In OpenLinux the *man* stands for *manual*.

At one time, the man pages were the only documentation that came with UNIX systems. Somewhere Maddog still has the thin book he received as a first-time UNIX user and systems administrator. The book contains only the man pages, and from those man pages Maddog was supposed to install a UNIX system. Years later, Maddog still looks first at the man pages to get a quick idea of what a command does and what arguments to use or what values to set on the command line.

This appendix shows you how to use the man(1) command, how to read and understand the man pages, and how to locate other man pages that may help you understand the OpenLinux command that you're investigating.

Viewing an OpenLinux Manual Page

To start using the man pages, follow these steps:

1. **With OpenLinux up and running, log in as a user (either a general user or root).**

2. **Type man.**

   The system asks what manual page you want. The syntax of the man command (like many other commands) requires at least one argument.

3. **Supply an argument by typing** man man.

   The first *man* is the command name, and the second *man* tells OpenLinux that you want information on the manual program itself. The system may tell you to wait a moment while it formats the page to your screen, and then it displays the reference page for the man command.

4. **If a colon (:) appears at the bottom of the screen, press the spacebar to see the next page, or use the arrow keys to maneuver around the pages.**

5. **To quit the program, press** q.

Sections in the man Pages

The man pages are found in several directories throughout your OpenLinux system:

- ✔ /usr/man
- ✔ /usr/local/man
- ✔ /usr/X11R6/man

Each directory is broken up into subdirectories representing sections of the manual, as follows:

- ✔ man1: User commands
- ✔ man2: System calls
- ✔ man3: Library functions
- ✔ man4: Special files
- ✔ man5: File formats
- ✔ man6: Games (look at everyone going to that section!)
- ✔ man7: Miscellany
- ✔ man8: System administration commands
- ✔ mann: nroff, troff, and groff (and now tk) macros

Note that most directories have more than one section.

Two sections may have an entry for a command of the same name. For example, section 1 has an open command, and section 2 has an open system call. To make sure that you're reading about the right section, you can specify the command on the man command line. For example:

```
[maddog@localhost maddog]$ man 2 open
```

Most sections of the man database (which is basically what man is — a database) have two parts:

- ✔ An intro page represented by a file called intro.*n,* where the *n* is a number that corresponds to the section number.
- ✔ All commands, calls, library names, and filenames, represented by files with the name command.*n,* where *n* is the section number name.

  If you use `cd` to change to the `/usr/man/man1` directory and issue the `ls` command, then you see files, such as `cat.1.gz` and `grep.1.gz`. Oddly, you don't find a file called `cd.1.gz`, because the `cd` command is built into the different shells, and its documentation is covered in the `bash.1.gz` file, or the `csh.1.gz` file.

Because man pages are actually a type of text file, they can take up lots of space. To conserve space on your system, all the man pages are stored in a compressed format, which is what the .gz ending indicates on the man page files. When you use the `man` command to view a man page, the file is decompressed as it's viewed. If you want to see what the raw man page text looks like, then try this command:

```
zcat /usr/man/man1/ls.1.gz | less
```

If you're using bash as a shell, then you can get information about the rest of the built-ins with this:

```
help
```

The intro page briefly describes the section of the manual and whether you need to know anything special about that section. Printing an intro page is simple by executing, for example:

```
man 2 intro
```

or

```
man 3 intro
```

Topics in the man Pages

Each man page is made up of several sections. In this part, we list the sections we think are most important in your quest to understand how to read man pages. Note that some man pages don't contain all these sections, and other pages contain more sections than those outlined here.

Name

The name is usually the command name, followed by a hyphen, followed by a one-line description of the command's functionality. This brief description of the command is usually what you see if you execute a man -k command or an apropos command. Either of these commands, when followed by a word, lists the name field from every manual page that contains that word. Type the following:

```
apropos cat
```

Your apropos command may produce few or no commands, perhaps because no one has generated the database made up of command names and descriptions. To generate the database, either you or your systems administrator must become superuser or root and then execute the following command line:

```
/usr/sbin/makewhatis
```

Synopsis

The synopsis is a shorthand way to describe what the command is looking for in an argument list. For example:

```
lpq [-l] [-Pprinter] [job # ...] [user ...]
```

is the synopsis for the lpq command (whose job is to show what's in the print queue). The command name (lpq) comes first, followed by a series of bracketed arguments. If an argument is enclosed in square brackets, then the argument is optional, which means the lpq command needs no arguments. If you type

```
lpq
```

you'll probably get a no entries message (meaning that nothing is waiting to be printed) or a list of people's jobs that are waiting to be printed on the default printer.

If you want to see what's waiting to be printed on another printer, then you use the optional argument -P followed by the name of the printer. For example:

```
lpq -Pzklpsa
```

Now if you type that command, you probably get a message, such as lpq: zklpsa: unknown printer, telling you that your system doesn't know about a printer named zklpsa.

In any case, the purpose of this section is not to show you all the functionality of the `lpq` command. Rather, the synopsis section shows in a shorthand way how the command should be used, including which arguments are optional.

Another confusing item you may see is the . . . notation. Looking back at the `lpq` command synopsis, you see this notation twice, once following the `job #` argument, and once following the `user` argument. This notation tells you that you can list as many job numbers on the line as you want, separated by spaces, and as many user names as you want, also separated by spaces.

Sometimes you see a command argument that begins with one hyphen (-) or two (--). These are technically known as *options,* whereas `job #` and `user` in the `lpq` command are *arguments*. Options tell the command how to manipulate arguments. You may see an option line that looks like this:

```
cat   [-benstuvAET]
```

or even this:

```
ls [-abcdfgiklmnpqrstuxABCFGLNQRSUX1]
```

Don't be overwhelmed. If you deal with the options one at a time, you'll understand how the command works. Take heart in the fact that much of the time, most people use only one or two options.

If you issue the `man ls` command, you'll see that `ls` has many more options. That's why `ls` has been described as "a command that went bad with good intentions."

Description

The description section is a brief introduction to the command's functionality, which then is expanded by what the options tell the command to do. The manual page for `man` itself is a good example of a description.

Options

As stated in the synopsis section, the options section shows how the command treats data in the arguments. Each option modifies the command's actions, drastically or subtly. The options also can pass information to the command about where to find files. The three types of options are

- ✔ No argument
- ✔ Attached argument
- ✔ Positional argument

No argument means the option has a hyphen followed by one or more single-character options. For example:

```
ps -ax
```

The a and the x don't have any other values they have to look at. However, in the following command

```
lpq -Pzklpsa
```

the -P option has to have an argument, which is zklpsa in this example.

Environmental variables

Sometimes, to cut down on the information you have to give the command, you can set an *environmental variable*. Each shell (or command interpreter) has an environment it works in. This environment (when created) consists of certain files that are open, have some memory, and almost always have some environmental variables.

Using the bash shell, type the following. (If you're not sure whether you're using the bash shell, type **bash** at the command prompt and then continue with the example.)

```
printenv
```

You see something like this:

```
HOSTNAME=localhost
LOGNAME=maddog
USERNAME=
_ETC_PROFILE=1
HELPPATH=/usr/openwin/help
MAIL=/var/spool/mail/maddog
PAGER=less
CLASSPATH=/usr/java/lib/classes.zip
TERM=xterm-color
HOSTTYPE=i386
PATH=/usr/local/bin:/bin:/usr/bin:/usr/X11R6/bin:/opt/bin:/op
        t/teTeX/bin:/opt/kde/bin:/usr/java/bin:/home/maddo
        g/bin
KDEDIR=/opt/kde
HOME=/home/maddog
SHELL=/bin/bash
USER=maddog
LESSCHARSET=latin1
JAVA_HOME=/usr/java
DISPLAY=:0.0
```

```
HOST=localhost.localdomain
OSTYPE=Linux
OPENWINHOME=/usr/openwin
SHLVL=2
_=/usr/bin/printenv
```

This list has lots of environmental variables, and we can't describe them all; but here are the most important ones:

- PATH tells the shell all the places to look for commands
- HOME tells cd where to go when you don't supply any arguments
- OSTYPE tells the shell and programs what operating system they're on

Different shells have different ways to set these variables (and create and set others) to tell the commands what to do.

Note that a variable not set to some value (null) is different from a variable that doesn't exist (unset), and these differences vary from command to command. For example, in the preceding listing, the first variable, USERNAME, is set to NULL. The fact that the variable is there at all is significant. The fact that the variable is set to NULL instead of some other value is also significant to various programs.

Diagnostics

Error messages or exit codes indicate that something has gone wrong in the program or the shell. Normally, UNIX error messages are terse. Sometimes things may seem to be wrong, but they're really okay. For example, most new users of UNIX think that when they issue an ls command in an empty directory, they should get an error message, such as directory empty or file not found. The problem? The ls command by itself can display the filenames in any order (as opposed to ls *, which displays the files in alphabetical order). Therefore, if you have a directory with three files named file, not, and found, which happen to print in that order, then you can't determine if the directory is empty. Granted, this example is contrived; but the UNIX developers thought that less is better than more (no, we're not talking about the command names less and more), and that silence is golden (which means something if you've ever heard those old, noisy, dot-matrix or daisy-wheel printers).

Most programs display an *exit code* that you normally don't see, unless it's a nonzero code (meaning that the program ended unsuccessfully). If you're a programmer, then you can test the value of the exit code to determine if an error has occurred; and if you write programming or shell script, then we encourage you to set and test exit codes.

Bugs/deficiencies

Yes, all programs have bugs, and most Linux people are good about correcting them. But some bugs are so arcane that they affect only one in a million people, and to try and correct them would mean redesigning the entire program. This type of bug is regarded, therefore, as a deficiency or a limitation and is listed in the man page.

Compatibility issues

If a new version of a command or a program comes out, the new version may work slightly differently than the old command or program. This difference can cause a *compatibility issue* with shell scripts that were written to use the old command or program. If the author of the command or program thinks there's a problem, then the problem should be documented here.

Caveats

Caveats are warnings that the programmer gives to the command or program user. Caveats may include things to think about before executing the command or program, security issues, or how much file-system space the program uses on large applications. For example, if a program is known to be a potential security risk but is still a popular tool (remote access tools like the rsh command are an example of this), then the Caveats section may warn you to be more security conscious as you use the program.

Disclaimers

Disclaimers are usually legal statements included at the insistence of the author's employer or the employer's lawyers, telling you that if you use this program and the program harms someone, don't come back to them. All programs in all operating systems have disclaimers someplace.

Authors

The authors are simply the people who wrote the command or program that the manual page describes. Often, this section also explains how to report bugs or discuss new features that you may want to see.

Acknowledgments

The acknowledgments section (which is much more pleasant than the disclaimers section) recognizes the work previously put into a program that has been expanded by the author. This recognition is the essence of Linux and the GNU Public License that allows and encourages people to build on the work of others.

Debugging options

Some programs, such as sendmail, have the capability to diagnose problems. If the manual page has a debugging options section, you can find information on setting and using these options to debug the program.

Configuration files

The program that a manual page describes can often be controlled in several ways. Some programs use command-line options; others rely on environment variables; still others use *configuration files,* sometimes known as *startup files.* This section of the man page describes any configuration files used by the program.

Configuration files may be in your home directory, a systemwide directory, or a sitewide directory. Often these files are looked for in a certain order. Sitewide files have the strongest influence; systemwide files and local-user (your startup) files have the second and third strongest influence, respectively. This ordering enables a systems administrator to set policies across companies and systems, while allowing you to tailor the program to your needs.

Examples of startup files are the `.bashrc` file (probably in your home directory) and the `/etc/bashrc` file (in the `/etc` directory). Note that the file in your home directory starts with a period. This type of file is called a *hidden* or *dot* file. Hidden files normally are not seen when you list your directory, unless you issue the `ls -a` or `ls .*` command.

Copyrights

People think that Linux code or other freeware code isn't copyrighted. This typically is not true. Authors of the code often take great care to copyright their code because they want credit for their work.

Copying permissions/distribution policy

Most Linux code is given away by the copyright holder through the GNU General Public License — the GPL. This license also is called *copyleft* or *OpenSource*. The GPL stipulates that those individuals holding a copy of the code can use the code for whatever purpose they want, as long as they make the code freely available to anyone who wants it. If they change the code, then they must make their changed code (including the source code) freely available to those who want it, as well.

Sometimes, other copying and distribution policies are associated with the command or program that the manual page describes. These policies can include the following types of permissions, where you may

- Use but not redistribute the code
- Use the code, but no source code is available
- Use and distribute the code as shareware, by paying a fee for continued use
- Have limited use, such as educational or personal (but not commercial) use
- Use the code on one machine only

If you've bought the operating system or a *layered product distribution* (a distribution that includes both the operating system and a commercial application) or both from a CD-ROM vendor, then the vendor's overall distribution policy is usually the strictest of any on the CD-ROM (that is, you're limited to installing the operating system on one machine only because of its licensed software), so you don't have to worry as long as you follow its overall licensing.

POSIX compatibility/standards conformance

In the dark days of computer science, each vendor went off to develop its own operating system with its own set of commands and programming interfaces. This approach created a Tower of Babel (not to be confused with the Tower of Hanoi, which is a puzzle game) among computer users and programmers. When UNIX systems first appeared, however, the systems were portable across different types of hardware. You could have the same operating system, commands, and programming interfaces whether you were programming a Digital Equipment Corporation system, a Sun Microsystems computer, an IBM computer, or others. Unfortunately, this portability lasted about ten minutes in the scope of UNIX's life, because after UNIX escaped from Bell Labs, it went to the University of California, Berkeley, and *poof:* Two different UNIX systems came into existence!

A little later, vendors started bringing out their versions of UNIX — with some vendors using System V as a basis, and other vendors using BSD (as the Berkeley version was called). Some vendors, such as Sun Microsystems, started out with BSD and then switched to System V (to the chagrin of their users).

In 1988, the IEEE developed the POSIX standard for operating systems. The IEEE is a great organization, and probably the greatest thing the organization has done is to build on UNIX rather than to start over from scratch with this specification. The interfaces are taken from the existing System V and Berkeley versions of UNIX.

If an operating system is POSIX compatible and a program is written to POSIX standards, then the program should be able to run with no problems on the operating system, and users should be able to use that operating system with little or no retraining from the last POSIX operating system that they worked with.

Although much work still has to be accomplished — both in defining POSIX and in vendors implementing POSIX — POSIX compliance and certification are worthy goals.

Other standards, such as for network communication and putting data on CD-ROMs, should be implemented and met by manufacturers, distribution makers, and developers (not necessarily in that order). Standards are both formal standards and informal de facto standards, both of which will help your system work better with the next system.

Linux was built with the goal of being POSIX compatible, so Linux follows many of the other POSIX standards. By following POSIX standards, Linux makes it easy to port code from one set of POSIX-compatible interfaces to another and from one POSIX-compatible operating system to another. POSIX compliance also allows OpenLinux interoperability with other operating systems. Many Linux people actively participate in the development of computer industry standards, such as POSIX, and the movement toward standards is generally supported in the Linux community.

Files

In addition to the startup or configuration files mentioned previously, sometimes the command or program that the manual page describes uses other files in the system and temporary files for holding intermediate work. Such files are listed in the Files section of the man page. If a command doesn't work, perhaps one of these files is missing, has the wrong file permissions (or the directory it's in has the wrong permissions), is owned by the wrong person, or has corrupt data.

Other places to look for help

You can find help in several other places on the system. First, try the info command. For example, enter info ls to learn about the ls command. Another place to look is the /usr/doc directory.

Note: Some system administrators conserve disk space by not loading /usr/doc on their systems. With the abundance of inexpensive disks, doing this creates false economy.

Documentation, such as the documentation found in /usr/doc, can be put on one system and then made available to everyone through the magic of the Network File System (NFS). Tell your system administrator to load /usr/doc on your system to share documentation. If you are your own system administrator, then go into a closet and give yourself a lecture!

Future work

The future work section lists the author's plans for the command or program that the manual page describes, often in an attempt to generate interest and help from other people.

See also/related software

The see also/related software section lists programs associated with the command or program that the manual page describes. Often, several programs make up a system of programs to do a particular task. Some programs have similar capabilities but are not quite the same. Some programs are the antithesis of the program you're looking at (for example, cut and paste). The *see also* often gives you an overall picture of what the program is supposed to do or leads you to the right program for the job.

Finding the Right man Page

If you don't know what command you're looking for, then use the apropos command followed by the word that interests you. The apropos command searches all the man pages looking for that word and lists the man command names along with one-line descriptions of all the commands containing that word. You probably should pipe the output of the apropos command into the less command:

```
apropos print | less
```

Note that `apropos` matches on partial words (called *strings*), which is why we suggest `print` instead of `printer`. The shorter your *keyword*, the more matches the command will find.

Then, after you have the pages you want to look at, execute the `man` command for each one. From the one-line description, you probably can decide which commands fit your needs.

Next, look at the description field, which gives you a better idea of what the command can do. If you're still not sure about the command's basic functionality, look at the see also section, to find out whether any other commands fit the bill.

After that, skip the synopsis section — it's usually a reminder of how to type the command — and go directly to the options section. Read through the options section, trying to apply the options to the basic description of the command.

After you read several man pages, you notice that the same options appear for similar commands.

All this is pretty passive work. To find out what a command really does, you can try the command out. Create a small test file using an editor, or use an existing file, such as the `/etc/passwd` file, as input.

Do not do this as root. You may inadvertently erase part of the operating system. Performing this experimentation as a nonprivileged, normal user is best.

From time to time, I read all the man pages in the system, concentrating on the command descriptions. I do this because I want to become familiar with new commands. Also, my memory isn't what it used to be. But to be fair to my failing memory, the system does have close to 1,000 general-user commands and about 260 system-administration commands.

Appendix C

About the CD

T he *Caldera OpenLinux For Dummies* CD-ROM contains the full distribution of OpenLinux 2.3 with the Lizard graphical installation utility. The CD doesn't include the PartitionMagic product, nor does the CD include commercial components, such as WordPerfect and StarOffice, that are available if you buy a complete boxed version of OpenLinux.

System Requirements

Make sure that your computer meets the minimum system requirements listed here. If your computer doesn't match up to most of these requirements, you may have problems using the contents of the CD:

- ✔ A PC with a 486 or faster processor.

- ✔ At least 8MB of total RAM installed on your computer. For the best performance, we recommend that people who want to use the X Window System and KDE have at least 16MB and preferably 32MB of main memory.

- ✔ At least 500MB of hard-drive space available to complete a default installation from the CD. You need less space if you choose the minimal installation option. Conversely, if you choose to install everything on the CD, you need about 1.4GB of hard-disk space. And keep in mind that the space requirements given here are only for the operating system and utilities. You want some additional space for other applications and your own data files as you work in OpenLinux.

- ✔ A CD-ROM drive.

- ✔ A 3½-inch floppy disk drive and a blank 3½-inch disk.

- ✔ A monitor capable of displaying at least 256 colors or grayscale.

- ✔ An IDE or a SCSI disk.

- ✔ A keyboard and a mouse.

- ✔ A modem with a speed of at least 28,800 Kbps if you want to go online.

Refer to Appendix A for a listing of all the hardware that's compatible with OpenLinux.

Using the CD

The instructions for installing the CD are in Part II. After you install the software, return the CD to its plastic jacket for safekeeping.

What You Find

The CD contains a Caldera Systems, Inc., OpenLinux operating system. You may view a lot of documentation on this CD through an HTML viewer, such as Netscape, which is installed by default. You also can print documentation from Netscape (if you have a printer connected to your system) or view the documentation directly from the CD by using another operating system, such as DOS, Windows, or UNIX, before installing OpenLinux.

We recommend that you review the README files in each of the main subdirectories before beginning the installation. These files contain valuable information about the product and guidelines for using the files in each directory.

Because the CD-ROM has a full implementation of OpenLinux, listing the hundreds of tools and utilities that are included in OpenLinux would take too much space. Briefly, the CD includes most of the software you need to access the Internet; write programs in several computer languages; create and manipulate images; create, manipulate, and play back sounds (if you have a sound board); and play numerous games. And, of course, all the source code is included.

If You Have Problems (Of the CD Kind)

Although we've tried to test various computers with the minimum system requirements, your computer may differ and OpenLinux may not install or work as stated.

The two likeliest problems you may face are not enough RAM for the programs that you want to use or hardware that OpenLinux doesn't support. Luckily, the latter problem occurs less frequently as more hardware is supported under OpenLinux. (Check out Appendix A for a list of compatible hardware.) Video cards (especially on laptops) are the most problematic pieces of hardware.

You also may have SCSI disks that use a controller that isn't supported by OpenLinux or a controller that's simply too new to have had the OpenLinux development team's proper support when the CD was pressed.

If you have trouble with what you think is a damaged CD, please call the IDG Books Worldwide Customer Service phone number: 800-762-2974 (outside the United States: 317-572-3993). Customer service, however, won't be able to help with complications relating to the program or to how the program works. Please see the Installation Instructions in Part II of this book.

Index

• V •

• W •

GNU GENERAL PUBLIC LICENSE

Version 2, June 1991

Preamble

The licenses for most software are designed to take away your freedom to share and change it. By contrast, the GNU General Public License is intended to guarantee your freedom to share and change free software—to make sure the software is free for all its users. This General Public License applies to most of the Free Software Foundation's software and to any other program whose authors commit to using it. (Some other Free Software Foundation software is covered by the GNU Library General Public License instead.) You can apply it to your programs, too.

When we speak of free software, we are referring to freedom, not price. Our General Public Licenses are designed to make sure that you have the freedom to distribute copies of free software (and charge for this service if you wish), that you receive source code or can get it if you want it, that you can change the software or use pieces of it in new free programs, and that you know you can do these things.

To protect your rights, we need to make restrictions that forbid anyone to deny you these rights or to ask you to surrender the rights. These restrictions translate to certain responsibilities for you if you distribute copies of the software, or if you modify it.

For example, if you distribute copies of such a program, whether gratis or for a fee, you must give the recipients all the rights that you have. You must make sure that they, too, receive or can get the source code. And you must show them these terms so they know their rights.

We protect your rights with two steps: (1) copyright the software, and (2) offer you this license which gives you legal permission to copy, distribute, and/or modify the software.

Also, for each author's protection and ours, we want to make certain that everyone understands that there is no warranty for this free software. If the software is modified by someone else and passed on, we want its recipients to know that what they have is not the original, so that any problems introduced by others will not reflect on the original authors' reputations.

Finally, any free program is threatened constantly by software patents. We wish to avoid the danger that redistributors of a free program will individually obtain patent licenses, in effect making the program proprietary. To prevent this, we have made it clear that any patent must be licensed for everyone's free use or not licensed at all.

The precise terms and conditions for copying, distribution, and modification follow.

TERMS AND CONDITIONS FOR COPYING, DISTRIBUTION, AND MODIFICATION

This License applies to any program or other work which contains a notice placed by the copyright holder saying it may be distributed under the terms of this General Public License. The "Program," below, refers to any such program or work, and a "work based on the Program" means either the Program or any derivative work under copyright law: that is to say, a work containing the Program or a portion of it, either verbatim or with modifications and/or translated into another language. (Hereinafter, translation is included without limitation in the term "modification.") Each licensee is addressed as "you."

Activities other than copying, distribution, and modification are not covered by this License; they are outside its scope. The act of running the Program is not restricted, and the output from the Program is covered only if its contents constitute a work based on the Program (independent of having been made by running the Program). Whether that is true depends on what the Program does.

1. You may copy and distribute verbatim copies of the Program's source code as you receive it, in any medium, provided that you conspicuously and appropriately publish on each copy an appropriate copyright notice and disclaimer of warranty; keep intact all the notices that refer to this License and to the absence of any warranty; and give any other recipients of the Program a copy of this License along with the Program.

    You may charge a fee for the physical act of transferring a copy, and you may at your option offer warranty protection in exchange for a fee.

2. You may modify your copy or copies of the Program or any portion of it, thus forming a work based on the Program, and copy and distribute such modifications or work under the terms of Section 1 above, provided that you also meet all of these conditions:

    (a) You must cause the modified files to carry prominent notices stating that you changed the files and the date of any change.

    (b) You must cause any work that you distribute or publish, that in whole or in part contains or is derived from the Program or any part thereof, to be licensed as a whole at no charge to all third parties under the terms of this License.

    (c) If the modified program normally reads commands interactively when run, you must cause it, when started running for such interactive use in the most ordinary way, to print or display an announcement including an appropriate copyright notice and a notice that there is no warranty (or else, saying that you provide a warranty) and that users may redistribute the program under these conditions, and telling the user how to view a copy of this License. (Exception: if the Program itself is interactive but does not normally print such an announcement, your work based on the Program is not required to print an announcement.)

    These requirements apply to the modified work as a whole. If identifiable sections of that work are not derived from the Program, and can be reasonably considered independent and separate works in themselves, then this License, and its terms, do not apply to those sections when you distribute them as separate works. But when you distribute the same sections as part of a whole which is a work based on the Program, the distribution of the whole must be on the terms of this License, whose permissions for other licensees extend to the entire whole, and thus to each and every part regardless of who wrote it.

Thus, it is not the intent of this section to claim rights or contest your rights to work written entirely by you; rather, the intent is to exercise the right to control the distribution of derivative or collective works based on the Program. In addition, mere aggregation of another work not based on the Program with the Program (or with a work based on the Program) on a volume of a storage or distribution medium does not bring the other work under the scope of this License.

3. You may copy and distribute the Program (or a work based on it, under Section 2) in object code or executable form under the terms of Sections 1 and 2 above provided that you also do one of the following:

   (a) Accompany it with the complete corresponding machine-readable source code, which must be distributed under the terms of Sections 1 and 2 above on a medium customarily used for software interchange; or,

   (b) Accompany it with a written offer, valid for at least three years, to give any third party, for a charge no more than your cost of physically performing source distribution, a complete machine-readable copy of the corresponding source code, to be distributed under the terms of Sections 1 and 2 above on a medium customarily used for software interchange; or,

   (c) Accompany it with the information you received as to the offer to distribute corresponding source code. (This alternative is allowed only for noncommercial distribution and only if you received the program in object code or executable form with such an offer, in accord with Subsection b above.)

   The source code for a work means the preferred form of the work for making modifications to it. For an executable work, complete source code means all the source code for all modules it contains, plus any associated interface definition files, plus the scripts used to control compilation and installation of the executable. However, as a special exception, the source code distributed need not include anything that is normally distributed (in either source or binary form) with the major components (compiler, kernel, and so on) of the operating system on which the executable runs, unless that component itself accompanies the executable.

   If distribution of executable or object code is made by offering access to copy from a designated place, then offering equivalent access to copy the source code from the same place counts as distribution of the source code, even though third parties are not compelled to copy the source along with the object code.

4. You may not copy, modify, sublicense, or distribute the Program except as expressly provided under this License. Any attempt otherwise to copy, modify, sublicense or distribute the Program is void, and will automatically terminate your rights under this License. However, parties who have received copies, or rights, from you under this License will not have their licenses terminated so long as such parties remain in full compliance.

5. You are not required to accept this License, since you have not signed it. However, nothing else grants you permission to modify or distribute the Program or its derivative works. These actions are prohibited by law if you do not accept this License. Therefore, by modifying or distributing the Program (or any work based on the Program), you indicate your acceptance of this License to do so, and all its terms and conditions for copying, distributing or modifying the Program or works based on it.

6. Each time you redistribute the Program (or any work based on the Program), the recipient automatically receives a license from the original licensor to copy, distribute or modify the Program subject to these terms and conditions. You may not impose any further restrictions on the recipients' exercise of the rights granted herein. You are not responsible for enforcing compliance by third parties to this License.

7. If, as a consequence of a court judgment or allegation of patent infringement or for any other reason (not limited to patent issues), conditions are imposed on you (whether by court order, agreement or otherwise) that contradict the conditions of this License, they do not excuse you from the conditions of this License. If you cannot distribute so as to satisfy simultaneously your obligations under this License and any other pertinent obligations, then as a consequence you may not distribute the Program at all. For example, if a patent license would not permit royalty-free redistribution of the Program by all those who receive copies directly or indirectly through you, then the only way you could satisfy both it and this License would be to refrain entirely from distribution of the Program.

   If any portion of this section is held invalid or unenforceable under any particular circumstance, the balance of the section is intended to apply and the section as a whole is intended to apply in other circumstances.

   It is not the purpose of this section to induce you to infringe any patents or other property right claims or to contest validity of any such claims; this section has the sole purpose of protecting the integrity of the free software distribution system, which is implemented by public license practices. Many people have made generous contributions to the wide range of software distributed through that system in reliance on consistent application of that system; it is up to the author/donor to decide if he or she is willing to distribute software through any other system and a licensee cannot impose that choice.

   This section is intended to make thoroughly clear what is believed to be a consequence of the rest of this License.

8. If the distribution and/or use of the Program is restricted in certain countries either by patents or by copyrighted interfaces, the original copyright holder who places the Program under this License may add an explicit geographical distribution limitation excluding those countries, so that distribution is permitted only in or among countries not thus excluded. In such case, this License incorporates the limitation as if written in the body of this License.

9. The Free Software Foundation may publish revised and/or new versions of the General Public License from time to time. Such new versions will be similar in spirit to the present version, but may differ in detail to address new problems or concerns.

   Each version is given a distinguishing version number. If the Program specifies a version number of this License which applies to it and "any later version", you have the option of following the terms and conditions either of that version or of any later version published by the Free Software Foundation. If the Program does not specify a version number of this License, you may choose any version ever published by the Free Software Foundation.

10. If you wish to incorporate parts of the Program into other free programs whose distribution conditions are different, write to the author to ask for permission. For software that is copyrighted by the Free Software Foundation, write to the Free Software Foundation; we sometimes make exceptions for this. Our decision will be guided by the two goals of preserving the free status of all derivatives of our free software and of promoting the sharing and reuse of software generally.

NO WARRANTY

11. BECAUSE THE PROGRAM IS LICENSED FREE OF CHARGE, THERE IS NO WARRANTY FOR THE PROGRAM, TO THE EXTENT PERMITTED BY APPLICABLE LAW. EXCEPT WHEN OTHERWISE STATED IN WRITING THE COPYRIGHT HOLDERS AND/OR OTHER PARTIES PROVIDE THE PROGRAM "AS IS" WITHOUT WARRANTY OF ANY KIND, EITHER EXPRESSED OR IMPLIED, INCLUDING, BUT NOT LIMITED TO, THE IMPLIED WARRANTIES OF MERCHANTABILITY AND FITNESS FOR A PARTICULAR PURPOSE. THE ENTIRE RISK AS TO THE QUALITY AND PERFORMANCE OF THE PROGRAM IS WITH YOU. SHOULD THE PROGRAM PROVE DEFECTIVE, YOU ASSUME THE COST OF ALL NECESSARY SERVICING, REPAIR OR CORRECTION.

12. IN NO EVENT UNLESS REQUIRED BY APPLICABLE LAW OR AGREED TO IN WRITING WILL ANY COPYRIGHT HOLDER, OR ANY OTHER PARTY WHO MAY MODIFY AND/OR REDISTRIBUTE THE PROGRAM AS PERMITTED ABOVE, BE LIABLE TO YOU FOR DAMAGES, INCLUDING ANY GENERAL, SPECIAL, INCIDENTAL OR CONSEQUENTIAL DAMAGES ARISING OUT OF THE USE OR INABILITY TO USE THE PROGRAM (INCLUDING BUT NOT LIMITED TO LOSS OF DATA OR DATA BEING RENDERED INACCURATE OR LOSSES SUSTAINED BY YOU OR THIRD PARTIES OR A FAILURE OF THE PROGRAM TO OPERATE WITH ANY OTHER PROGRAMS), EVEN IF SUCH HOLDER OR OTHER PARTY HAS BEEN ADVISED OF THE POSSIBILITY OF SUCH DAMAGES.

END OF TERMS AND CONDITIONS

IDG BOOKS WORLDWIDE BOOK REGISTRATION

We want to hear from you!

Register This Book and Win!

Visit **http://my2cents.dummies.com** to register this book and tell us how you liked it!

✔ Get entered in our monthly prize giveaway.

✔ Give us feedback about this book — tell us what you like best, what you like least, or maybe what you'd like to ask the author and us to change!

✔ Let us know any other ...*For Dummies*® topics that interest you.

Your feedback helps us determine what books to publish, tells us what coverage to add as we revise our books, and lets us know whether we're meeting your needs as a ...*For Dummies* reader. You're our most valuable resource, and what you have to say is important to us!

Not on the Web yet? It's easy to get started with *Dummies 101*®: *The Internet For Windows*® *98* or *The Internet For Dummies*®, 6th Edition, at local retailers everywhere.

Or let us know what you think by sending us a letter at the following address:

...*For Dummies* Book Registration
Dummies Press
10475 Crosspoint Blvd.
Indianapolis, IN 46256

™

...FOR DUMMIES

BESTSELLING
BOOK SERIES

Installation Instructions

The *Caldera OpenLinux For Dummies* CD-ROM contains the full freeware distribution of Caldera OpenLinux.

Important Information about Using Linux: Linux supports many IBM-compatible PCs, but some PCs and components aren't supported. Appendix A lists the hardware compatible with OpenLinux. Please review that appendix before attempting to install OpenLinux from the *Caldera OpenLinux For Dummies* CD-ROM.

The Linux operating system and its applications are collaborative products of a worldwide community of independent users. IDG Books Worldwide, Inc., doesn't guarantee the fitness of the Linux operating system, Linux applications, or the *Caldera OpenLinux For Dummies* CD-ROM for any computer system or purpose. IDG Books Worldwide, Inc., doesn't provide additional installation support or technical support for the Linux operating system, Linux applications, or the *Caldera OpenLinux For Dummies* CD-ROM.

Part II of this book describes the installation process for Caldera OpenLinux.

Limited Warranty